# WINNING
## AGAINST ALL ODDS
### DISCOVERING THE TRUE WARRIOR WITHIN

# KEVIN PARKER

GMCP

First edition

Edited by Caitlin Freeman

Published by Global Mentoring, Coaching and Publishing

ISBN: 978-0-9996791-3-5

# DEDICATION

I dedicate this book to my stepmother Debbie, may she rest in peace. She inspired me to write this book, and I am forever grateful for her encouragement, her faith in me, and her belief that I could use my story to inspire others to win against all odds. I also want to thank Jesus Christ for saving my life and allowing me to become the true warrior that I am today. All the glory goes to God.

# TABLE OF CONTENTS

# FOREWORD
## *by Dr. Cali Estes, MCAP, ICADC*

"Tiger's Blood and Winning."

You probably recognize both of those terms, coined by Charlie Sheen amidst his crack cocaine and alcohol infused meltdown a few years ago. In fact, most everyone can remember the public spectacle that cost him his job, his career, and his kids.

Or the times that Britney shaved her head and beat the Paparazzi car with her umbrella in a rage. We all had ringside seats to that crazy adventure!

*But did anyone actually do anything about it?*

As a Celebrity Addictions Coach, I work with clients that have addictions and troubles of all kinds. It's my business to know their struggles, vices, and negative outcomes. I have held the hair of celebrities as they puked into the toilet. I have helped more than one top executive recover from crippling addictions that cost them their job, their spouse, even their kids. I show up at people's homes, offices, and even tour buses, and I get right to the core of their issues.

My work is a calling. I watched my husband overdose three times on heroin and fentanyl. I endured the feeling of powerlessness as he got our

BMW carjacked and wound up nearly dying in the ER. As I say in my book, *I Married A Junkie*, we too often feel hopeless, helpless, and powerless when we watch our loved ones spiral out of control. Not anymore. There is help.

No matter what any of the people I have worked with have lost—from money to loved ones—it cannot compare to almost losing your life or waking up to find your body parts are just...missing. I cannot even imagine the horror and pain that Kevin Parker endured during his addiction and recovery. Many of my clients would have simply given up and checked out.

From the minute I met Kevin Parker, I knew he was a True Warrior. Not many people can survive an addiction as harrowing as what he went through, let alone come out on top and tackle life with a vengeance. I have seen his resilience firsthand. He has an ability to help others heal on a level that most people can't even comprehend.

Kevin came to my school, The Addictions Academy, to train in Recovery Coaching and wound up becoming a stellar faculty member. The students in the program look up to him as a mentor and respect his leadership. He is a trainer of trainers and an amazing public speaker, but I don't have to tell you that—you are about to discover that for yourself.

Have you found yourself stuck in addiction, and you just feel lost? Or have you watched a loved one slowly kill themselves with drugs and alcohol? Then you need to pick up Kevin's book and read his story. He will inspire you to fight for a second chance at life.

– Dr. Cali Estes, MCAP, ICADC
Celebrity Addictions Coach
#1 Best Selling Author of *I Married A Junkie*
www.TheAddictionsCoach.com, www.TheAddictionsAcademy.com

# CHAPTER 1

~~

Where was I? I couldn't recall exactly. I had no memory of how I'd arrived here, wherever "here" was. I opened my eyes to look around. I smiled. Now I knew—I was in paradise. I was lying on a tropical beach with white sand, twisted palm trees, and a warm breeze blowing over my body. The sun was beating down on my face, and I could smell the refreshing spray of saltwater in the air. I was lounging in a wide, reclining beach chair with a drink in my hand and a smile on my face. I looked over and saw my friend Taylor lounging in a chair next to me. We grinned at each other, like we couldn't believe we were in such a beautiful place. The beach was peaceful and serene, and I remember thinking to myself that life just can't get any better than this. I felt as blissful and free as a bird. I could spend the rest of my life on this beach and not regret one second of it.

As I was lying there, stretched out on my chair, I turned my head to gaze at a nearby palm tree that was swaying in the breeze. I could see an appealing, mango-like fruit that was hanging from one of the branches. I wanted to know what that fruit tasted like. I got up and walked over to the tree, the white sand warming the soles of my feet. I reached for the branch, but it was about ten feet up, too high for me to jump. I still hungered for the fruit, so I bear-hugged the trunk and shimmied up the tree until I got to the branch. I stretched out my arms, and I was able to grab the fruit and twist it off the tree. My prize in hand, I slid back down the trunk. A sweet aroma filled my nostrils. I'd never seen a fruit exactly like this, but it looked edible and smelled ripe. I suddenly realized that I was holding a knife, so I cut open the skin and took a huge bite of the sweet, juicy flesh. It was so delicious that I devoured the entire thing in minutes, enjoying every last bite.

When I was done eating the fruit, I glanced over at my friend Taylor, who was still reclining in her beach chair. I thought to her, "Let's go surfing." Taylor heard what was on my mind, and I remember thinking to myself that she must have become telepathic. We looked at each other with the same joyful expression on our faces, and we ran across the beach to a place where there were two surfboards that were stabbed into the sand. We grabbed the boards and ran into the waves, swimming further and further out to sea. The turquoise water was so clear that I could see all the way to the ocean floor. Little, colorful fish were darting this way and that, creating trails of bubbles below me. Taylor and I paddled about 200 feet from the shore, hoping to catch the perfect wave. I remember grinning as I sat there on my surfboard with my friend, feeling the warm breeze and the swell of the waves. I was serenely calm. I looked up at the beautiful blue sky and thought to myself that this felt like heaven.

As I gazed upwards, I saw a few clouds roll in, followed by a few more. It was becoming overcast, and I could no longer feel the warmth of the sun on my face. The gentle breeze died down, and the ocean waves grew flat and motionless. I looked to the shore and saw that the coast was now so far away that I could barely make out anything on land. I sat on the surfboard and glanced back toward the ocean, hoping that my wave would come soon. I suddenly felt alone. I turned around and realized that Taylor was gone. She was nowhere to be found. I looked back to the shore and the coast had completely disappeared. I was alone and adrift on the open ocean.

I felt empty inside. I had an abrupt pain in my chest, almost like a panic attack but without shortness of breath. The feeling was crippling, and it rendered me totally immobile. I was stuck, and I slowly fell backwards onto the surfboard. I didn't know which way was up or down, and it felt like my body was beginning to seize. I remember thinking, "Why the hell did I eat the damn fruit from that tree? It must have been the forbidden fruit they warned Eve about. At the very least, it must have been poisonous." All I knew was that I had made a mistake and I was going to pay dearly for it. I was now floating in the middle of the ocean, far away from land and completely helpless. I thought to myself, "I'm going to die out here." I was at the mercy of nature. Wherever the current took me, that's where I would go, and there was nothing that I could do about it.

At this point, I knew that my life was no longer in my hands. I surrendered to the ocean and to God. I let go and allowed myself to be at peace with my fate as I drifted further and further out to sea. I remember looking into the sky and seeing a movie reel of my whole life flashing before my eyes. All the things I had lived through, the good times and the bad, flowed together in a long, twisting flashback. It felt like an eternity drifting beneath the beautiful sky, and eventually my eyes started to close from pure exhaustion. I gave up and allowed myself to drift off.

As I approached oblivion, I began to hear some sort of commotion. Among the various sounds, I recognized voices, although I couldn't make out what they were saying. They sounded like they were talking in some foreign tongue. I realized that I had washed up on the shore of an island. I was surrounded by indigenous people speaking a language that I couldn't understand. The islanders rushed over and picked up the surfboard with me on it. They lifted me up and marched inland. They carried me a long way from the shore. I had no idea where they were bringing me or what they were going to do to me when we got there. All I knew was that I was no longer floating helpless and alone in an endless ocean abyss.

The islanders carried me to a tiny straw hut. It was dark and dirty inside, and I could barely make out my surroundings. They placed me on top of a high, flat surface, and I realized in horror that it was a shiny metal operating table. They strapped me down to the table and suddenly the darkness of the room was pierced by a bright white lamp that shone directly into my eyes. I was on the verge of panic as I tried to pull against the straps that restrained my arms and legs. I couldn't see anything but the blinding light over my head and dark shadows in my peripheral vision. I didn't know where I was or who these people were, and I couldn't make out a word that they were saying. I couldn't even see their faces. I struggled to move my body, but I discovered that I was completely immobilized. I felt trapped and alone.

Most of what the islanders said sounded like gibberish to me. I was scared of them at first, but over time I realized that they didn't mean me any harm. I still didn't know where I was, but I was glad to have company. The spotlight above my head began to feel soothing, so I chose to focus on it. I still couldn't comprehend any words that the people were saying, but after a while I could tell that someone was singing a song. I had never heard the song before, but for some reason the voice that was singing it brought me great comfort. Slowly, I was able to pick out the lyrics. The song went, "There was a man right here, his name was Paul Revere, can do, can do." Even though I could understand the words of the song, I couldn't make out a single thing that anyone else was saying. It seemed odd to me that this little third world hospital would have a strange English song playing in the background. It wasn't a particularly good tune, but it was reassuring, and I listened intently as it repeated over and over.

I wasn't sure how long I was lying there on that operating table, but I began to wonder if these islanders would ever allow me to return home. I missed my family and friends, and I worried that I would never get to see them again. I prayed to God, begging Him to let me return to the ones I love. As I was praying, a miracle occurred—suddenly I could hear my father's voice. Then I heard my mother and both of my stepparents. My wish had come true! I had been reunited with my family. I was so excited. I couldn't have been more thankful and relieved to hear such sweet sounds.

As their voices grew closer, the blinding light above my head began to dim and the peripheral darkness became brighter. Slowly, the two areas merged into on another, and bam! The picture cleared, my vision returned, and I realized that I was lying on a bed in a hospital room. I had indeed heard my family's voices. I now could see that my mother, father, brother, stepfather, and stepmother were all huddled around me, trying to get me to respond to them. They looked distraught and broken. I didn't know what was happening. I just knew that I was in a hospital, my family was upset, and I had no idea how I had gotten here.

My mother looked like she had aged ten years since the last time I had seen her. I could tell that she was terrified, but she also looked relieved. She asked me with tears in her eyes if I could hear her. I tried to respond, but nothing came out. I started to panic. I looked around and saw that I was surrounded by a dozen different machines that were making beeping and breathing sounds. I realized with horror that there were tubes going into my throat and tubes coming out of my chest. I was unable to move or speak. I couldn't even breathe on my own.

I had never seen my family so devastated before. Despite the sorrow in their eyes, their faces seemed to glow with a glimmer of hope now that I was awake. "WHAT THE HELL DID I DO?" This was the question that raced through my mind. What the hell could I have done to put the people I care about most through such a horrible ordeal? I realized that I must have really screwed up this time. This was the worst moment of my life, and it will haunt me for the rest of my days. I knew that I had hurt my family in the most devastating way possible, and I couldn't even speak to ask for their forgiveness. Not that any apology I could have offered them would have made a difference. I had caused my family unimaginable pain and agony, and I wouldn't wish it on my worst enemy.

I stared down at my body, trying to gather clues about what had happened to me. In addition to the tubes going into my throat and my chest, there were tubes coming out of the bottom of my hospital gown and running off the bed. Looking further down, I saw with a shock that my feet were blackened and swollen up like balloons. I couldn't move any of my limbs. I was in immense pain and sweating profusely.

Shifting my gaze to the rest of the room, I saw that I was hooked up to about ten different machines. In fact, the entire room was filled with equipment. My family members were huddled together at my bedside, practically on top of one another, and there were two doctors and a nurse standing there as well. It dawned on me that I might not make it out of this situation alive. Certainly, I could tell from the worried looks on my parents' faces that they were scared I wouldn't survive. I heard the doctors talking to my family. They said that I had a high temperature and that my brain was frying. They warned my family not to get their hopes up because I probably wouldn't make it through the night. I started panicking. I wanted to scream, "I can hear you! I'm right here!" However, the tube in my throat prevented me from making any sound. Everybody was crying, and I was overwhelmed by the seriousness of the situation. This was more dire than anything I could fathom.

As I lay there in the hospital bed, I kept racking my brain, trying to figure out how I had gotten here. I knew that I must have done something awful to end up in such a terrible state. Eventually, I was able to put the pieces together. I had apparently overdosed and choked on my own vomit. As my body shut down from lack of oxygen, I had descended into a coma, and I'd been on the brink of death for several weeks. I learned this from listening to the conversations that went on between my family, the doctors, and my friends who came to visit. No one spoke directly to me about what had happened. They all thought I had suffered brain damage and couldn't understand them. The doctors told my family that my steady 108-degree temperature had likely caused cognitive impairment. They warned my family not to get their hopes up. Even if I survived, I would be a complete vegetable, and my parents would have to care for me for the rest of my life. They would have to feed me, bathe me, and change me every day. I would likely lose both of my legs, and I could possibly lose my arms, too. I would never be the son they once knew. I was going crazy from watching my family suffer and cry over me. All I wanted was a way to communicate with them. I longed to let them know that I loved them and that I wasn't braindead; however, the only signal I could give them was to slowly blink my eyes.

I was terrified, angry, ashamed, and on the verge of giving up. I reflected on the past twenty-five years of my life, trying to figure out how I had reached such an extreme low point. Where had things gone wrong? As I asked myself these questions, I understood that it wasn't a single choice or event that had ruined my life. It was a culmination of harmful experiences, bad influences, and poor decisions that had led me down this path. If I was going to survive this nightmare, I knew that I needed to make a serious reevaluation of my existence and figure out how to change my future. However, to understand how this happened to me, how I could have been so blindsided by my life, I'm going to have to take you all the way back to the beginning...

# CHAPTER 2

M y earliest memories have to be from when I was about three years old. I was living with my mother in a small apartment above a bar in St. George, Staten Island. It was just me and my mom. She had a job as a bartender downstairs, and in the afternoons, she would carry me with her down the creaky, worn out staircase and go to work. At that time, she was single, and the money she made was to provide for me. I remember it being an old people's bar, or at least the customers seemed pretty ancient to me. Led Zeppelin or some other classic rock band was always playing on the jukebox. There was an old-timey cigarette vending machine in the corner. You would grab the handle, give it a pull and a push, and the machine would deliver you a pack of smokes. I remember this machine fondly because my mom let me play with it in the daytime to keep me occupied. To my three-year-old self, that vending machine was like a giant, fancy toy. It reminds me of how old I really am to think that I lived in an era where cigarette machines were everywhere. Oh, the good old days.

My mother Barbara is one of the most beautiful women I have ever known, with baby blue eyes, blonde hair, and a slim figure. She always made sure that I was fed and had a roof over my head, but we lived within very modest means. In retrospect, I'm grateful for this humble upbringing because it taught me to always appreciate the things I have. No matter what was happening in our lives, my mother made me feel safe, and I knew she loved me with every fiber of her being. She is a caring, generous woman, and she excels at understanding what other people need. A lot of who I am is because of my mom. She taught me how to be affectionate and creative, and she gave me the emotional intelligence that I have today.

My mother and my father separated when I was about one year old. Growing up, I had the typical two-family childhood. I would see my father on weekends and holidays, and during the week, I was with my mom. Even though my parents weren't together, they both worked hard to make sure I was a happy child.

My father Kevin is a solidly built man with a goatee and a bald head. He has piercing blue eyes and a contagious smile. He is one of the strongest, wisest, and most charismatic men that I have ever known. He was never formally educated, but he made up for it with well-developed street smarts. He has a keen ability to read people and situations. He's the guy that you ask to have your back in a tough spot. When I was growing up, I remember realizing that my dad must be a really special man because everyone wanted to associate with him. He was loved by most, feared by some, and respected by all who knew him. I can attribute a lot of my personality and charisma to my father. Even as a young boy, I knew I wanted to be just like him. He didn't take shit from anybody, but he was loyal and caring to the people he loved. I wouldn't have gotten as far as I have without his footsteps to follow in. He's always been my lighthouse guiding the way.

About a year after they separated, my mother started dating again. My father was dating someone as well. As I grew up, I came to know these people as my stepparents. My mother met a firefighter named Gene who had two boys from his first marriage, Tim and Chris. Tim was a toddler my age, and Chris was seven years my senior. My mother and Gene clicked right away, and not long after, they moved in together and combined their households. Gene's sons became my stepbrothers, and since Tim was my age, they naturally paired us together.

When my mom and I moved in with Gene and his boys, Tim was recovering from a recent dog attack. It was a freak accident. The animal was a massive wolf-dog hybrid, and it had mauled his face, ripping off half his scalp and one of his ears. It was horrific. No two-year-old baby should ever endure such a traumatic experience. As much as the attack scarred him physically, I think it caused even greater emotional wounds that have taken far longer to heal. Tim grew up believing that the world is an inherently violent place. He was always defensive and strived to be tougher and meaner than the next kid. Life had taught him that he had to attack first if he wanted to survive, and that core belief played a big part in who he became as a person.

Tim was one of the people I looked up to the most as a boy. Even though he was my age, he was like my big brother. He was a promising athlete, and he could run faster, throw farther, and punch harder than me or any of the other little kids we knew. He often used his physical toughness to get what he wanted. I now know how much he loved me when we were young, but at the time, I experienced this physical intimidation as bullying. When we would roughhouse, he would whale on me, call me names, and tell me that I wasn't welcome in my stepfather's family. This played into my insecurities as a child of a combined household. Like many stepchildren, I had a deep-rooted anxiety that I didn't belong, and I often felt that I wasn't good enough.

My stepfather Gene has been a huge influence on my life. My mom and he had primary custody of me during the week, so I grew up under his roof. He took me under his wing and taught me almost everything I know. He showed me how to be responsible and encouraged me to be determined and independent. Many of my good habits, skills, and talents are a byproduct of his persistent teaching over the years. Without his guidance, I wouldn't be half the man I am today.

He seemed like a massive, imposing grownup to me at the time, but looking back, my stepfather was just a young man in his early twenties. He loved kids, and he always found the time to play with us. His house had a huge backyard, and he made sure that my brothers and I had plenty of activities to keep us entertained. He built us a basketball court that lit up at night so we didn't have to play in the neighborhood, which could be sketchy after dark. He also set up a wiffleball stadium, and when the weather turned warm, he would fill up the large pool that he had built. I used to spend the summers playing with my stepfather and my stepbrothers in the pool. Tim, Chris, and I would take turns climbing on my stepdad's shoulders and slugging it out with each other. This game was called Chicken, and the objective was to pull your opponent down from the adult's shoulders and drag them into the water. Sometimes we would play basketball in the pool, and my stepfather and older brother Chris would dominate. One of our favorite games was turning the water into a giant whirlpool. My stepdad would decide what direction to swim, and we would all circle around and around until the center of the pool started to rotate. Once it was strong enough, my stepfather would yell, "Alright, reverse!" We would try to swim the other way, and then we would inevitably get pulled off our feet by the current, laughing, splashing, and sputtering.

My stepfather was extremely athletic, and he wanted to make sure that we got into sports, as well. In addition to basketball and wiffleball in the backyard, he also equipped the basement with a ping-pong table, a workout area, and a batting tee. As kids, part of our homework each night was to swing our little baseball bats and hit the ball one hundred times before we went to bed. My stepdad was a baseball coach, and he had big dreams for Tim and me. It was his mission to train us for the big leagues, and with enough practice and a touch of luck, he thought maybe we could get there someday. In the meantime, he was determined to coach us as hard as he could.

I didn't just train for baseball in my stepdad's house. He also made sure that I knew how to fix and maintain a home. He was like Geppetto. He could create anything with his hands. His house was built in the 1920s, and he replaced all the moldings with exquisite, handcrafted elements. He rebuilt that house from the ground up. Every single piece of wood was sanded, finished, and coated in polyurethane to a beautiful standard. I would tag along for these adventures in craftmanship, and he would allow me to hand him his tools one by one. We did everything from laying concrete to woodworking to repairing appliances. If he noticed that anything had broken, he would fix it. He would take apart the smallest components, whether they were from a vacuum, a TV, or a hot water heater, and he would figure them out. His favorite quote was, "It's not magic." He showed me that there is no problem too complex to solve. If you take your time to understand the underlying mechanism, you can accomplish anything.

As much as my stepfather showed me how to be a man, my mother taught me the importance of being a gentleman. My mom is sweet, creative, and empathic. Anytime I do something kind or thoughtful, you can thank her for that. She showered me with unconditional love, and she taught me to have compassion for those less fortunate than me.

My mom has always been gifted artistically. I will never forget the time that my second-grade teacher gave us the seemingly impossible task of sculpting a bust of Albert Einstein. I felt lost. I didn't know what to do, so I brought the assignment home and asked my mom to help me. She dropped what she was doing and took me to get some clay and sculpting tools. I don't know how she did it, but she created a perfect likeness of Einstein out of the clay. It looked just like him, from the nose to the hair to the funny expression on his face. She had an eye for artwork, and it was breathtaking how good she was when she put her heart and soul into a project.

When I was growing up, my mom liked to cook, clean, and make everything look tidy. She took pride in making our house feel warm and comforting. She also loved to take me exploring with her. She grew up in the Stapleton neighborhood of Staten Island. It's a rough area now, but when she was young, she used to go on fun adventures with her girlfriends. Sometimes she would tell me about the times that she would sneak out of her bedroom window and shimmy down one of the trees in her yard so she could hang out with her school friends at night. Then she would drive us to her old house and show me the trees she used to climb and the places where she and her friends liked to spend their time.

She would often bring me to Silver Lake Park or take me on adventures in the woods where she would reminisce about making huts, forts, and treehouses as a girl. Sometimes we would sneak into places where we weren't supposed to be, like the old Army Fort. Other times, we would stand on the waterfront and look for the perfect flat rock to skip out on the bay. I was an outdoorsy kid, and I connected with my mom over our shared love of nature. We could honestly have an awesome time with nothing more than a big stick and a couple of rocks.

One of our favorite spots to visit was a place called Horrmann's Hill. We would hike up the hill, and I remember the beautiful view that greeted us when we reached the top. Of course, Horrmann's Hill is no more than one hundred feet tall, and from an adult perspective it looks small and eroded. Still, I am grateful to my mother for making that hilltop seem as impressive as climbing Mount Everest. She made me feel like I was on top of the world, towering over Staten Island and proudly surveying the land below.

While my mom was beginning her new life with my stepfather Gene, my dad was dating a woman named Debbie, who would become my stepmother. Debbie was a true light in my life, and she adored me as if I were her own son. Love poured out of her eyes every time she looked at me. I used to call her my momma with the black hair. She loved me with so much intensity. She was passionate, to say the least, and she adored kids more than anything. My stepmother always believed in me and told me I could accomplish anything I set my mind to. So much of my confidence comes from the shower of genuine compliments she would bestow on me and the glimmer in her eye when she would talk about me to others.

My father and stepmother taught me the power and importance of family. When I was about three and a half years old, they brought my little brother, Sean, into the world. Sean and I were raised to love each other unconditionally, and to this day we are best friends. My stepmother would tell me, "It's you and him against the world. Remember, you are brothers, not half-brothers. You're my son just as much as he is."

My stepmother made sure that the two of us were inseparable, and as soon as he could walk, Sean started following me everywhere. He was like my shadow. I couldn't breathe without him popping out of the woodwork, wanting to play. As we got older, we would wrestle and fight, and sometimes we would come to blows. We would curse each other out, swing at each other, and then five minutes later, we would be hugging each other and laughing. We were both stubborn bastards with everyone else we knew, but when it came to each other, we were more likely to say, "Sorry, bro," and make up. We always had an amazing bond.

My father had a house with a pool and a beautiful backyard right next to the train station. As a child, I would climb onto the fence near the train trestle to pluck honeysuckle flowers and eat the nectar inside. They were delicious, and I would eat hundreds of them until I got a stomachache. I was a curious kid, and I took a special interest in observing my father. I remember thinking that I wanted to be just like him. One day as I watched him paint the house, I got an idea. The next morning, I grabbed a paint brush and some maple syrup, and I covered the entire wooden dining room table with a fine finish of sticky maple sweetness. I was so proud of my work that I woke my father and stepmother to show them what a great job I had done. To my dismay, they weren't as happy as I was expecting they would be, but now my dad and I laugh about it. It's become one of our favorite memories from my childhood.

I was a good kid growing up, but definitely a handful. I used to love playing hide-and-seek, and I was brilliant at it. Most of the time, the seekers could never find me. I remember the day I found the perfect hiding spot under the kitchen sink. I removed all the products from the cabinet under the sink, shimmied into the spot behind the pipes, pulled the bottles and boxes back into place, and closed the cabinet doors. I could hear my dad and stepmother searching, but neither of them found me. As I lay there, curled up in that dark, secure spot under the sink, I started getting sleepy. Before I knew it, I had dozed off. I awoke four hours later to my parents hysterically searching for me. They had looked everywhere, even under the kitchen sink, but my hiding place was so good that they couldn't see me. They feared that I might have hidden outside and then been nabbed by a kidnapper. They'd even called the cops. Eventually, I crawled out from under the sink, rubbing the sleep from my eyes like nothing had happened, thinking how slick my hiding spot had been. Little did I know I almost gave my parents a heart attack. My four-hour nap had turned into the longest four hours of their lives.

Experiences like this taught me early on that I could beat the adults at their own games. My stepmother would tell me that if I didn't clean my room, I couldn't go out and play. She explained that she would sit and watch me until I tidied, made my bed, and put away my toys. I thought to myself, two can play this came. Being the smartass I was, I told her, "Well, if I can't go out, then you can't go out, because you have to watch me." She got so mad that she became red in the face. She stomped off to the porch outside, just to show me that she could do whatever she wanted. Deep down, though, I think she knew that I had trapped her in a stalemate.

Another time, she told me that if I didn't pick up my toys, she would put them all in bags and give them to "The Man." I looked her straight in the eye and told her, "I'm not cleaning my room, so you can give them to the man if you want." True to her word, she bagged up my toys. She didn't give them away, but instead hid them in the garage. I wasn't expecting her to call my bluff, and I pouted around the house for most of the day. We took a walk later that afternoon, and along the way, we saw an older man strolling in our direction. He greeted us as he approached. My stepmother said hello, and then told me, "Say hi to the nice man." I crossed my arms, shook my head, and refused to greet him. Instead, I wordlessly stared him down. My stepmother looked at me aghast. She asked me, "Kevin, what on earth is the matter with you?" I looked at her, then I turned my gaze to the man. I pointed my finger at him while giving him the most stone-cold glare I could muster. I said, "Are you the man?" He was confused, but he humored me. He smiled, "Sure, kid, I'm the man." I took a deep breath and bellowed, "Are you the man who stole my toys?!" My stepmother must have finally understood my train of reasoning because she started laughing and then explained to this stranger what had happened. He chuckled and shook his head, "No, son, I didn't steal your toys." I was upset with both of them, of course, but in response to my glares, they gave me amused looks of respect. Here I was, all of four years old, mustering up the courage to confront this stranger about stealing my toys, when they were really in the garage the whole time.

I was a precocious child, and I wanted to take part in all the things that the grownups got to do. I loved getting dressed up in a suit, going to parties, and eating fancy food. I was well behaved at social events and always hung out with the adults and my older cousins. I loved observing my family members and figuring out everything that was going down. I was always a little too curious for my own good.

As a kid, I was fascinated with finding out how things worked. One time, I snuck into my dad's Jeep and tried to get it to start. Luckily for me and everyone, I didn't have the keys; however, in my efforts to drive the car, I pulled the emergency brake. Our driveway was on a slant, and with the wheels now free to turn, the Jeep rolled into the middle of the street and hit a parked car. My father had the keys with him at his bar where he worked, so the truck just sat there blocking traffic for several hours until my dad got home.

Another time, I remember wanting to go play with a little blonde neighbor girl who lived on the corner. That day, I decided to pick her up in my red, electric-powered toy Jeep and take her for a joy ride. I got in the car with my girl and started driving up the block. My stepmother had just gotten out of the shower, but she must have looked out the window and noticed me going farther than I was supposed to. She opened the front door dressed only in a towel and yelled at me to turn around. I looked back at her with a grin on my face, put my arm around my girl, and clicked into high gear. My stepmother ran out of the house, barefoot and wrapped in her towel, and tried in vain to catch me. I crossed a major boulevard, drove into town, and parked right next to my dad's real-life Jeep at his bar.

As far back as I can remember, I lived two separate realities in two separate households, and they rarely coalesced with each other. I lived one life with my mother and stepdad, and I lived a completely different life with my father and stepmother. Despite all the negative stigma that often surrounds broken families, I think the good ultimately outweighed the bad. After all, I got to celebrate two birthdays and two Christmases every year.

When I was at my father's house on the weekends, my little brother Sean treated me like I was Hercules. I was a god to him, and as far as he was concerned, I could do no wrong. I loved seeing myself through Sean's eyes. During the rest of the week, I lived with my mom, my stepfather, and my stepbrothers, and my dynamic in their family was quite different. In my relationship with Tim, I often felt like I had no power at all. When we would tussle, our playfighting would frequently become unsafe. When we weren't wrestling, he would call me names and remind me that I was weaker than him. Sometimes, I would touch his head, and he would punch me square in the face. He was understandably protective of his scalp, and if you touched him anywhere near his injury, he would just snap. Of course, he had no problem punching or slapping anyone else unprovoked, and most of the time that person was me.

It's important to understand that children lack the number and diversity of experiences that we adults possess, so events that we might consider trivial can be profoundly painful to a child. Nowadays, if someone told me "you're worthless," or "nobody loves you," I could easily tell them to get lost and go on with my day. I have amassed enough life experiences to know that I am a worthwhile person—God loves me, and plenty of amazing people think that I'm pretty great, as well. However, when I was a child with few external references and a fragile self-concept, insults were extremely damaging.

I now know that as much as he bullied me, Tim loved me to death and still loves me to this day. At the time, he didn't realize how much his verbal and physical attacks were traumatizing me. He often stood up for me when I was being bullied by other kids. He would tell any would-be attackers, "That's my brother—don't you dare touch him," and he would beat up anybody who tried to put their hands on me. This didn't make me feel particularly safe, however. His way of expressing love was sometimes like a crushing weight, slowly pressing me into the identity of a loser and a loner who was too weak to fight back against the taunts of bullies. Tim made me acutely aware of how much I craved the recognition of my peers. What I didn't yet realize was how far I would go to get their approval and respect.

# CHAPTER 3

W̲e all have pivotal experiences in childhood, moments that create a clear distinction between *before* and *after*. We look back and realize how much that single event changed our lives. I remember one such day when I was in third grade. Tim and I along with a few of our friends had arrived early to school that morning. We were all hanging out in front of the building, waiting for the day to start. We were bored and restless, and before long, my buddies started wrestling with each other. I was a bit of a shy kid, so as their fighting escalated, I took out a book from my bag and started reading. Pretty soon, I was engrossed in the pages. One of them yelled at me, "Hey Kevin, wanna play?" I shook my head. "Uh-uh, I'm reading." He didn't take no for an answer. "C'mon, Kevin! Play with us." I shook my head again and turned my back on them. As I was standing there, facing one of the large cement pillars that lined the front of the school building, Tim snuck up behind me and kicked me in the back. I went flying and ran nose first into the pillar. I smashed my head and saw stars dancing before my eyes. The right side of my face started to throb as a stream of blood flowed freely from my nose. I'd have a black eye for sure.

I threw my book and backpack to the ground and spun around in an absolute rage. I swung my fist out in front of me, and I tried to punch Tim with the biggest haymaker I could muster. Unfortunately for me, he was prepared. As my right hook crossed his face, he leaned back, and my knuckles only managed to graze his nose. The force of my swing twisted my body to the left. I was leaning forward with my arm contorted across my chest, completely defenseless. At the same moment, Tim threw a right hook with all his might, driving his fist squarely into my left eye. I fell to the ground, knocked out cold. When I woke up, I had two black eyes and a badly bruised ego. I made a pact with myself after that. Nobody was ever going to best me one-on-one like that again. If they wanted to take me down, they would have to bring backup.

I wasn't very popular as a kid. I was quiet and mostly introverted, and I could play by myself for hours. I would build forts in the woods and go on adventures with my toys. Video games were my best friend. I had buddies, don't get me wrong, but they were all quite popular, and I often felt like I was the low man on the totem pole. At times, my mother literally had to kick me out of the house to get me to go out and play. At least my friend group was known for going on fun adventures. Some days, we would build tree forts in the woods with discarded two-by-fours that we'd take from construction sites. Other days, we would borrow a baby pool and some hockey sticks, and we'd go rowing in the swampland, looking for wildlife. I can't tell you how many times we fell or threw each other into that disgusting swamp water.

Tim and I would often get ourselves into mischief. Luckily, many of the adults in the neighborhood knew us, and they would keep an eye on us to make sure we weren't in any real danger. There were only two hard and fast rules that we had to follow. The first rule was that when the streetlights went on, we had to come back to the house and check in. If it was a school night, more likely than not we had to stay in for the rest of the evening, unless we were at a friend's house. The second rule was that if my mother whistled, we'd better get home immediately. If we couldn't hear her whistle, it meant we were too far away, and we'd be in deep trouble when we got back. This wasn't too restricting for the simple fact that my mother is the world's loudest whistler. She would go to the top floor of our house and whistle as loud as she could. The echo would carry nearly ten blocks in each direction. There were only a few times in my life when we didn't hear her whistle, but each time we got our asses handed to us.

Two of my closest friends were twin boys—Benjamin and Kyle—who lived directly behind us. Even though they were twins, Kyle was much bigger than his brother. Benjamin was small like me, and that made us automatic friends. We would often team up against Kyle and Tim, who were much bigger than either of us. They would chase Benjamin and me through the neighborhood and throw rocks at us, try to trap us, and beat us with sticks if they could. It was all meant in good fun, but Tim and Kyle were rough, and when they would get too close, Benjamin would yell out, "Get away! Get away from me!" The two of us were much better at climbing, so we would shimmy up trees, scale rooftops, and clamber over fences—anything we could do to escape the fists of our brothers. My biggest skill was hiding. I was a slow runner, but I had the near mythical ability to dip into little clandestine spots and hide in plain sight. I would conceal myself in people's swimming pools, on top of roofs, even in people's cars—anywhere that I wouldn't be caught. I felt a kind of pride when Tim and Kyle would be yelling for me only a stone's throw away, and yet no matter how hard they searched, they couldn't find me.

One of our favorite games was manhunt. When we would play, the whole neighborhood within a three-block radius would get involved. We played full-out. Within the area of our game, there were no rules or boundaries. My parents would occasionally get involved. I remember one time, my stepdad Gene got a water gun and started chasing Tim, me, and three of our friends. We all ran to my house with my stepdad in hot pursuit. He nearly cornered us as we raced through the front door and dashed up the stairs. We barricaded ourselves in the upstairs bathroom and tried to hatch a plan. My stepdad pretended to be a big, bad ogre on the other side of the door, and when that didn't scare us into coming out, he got my mom and told her to distract us.

Meanwhile, we gathered some balloons from a bathroom drawer and filled them with water, preparing to defend ourselves. We soon realized that my stepdad had gone outside, grabbed an extension ladder, and was in the process of climbing up to the roof so he could sneak onto the balcony outside the bathroom window. As soon as we heard him reach the rooftop, the five of us grabbed our water balloons, opened the window, and fired our weapons up at my stepdad's face. Boom! Boom! Boom! The balloons hit him, and he lost his grip, tumbling off the roof. Thankfully, the balcony below caught his fall. He landed on his back with a thud and a groan, and he wheezed at us, "Okay, game's over!"

My stepdad was always a lot of fun. Every year, we would have a giant 4th of July party. He would buy rows of fireworks and line them up from one end of the street to the other. He would set them off and they would shoot into the sky. Pow! Pow! Pow! We kids got to light bottle rockets and Roman candles as we chased after each other with sparklers. It was awesome. Late in the evening, my stepdad would build a massive bonfire in the backyard. His job as a fireman had taught him how to handle flames. He would put on his firefighter uniform, and he'd build the fire bigger and bigger until it was roaring at least ten feet high. He was an authoritative figure, and he always made sure the situation was under control, but after an hour or so, someone from the neighborhood would inevitably call the police. A fire truck would pull up in front of the house, sirens blaring and lights flashing. My stepdad would walk calmly out of the front door, still wearing his uniform, and shake hands with the guys as they jumped down from the truck. He knew many of them from the job, so he would invite them to the backyard for hotdogs and watermelon. They would usually say, "No, we're just stopping by. It's a routine call. Just try to keep it down a bit, okay?" Then that would be that. It was the 90s, and the culture was much more live and let live back then.

My stepbrother Chris was seven years my senior, but he was more like another adult in our family than an older brother. Tim's accident had forced Chris to grow up fast. He would babysit Tim and me, and my dad relied on him to be like an honorary grownup. As soon as he was old enough, Chris started making plans to venture out on his own and start his life. He was focused and driven. That didn't stop my stepdad from teasing him. Gene made sure there was plenty of joking in my family.

I remember one time when Chris brought one of his first girlfriends home for dinner. I was about eight at the time, so Chris must have been fifteen. We were having steak, baked potatoes, and broccoli, and my stepdad managed to find a rock that looked just like a potato. He heated the rock in the microwave, and as we all sat down for our meal, he served the potato-rock to the new girl. It was a "welcome to the family" gesture. She tried to cut into it for several minutes while we all watched, trying not to giggle. Eventually, she picked it up and gingerly announced to the table, "Um, I don't think this is a potato." We burst out laughing while Chris turned beet red and his girlfriend tried to chuckle along.

Chris stayed with us for another few years, and then as soon as he turned seventeen, he moved down to Florida and started venturing out on his own. He began hustling at many different jobs. He became a firefighter, he owned a pool hall, he invested in real estate, and now he flips houses in Arizona. He's always known how to make money, and he's done very well for himself over the years. I've looked up to him my whole life, and I remember as a kid wanting to follow in his footsteps as a successful, independent businessman.

A huge pillar of my early life was baseball, and I had the best coach in the world. My stepdad was Mr. Baseball, and he coached Tim and me throughout our childhood and into our teenage years. He was a star player growing up, and he had a deep passion for teaching young kids the game. He put so much of his time and effort into making us the best baseball players we could be, and I couldn't have asked for a better mentor. When I was a little kid, I didn't even know how to run properly, let alone how to be an athlete. I pranced around using a weird skipping gate until I was about seven years old. That's when my stepfather showed me how to put one foot in front of the other and run like the rest of the boys.

My stepdad dedicated all of his spare time to practicing with us and showing us the fundamentals of the game. He would coach a two-hour practice session for all the kids in the league, and then he'd spend another few hours giving Tim and me extra attention and training. He built us a pitching screen, and in order to give us enough baseballs to practice with, he would roam the nearby swamps and woods behind the Little League field to hunt for lost balls. We had buckets and buckets of baseballs, and he would pitch to us every afternoon until the sun went down to help us refine our swing. We ate, slept, and dreamt baseball every day for years.

Thanks to my stepdad's coaching, I made the all-star team every year, and it was my one claim to fame as a child. No matter how good I got, however, Tim was always light years ahead of me. He was a natural, and he got better and better every day. He was the best kid in the league, and it was truly mesmerizing watching him play. When he got up to bat, it was like the clouds would part, the sun would shine, and the gods would smile down on him from above. If things had gone differently in our lives, I honestly believe he could have had a Major League career, and I think everybody in the family was betting on it.

I'm glad I had baseball in my life because it was one of the few things I was respected for. There were several kids that would bully me almost every day. It wasn't that I couldn't hold my own in a fight. I was growing into a strong kid who could look after myself. It was the mental and emotional aspect of the abuse that was particularly demoralizing. The difference between bullying and roughhousing became clear to me when I got to spend weekends with my brother Sean and my cousins. We would wrestle and fight all the time, but none of us felt bullied. There is often a fine line between the two, and it ultimately comes down to intent and perception. My cousins, my brother, and I would beat each other black and blue, but we didn't mean anything by it, and we never felt it as mistreatment.

At the time, I was heading into middle school. My father had recently split up with my stepmother Debbie, and she had moved with Sean to the Poconos. My father is one of eleven kids, and two of his brothers lived nearby in rural Pennsylvania, so every weekend, he would drive me up to spend time with my stepmom, my brother, and my cousins.

Those car rides with my dad were some of my favorite times. We would cruise along the road with the windows cranked down as my dad blasted "Gettin' Jiggy With It" and rapped along to Will Smith. I remember looking at him with quiet reverence as he nodded his head to the music, thinking that he was pretty cool for a forty-year-old. As easygoing as my dad was, he was a stickler for car safety. He insisted that we always wear our seatbelts, and he made up a game that he would play with me and my brother to make sure that we didn't forget. The rules were that anytime we got in the car, if we noticed that one of us had forgotten our seatbelt by the time the engine had started, we had his permission to wrestle that person and punch them in the chest. That included allowing us kids to wrestle and punch him, which of course was the most fun. I still remember bouncing in my seat, excited for a road trip, when — bam! — my little brother's fist would knock the wind out of my chest. I would wheeze, buckle my seatbelt, give my brother a shove, and then the three of us would laugh together at our game.

When my cousins and I got together, things would get crazy. We were all fighters, and we would wrestle, box, and literally beat the crap out of each other all weekend long. It got to the point that my younger cousin Pat wasn't allowed to hang out with us anymore because he would always come home with a black eye. I liked to fight my older cousin Jimmy, who was twice my size and was like a big brother to me. We would have pillow fights, but instead of pillows, we would fill the pillowcases with plastic toys in order to pack more of a wallop. We were always whaling on one another, but it really toughened us up. My little brother Sean often got it the worst, but he was a maniac, and he never gave up. We used to beat him bloody and swollen, but he would just keep fighting back. He was a glutton for punishment. Sean was frequently the instigator of our brawls. We had bunk beds in our room, and I remember lying on the bottom bunk when all of a sudden, Sean would drop down from above and tackle me. We would roll around on the bed like it was a wrestling mat, and I would pin him down until he gave up, though not before he got in a few good punches and kicks.

Sean loved me and my cousin Jimmy, and he would hang around us like he was our shadow. Jimmy and I would smoke whenever Debbie was out running errands, and as stealthy as we tried to be about it, Sean saw what we were up to. One day when we were wrestling with Sean, we got too rough, and he started crying and threatened to tell on us. We didn't want him ratting us out, so we stripped him naked and locked him outside in the freezing cold winter until he stopped making a fuss. When we let him back in the house, he went crazy, kicking and punching us. He gave us back every ounce of what we dished out to him. In retrospect, some of the stuff we did to Sean was pretty messed up, but he thanked us later, because it helped him become the strong guy that he is today.

Meanwhile, in my Staten Island middle school, all my friends had started kissing girls, and some were fooling around and getting to second or third base. This made me feel even more insecure; I was terrified to kiss a girl, let alone touch her more intimately. I remember in fifth grade, one of the girls in my class had a crush on me. She would run after me on the playground and chase me up trees. I would hide from her after class because I was terrified of her advances. The other kids laughed at me and called me a "prude." By now, my friend group had graduated from games of tag to playing spin the bottle, but whenever the bottle pointed to me, I was met with giggles or repulsion. The girl would inevitably say something like, "Eww, I'm not kissing that kid." I began to despair that no girl would ever like me enough to want to kiss me, and I questioned what any girl would find attractive in me, anyway.

In sixth and seventh grade, I was bullied on a weekly basis, and some weeks, the attacks came every day. As the taunting and teasing grew more constant, I started to accept it as my lot in life. There were even a few girls who would pick on me. One girl pushed her desk at me and then started swinging her fists in my face. It wasn't that I couldn't physically defend myself. After all, I was able to hold my own against my cousin Jimmy, who was bigger than any of these middle school kids. However, I was terrified of beating up my tormentors because I didn't know if my parents would punish me for getting into a fight. I had developed a kind of learned helplessness, and I was keeping myself trapped in the self-definition of victimhood. I was a submissive kid, and I accepted whatever insults or physical blows the other kids hurled at me. I had come to believe that this was all I deserved. I did well in school, and I was enrolled in mostly honors classes; however, I was also a huge nerd, and academic achievement is rarely a path to popularity. I had braces, buck teeth, and acne, and I was still sporting the same flattop haircut that had been out of date when I'd begged my mom to let me get it back in the third grade. In reality, I was just going through an awkward phase, but at the time, it felt like I was doomed to a life of torment and ridicule.

As I approached the end of eighth grade, I knew I would have to make some major changes in my life if I wanted the bullying to stop. I needed to reinvent myself and somehow transform into one of the cool kids. I didn't have a clear plan for how to do that, but if I played my cards right, the summer before high school might give me the perfect opportunity.

I started hanging out more often with my cousin Jimmy. He was the toughest, coolest kid I knew, and girls absolutely loved him. If I emulated him, I could become the person I'd always wanted to be. I would have lots of friends and finally get noticed by the pretty girls who had either ignored me or laughed at me all these years.

In addition to Jimmy, I also hung out with Tim that summer. My stepbrother was very popular, and I figured that if I just started doing whatever he did, I would become well-liked. Tim had begun smoking cigarettes, and I mirrored him and picked up the habit, as well. We had our own little club house in the woods, and we'd often skip school and go there to smoke cigarettes that we stole from our parents. We felt very grown up. Then one day, Tim brought something new for us to smoke. It was pot. He lit up, took a hit, and handed me the joint. I was determined to be cool, and I was a curious kid. I wanted to see what all the fuss was about. I inhaled the strange-smelling smoke and tried to hold it in like I'd watched Tim do, but I immediately coughed it back up. I fought to suppress a coughing spell, and after a minute, I brought the joint back up to my lips and took another hit. I felt an odd feeling of peace come over me. Although I didn't understand it at the time, I was trying to fill some kind of void deep within me. It had been growing and festering inside for many years. I didn't know why I felt so empty and alone, but maybe, just maybe, pot would help me feel more whole.

Nearly every day, Tim and I would go out to our club house, smoke a joint between us, and get high as a kite. Back then, a few hits would be enough to keep us stoned all morning. It was my first experience of being a rebel and not doing what I was supposed to do, and I was enthralled by the forbidden nature of it all. I started smoking pot on the weekends and even at night during the week. I was terrified that my parents would realize that I was stoned so much of the time, so I stashed Visine and cologne outside of the house to mask my inebriation. Of course, I was a good kid, so my parents wouldn't have fathomed that I was smoking, but I was paranoid. I loved getting high. For the first time that I could remember, I was feeling comfortable in my own skin. I was less uptight, and I found it easier to be silly and playful. Tim and I would laugh for hours at stupid shit until our stomachs hurt. Then we would run over to Taco Bell and eat ourselves into a coma. We had a tradition every Friday night. We would all get dressed up, roll a dime in one joint, and smoke the fattest doobie while walking through Miller Field. By the time we got to the other side, we were stoned out of our minds. There was a movie theater across the field, and we would often go watch a movie when we were done with our joint. It didn't matter too much what we saw—anything was funny when we were that high. We rarely paid for our tickets. We had friends that worked in the theater, and they would let us in the back door.

About halfway through that summer, my teenage life changed forever. It started when I finally got my braces off and realized that I had a dazzling smile underneath those metal tracks that had all but destroyed my confidence. At around the same time, my face started to clear up from my persistent acne. Then my cousin Jimmy took pity on me and gave me a new haircut. I went from a spiky flattop to a crisp, faded Caesar. Jimmy also gave me his dragon medallion on a silver chain to wear around my neck, and within the space of a week, I was a completely different person. When I looked in the mirror, I saw no trace of the little kid that had caused the girls to giggle with pity or disgust. Now all I saw was a confident young man with his shoulders held back, wearing a cocky smile that he wasn't afraid to flash at anyone. I was ready to become the cool kid that everyone wanted at their party, the guy that all the girls wanted to be with.

The next weekend, Tim and I took our usual stoned path across Miller Field and snuck into the movie theater courtesy of our buddies to watch whatever film was hot that week. I don't recall what we saw, but I remember the rest of the night like it was yesterday. We all met up behind the theater after the movie was over, and just like every other evening, there was a group of girls who hung out with us. Yet unlike all those other times, I distinctly remember that the girls were staring at me as if they were noticing someone for the first time. They actually appeared to see me—I wasn't just a background player or a nonliving entity like I'd been before. One girl named Nora was giving me a particularly suggestive eyeing down. She was smiling at me and flirting with me hard. This was completely foreign to me, and I had no idea how to act. One of my asshole friends caught on to what was happening and blurted out in a teasing manner, "He's a prude!" All the girls started giggling, and I got quite embarrassed. My face turned beet red. The girls teased me and asked me if it was true that I had never kissed a girl before. I shook my head no, completely humiliated.

I thought to myself, this girl is never going to kiss me now that she knows. Yet despite all this, Nora asked me to follow her behind the dumpster that was in back of the movie theater. As I walked after her in a daze, I vaguely remember thinking that this wasn't how I'd pictured my first kiss, but I quickly put that thought out of my head. I was so eager to do it that I didn't care how it happened. Thankfully, I recalled the kissing technique that some of my friends had shared with me. Looking back, it makes me laugh because it was clearly the fantasy of inexperienced boys. Yet at the time, I clung onto those instructions for dear life: I closed my eyes, made lip contact, and twirled my tongue clockwise to massage her tongue. We must have kissed for only thirty seconds, but it felt like a lifetime. I'd finally done it! I didn't get to enjoy the moment very much because I was too focused on not screwing it up. The last thing I wanted was to be branded a bad kisser. When we unlocked our lips, I saw a twinkle in her eye that I'd never seen from a woman in my life. She liked me, and she'd actually enjoyed the kiss. I felt as though an immense weight had been lifted from my shoulders. I had taken the first real steps toward becoming the man I'd always wanted to be.

I learned a priceless lesson that night. The way you feel about yourself and carry yourself profoundly affects how other people perceive you. I learned that confidence is an essential element of self-perception, and so long as you are bold and courageous, you can accomplish anything. Even if I were trembling in my boots, from that point on, I would try to appear confident because it's more powerful than looking insecure or scared. Sometimes you just gotta fake it until you make it. After that night, I realized I wasn't a freak or an outsider, but merely a kid who hadn't known how to believe in himself before. This was all the validation I needed to transform myself into the legend I had dreamed of becoming in high school.

Fear is usually scarier than actual events. When we are afraid, we play the worst possible scenarios in our minds, and 95% of the time, things turn out not to be as bad as we've imagined. That night, I realized that by living in my head, operating from a constant state of fear, and worrying what everybody thought about me, I had been holding myself back for years. Maybe to some people, kissing a girl might seem like a tiny milestone. I mean, everybody does it eventually, right? But for me, it was a big learning curve. I went into high school that fall with a fearless attitude. I had built a brand-new persona, and I walked with a new kind of strut. I was a guy who had kissed a girl, who smoked weed, and who wasn't afraid to beat up any kid who gave him shit. I was the same person, and yet I was completely different. I saw my change in self-perception reflected in the eyes of my classmates. As I looked around, I realized that there was a whole new world here, just waiting for me to own it.

# CHAPTER 4

T he first morning of high school, I woke up two hours early, both excited and nervous to start the day. I got dressed in my favorite outfit, sat in front of my bedroom mirror, and tried to psych myself up enough to leave the house. I would need all the confidence I could get. A few weeks before, my cousins and I had hit the mall and picked out some new, trendy clothes so I wouldn't embarrass myself on the first day. I normally shopped at K-Mart or Old Navy, whatever was the cheapest, but I knew that if I wanted to get the respect I craved, I would need to dress the part. I was about to start a new chapter of my life. I wasn't exactly sure what the new me was going to look like, but I welcomed the change.

I loaded my Walkman with a mixtape CD I'd made, gave my appearance one final check in the mirror, and set out for school. My high school was a twenty-minute walk from my house. As I drew near to the building complex, I saw thousands of kids outside, hanging around and waiting for school to start. There were nearly four thousand kids at this school, many more than at my middle school. I was nervous and unsure how this was going to play out, but I kept walking, getting closer and closer to the front gate. As I approached, I began to notice clear distinctions between the social groups. There were the rockers, who dressed grungy and gothic and hung out around a tree on the outskirts of the property. Then there were the jocks in their football jerseys who crowded together near the front of the building and called to each other so loudly that their voices could be heard across the school yard. Many of the seniors were standing around in the parking lot, leaning on their cars and catching up with one another after the final summer break of high school. At last, I reached the front gate that separated the school grounds from the roadside. As I was about to pass through, I saw a row of freshmen who stood there anxiously, heads down, unsure if they should go in or not. There was a clear social hierarchy in this new environment. I didn't yet know where I fit in, but I knew one thing—I was going to make a name for myself in this place. I was determined not to repeat the mistakes I had made in middle school. I strode through the gate, leaving the nervous freshmen behind me, and walked up to the school building with my head held high.

My first day of high school went better than I could have ever imagined. I had placed as a freshman honors student, but the kids who'd bullied me in middle school had not, so they weren't in any of my classes. I did recognize some kids from my old school, but they didn't give me grief. In fact, when I arrived at my first class, a few girls that I knew from the previous year did a double take as I walked through the door. They seemed to be in shock that I was the same guy they had known in middle school. As their gaze lingered on me, I realized that they were checking me out. I walked over to an open desk and looked around. I couldn't believe my luck that there were so many beautiful girls in my class, and for the first time, they seemed to be attracted to me as well.

High school was very cliquey. Within the first few days, you had to establish who your friends were and what role you were going to play. I'd always had a comedic personality, but when I was in middle school, I'd never let that part of me shine through. Now that I was a freshman, I was determined to change all that. After all, I was a guy who smoked weed and didn't take shit from anybody. I broke out of my shell and established a new reputation. I was no longer the scapegoat that was easy to pick on. Now, I was the kid who had a one-liner in response to everything the teacher said, the guy who sat at the back of the room and cracked jokes with the cool kids. I became a class clown.

On that first day of high school, I met my best friend, Daniel. He was a handsome Italian kid from the South Shore with a big nose and a real sense of style. He was very metrosexual. Daniel was the type of guy who took forty-five minutes to do his hair and would freak out if you even joked about touching it. His family had a lot of money, and he wasn't afraid to show it off. He wore fancy, name brand clothes, and his outfit on any given day cost more than my entire wardrobe. Daniel wasn't anything like what I was used to. He was the funniest, coolest kid I'd ever met. I couldn't believe my luck when I found out that he also played baseball and was going to be on the team with me. Finally, I would have one of the most popular kids at school in my corner.

Along with Daniel, I met another kid, Dean, who was a great student and super smart. He was also trying out for the baseball team. He was a handsome if somewhat stocky guy who looked like he'd gone through puberty about three times, what with his deep voice and his broad chest that was covered with a werewolf-like amount of hair. The three of us were complete opposites in terms of personalities and looks, but despite our differences, we developed a close friendship. We quickly became the talk of our freshman class. It seemed like every girl we met had a crush on at least one of us.

At the end of that first day, I walked home on cloud nine. Within a matter of hours, I had made friends with two of the coolest guys in my grade, and I'd caught the eye of at least a few popular girls. This was a complete 180 from what I was used to, and I was absolutely pumped to see how this whole high school thing would play out. I arrived home, went up to my room, and fell back onto my bed with the biggest smile on my face. For the first time ever, I couldn't wait to get back to school. I barely slept a wink that night. I tossed and turned until morning, filled with adrenaline and anticipation for what the next day would bring.

Reality kicked in when I arrived at school the following morning. Some of my classmates were whispering stories about Freshman Friday, which was coming up at the end of that first week. Freshman Friday was a day when all the upperclassmen would beat up, bully, and rob the incoming freshman to teach them their place on the totem pole. It was a stupid tradition, but it had been going on for who knows how long, and it wasn't about to stop for my class.

I've never really understood bullying. What can someone possibly get out of abusing a person who is weaker than them? If you think that taking someone down a peg will magically make your life better, I'm here to tell you that you're mistaken. I know the ramifications of what bullying did to me, and it didn't elevate the lives of anyone who mistreated me. Nowadays, I've come to feel grateful for all the times I got beat up because it gave me empathy for anybody that was different than me or who didn't know how to fight back. Don't get me wrong, I was always a ball breaker, and I used to tease my friends all the time. However, they stuck up for themselves and returned whatever shit I gave them as fast as I could dish it out. We loved to roughhouse, and we would always joke with each other in a light-hearted way. I think it's important to make a clear distinction between play-fighting and bullying because kids need to be able to play in the dirt, skin their knees, and tussle with each other. The difference was that our actions weren't malicious or intended to cause each other harm.

As soon as I heard about Freshman Friday, I was nervous that some senior jerk was going to beat me up and push me back into the same old pattern of being picked on and harassed. I made up my mind that I was not going to let that happen again. I was sure I could fight off most of the senior guys if it came down to it, but I was nervous to do it on school property for fear of getting suspended. I also knew that having a perfect disciplinary record wasn't going to mean shit if people thought I was a coward. I would just get labeled as the school scapegoat again. It was time to make a decision and take a stand. I told myself that if anyone put their hands on me, I would make sure they'd be too afraid to lay hands on me again.

Friday finally arrived, and one by one, the seniors and some of the juniors started picking off the weakest freshman kids. They made a big game of it. They would scan the crowd, choose a victim, and then trip them, give them a wedgie, steal their money, or inflict on them any other number of humiliations. Once they'd had their fun, they would run off, laughing and high fiving each other. I got through nearly the whole day without someone pushing me around. Around seventh period, I was walking over to my next class when one of the seniors came up from behind and kicked one of my feet out from under me. I think he was trying to do a two-leg sweep to make me fall on my face. However, all he managed to do was make me trip and stumble forward. I don't know what changed in me, but all of a sudden, I snapped. Red clouded my vision and instinct took over. I threw down my backpack and whipped around to face my attacker with an enraged glint in my eye. I must have looked crazy. I yelled, "TOUCH ME AGAIN AND I'LL BREAK YOUR FUCKING NOSE!" The guy who had tried to trip me was a kid not much bigger than I was. He was standing next to his friend—an accomplice, no doubt—and both boys were stopped dead in their tracks, mouths slightly agape, stunned into silence. It was clear that he was not expecting me to react the way that I did. He actually looked frightened. After a moment, he apologized and said, "Hey man, it was a joke. I'm sorry." Then he turned and walked away with his friend following behind him.

Now it was my turn to be at a loss for words. For the first time in my life, I had not only fought off a bullying attack, but I had managed to intimidate the other guy. This was one of the most empowering moments of my young life. I'd stuck up for myself, and it had actually worked! I realized that all I had to do was fight back hard enough, and no one would get the better of me. I took on a new self-definition that day. I was no longer a guy who was afraid of someone bigger and stronger than me grinding me under their heel. I was no longer the victim of other people's abuse. The new Kevin was a tough kid who always stuck up for himself, who never backed down from a fight, and who didn't let anyone get the jump on him.

The next few weeks of high school passed without incident. I was doing well in my classes and meeting lots of amazing new friends. Without quite knowing how it had happened, I had become one of the popular kids in my grade. One of the people who was instrumental in my newfound reputation was a girl named Katie. She quickly became a close friend of mine. Katie was super sweet to me, but she could be a real bitch if she didn't like you. She was good friends with just about anyone who mattered in high school, and everyone knew her. She was lots of fun to be around and was always down for whatever crazy new adventure we concocted. I first connected with her in gym class. We used to smoke cigarettes and joints around the track instead of doing exercise. It was a bonding experience. Katie introduced me to some really cool people that I would never have had the guts to make friends with on my own. She was the glue that brought many people together.

In freshman year, my friends and I all had band class together. It was an extremely rowdy room, and the teacher had no control over us. We would laugh and joke around all class long. When things got quiet, Daniel would reach over and smack one of the girls on the ass. I don't know if the girls liked it or not, but I could tell that they loved him. Some friends and I used to hang out in the back where there were soundproof booths. Sometimes I would bring little bottles of chocolate liqueur with me to class and invite a couple of the girls to drink them with me back in the sound booths. Other times, we would smoke cigarettes and even sneak a few hits from a joint. We were little rebels, and we had so much fun in that class.

One of my favorite periods in freshman year was math. I didn't care much about the subject matter, although I always managed to get good grades. What made the class amazing was the disproportionate number of incredibly hot girls. I was in my happy place. It was right after lunch, so I usually went out to smoke pot before class began. Math was much better stoned.

Math was also the class where I met Lily, the girl who would become my first high school sweetheart. We used to flirt hard with each other. I thought she was the cutest, sweetest, smartest girl I'd ever met, and I always made sure to sit right behind her so we could pass notes. Well, at the time I was passing notes with about five different girls on any given day, but Lily was my main focus. I was a stoner and I hated doing homework, so I would usually get some of these girls to do my homework for me. I didn't see any point in trying to deceive the teachers about what I was doing. I would turn in homework that was clearly written in a girl's flowery handwriting. The math teacher disliked me. She thought I was a distraction, and she suspected I was cheating on my tests. The truth was, I was too lazy to cheat. Regardless of how little I paid attention, I always managed to get decent grades. I was a smart kid. I never studied for a single test in high school, and I never did any homework, but I still got an 80 average. I had goofing off and breezing through school down to a science. Looking back at that time, I really wish I had applied myself. There's no limit to what I could have accomplished if I had taken school seriously. At the same time, I would have missed out on so many pivotal life experiences, and I wouldn't be half the man I am today. I don't regret the way things ultimately turned out, but I certainly could have made far wiser decisions along the way.

I smoked a ton of weed in high school. Nowadays, I'm neither for it nor against it because there are so many medicinal uses for CBD oil as well as THC. What I can say undeniably is that no child or teenager should ever smoke weed. It destroys your motivation to accomplish anything in your life. You become lazy, and soon you are content with just getting by. Children should never be exposed to a substance that robs them of their ambition. Kids should be shooting for the stars and striving every day to accomplish their goals. As for me, my daily goals had been reduced to making sure I got high. I would usually smoke on my way to school, and if I didn't have anything that morning, I would meet someone outside. Then I would smoke during lunch and PE, and I usually schemed a way to be marked present so I could cut a class or two. I would hang out with a few friends of mine at the nearby bowling alley or in the woods behind the school, and we would have little smoking sessions there. Finally, I would smoke on my twenty-minute walk back home. Pretty soon, my entire life revolved around getting high with my friends.

The more I smoked, the more expensive my habit became. This quickly grew to be a problem because my allowance was $20 a week, and I couldn't get a job. Not only was I only fourteen, but I also played baseball practically every day after school, come rain or shine. That all changed when I met a guy at school who was buying ounces of weed and would sell me quarters. He would bag up twenty dimes for me at $10 a pop and charge me $110, which meant that if I sold just a little over half of my stash, I could smoke the rest for free. I didn't start selling weed to make money. At first, it was just a means for me to support my habit and maintain my newfound social life. Within a few months, however, it turned into a thriving business. Every day, I was earning $50 to $70 and smoking for free. It was the early 2000s, and that was a lot more money than I'd ever made. I was starting to feel like a big shot. Not only was I a popular kid in my freshman class, now I was making a name for myself among the upperclassmen. For a kid who'd been bullied and ignored throughout middle school, this sudden recognition and notoriety became highly addictive, and I sought it out every chance I could get.

Each day, I would meet up with my friends in the woods behind the school. I would sell them pot and then we would all smoke together. Making money and smoking weed were my two favorite activities back then, so those were some good times. The woods separated the high school from the police station, and in fact, our smoking spot was in full view of the station's back wall. We used logs to build lookout seats so we would be able to see if the police were coming. They knew we were up to something, and they would occasionally try to sneak up on us. A few people actually got arrested and brought to the high school delinquency office, but I was too quick and clever for that.

The woods turned out to be a great place to meet new friends. I met one of my favorite people in high school that way. Her name was Brooke, but I called her "gangsta." She was a short, eighty-pound lesbian who rocked a bandana and carried a knife on her waistband for everyone to see. She didn't care what anybody thought, and she would scare the biggest guys at school. She was a hippie at heart, and she loved smoking weed and doing acid. She was more of a lover than a fighter, but she was definitely someone you didn't want to mess with. It always amazed me how good she was at picking up women. Straight, gay, it didn't matter. She was certainly a little pimp, and I used to ask her how she did it. She would just laugh, shake her head, and say, "I love you, Parker." She rarely came to school. I think she would only go to class if she were tripping on LSD. Quite often, we would end up at her house, smoking in her bedroom or back yard. The only other time she regularly came to school was when we had gym together, and we would smoke around the track. Once in a while, I'd see her roaming the halls or walking right into the lunchroom regardless of what period it was.

The security at my high school was a joke. We smoked cigarettes everywhere, even though it was supposed to be prohibited. We smoked in the bathrooms, in the locker rooms, and in the school yard. We smoked out the windows or went outside the lunchroom. I would even smoke my one hitter pipe inside the lunchroom. I would take a hit of weed, blow it out, and then move to a different table. The lunchroom monitors would be trying to figure out where the smell was coming from, but I never got caught. Sometimes, my friends and I would leave in the middle of the day and walk to the store to get cigarettes and junk food. The school doors locked behind us when we left, but it was easy to get around that. When we got back, someone would usually open the door for us, or occasionally we would just jam the lock so we wouldn't get shut out. Even the school security guards were our friends. We would usually buy some extra food and drinks when we were out, and we'd give some to the guards for looking the other way. I was friendly with four of the main security officers, and they never reported me. I actually used to smoke weed with one of them.

I was feeling like a badass from all the respect I was receiving from the delinquents in high school. Then my brother Tim introduced me to some older kids in the neighborhood who didn't bother going to school at all. I would often cut class to hang out with them. Some weren't even kids anymore; they were just low-life drug addicts in their early twenties. There were usually ten or fifteen of us who would meet up at this old house with a wooden front porch where Tim's friend Keith lived. To get to Keith's house, you had to walk down a long alley behind another house, so it was the perfect place to stay away from the cops. Keith's mom would often sit with us and smoke our weed and pop our pills while we were all hanging out. Looking back at that house, it was no place for a fourteen-year-old kid to spend his afternoons. When I hung out there, however, I felt a sense of belonging and protection. I knew that these kids would have my back if I ever got into a fight. I grew up in a rough neighborhood where people got jumped, robbed, and stabbed every day. Being Tim's brother gave me all the street cred I needed to move freely without anyone giving me a hard time.

I took a liking to one kid in particular, a guy named Nico. He was my age and lived two blocks from my house. Nico was a funny kid with a big mouth, and he always had a wisecrack on the tip of his tongue. I'm grateful I made friends with him because I was green behind the ears and quite naive when it came to street life. I was always an observer growing up. I would watch how he interacted with the other people in the neighborhood. I learned on the streets that everyone wears a mask and has their own intentions. There was so much lying and scheming between friends that I never really knew where anyone's loyalty lay. I would see Nico tell one kid one thing and another kid something different. It was a game of leverage, and a constant struggle for control. I learned what it meant to keep my friends close and my enemies closer. I realized that even though my friends might help me out situationally, the only person that truly had my back was me.

I got into more and more mischief. I was hustling and making money. I started making a name for myself and getting attention from all the wrong people. Word got out in the school that I was making a lot of dough dealing pot, and that sparked jealousy. It put a huge target on my back, and everyone wanted a piece of me. Fortunately, I was sharp and clever, and I had inherited my father's gift for reading people. I was constantly being set up to be robbed or jumped, but I always managed to outsmart the plot and stay one step ahead. I got into many fights in high school, but I won every single time. One day during a fire drill, I was walking outside by myself. I was in a crappy mood, and I saw three kids ahead of me walking deliberately and obnoxiously slow. I didn't feel like waiting, so I squeezed by them, grazing one of the kids on the shoulder as I passed. I glanced back and apologized, "My bad." I recognized from what they were wearing that they were part of a gang called the Bloods. They were flagged up in their red colors, and many people were afraid of them. I could care less. I had my headphones on, trying to tune out the day. Before I knew what had hit me, one of the kids walked up behind me and rammed me with his shoulder, trying to knock me over. I spun around with my hands up, ready to fight. They didn't expect me to stand up to all three of them. We started getting into a heated argument, and just as we were about to start swinging at each other, the smallest guy in the group got in between us and made peace. I thought it was all over, so I proceeded to walk away and headed back into the school building. I climbed up the stairs to the second floor, still wearing my headphones. Out of nowhere, I was hit with a right hook on the side of my head, knocking my headphones off. In one swift motion, I spun around and clocked the kid who hit me, knocking him down. Meanwhile, the other two guys grabbed my backpack because they knew that was where I kept all my weed. They pulled my jacket over my head and wrestled me to the ground as all three kids stomped me out. I finally got my jacket off, and just then, I saw that one of the kids was about to kick me straight in my face. I swooped his leg with my hands, and he stumbled into one of his buddies. That gave me just enough time to get onto my feet and slam the other kid into the wall. When he hit the wall, I slugged him with a three-piece, knocking him out cold. I turned to the kid who was still holding my backpack, and I gave him the most vicious glare. As I stared him down, he proceeded to clutch my bag, turn around, and run down the hallway, looking back in fear. I followed in pursuit, and as I caught up with him, I hit him with the hardest right hook I had in me. He toppled backwards and landed with a thud on the linoleum. I bent down and ripped my backpack from his hands, and as I did, I looked up at the third kid. He didn't even try to fight. He abandoned his two friends and ran away.

After that incident, my reputation preceded me everywhere I went. People either feared me, respected me, or wanted to fight me to prove their mettle. Regardless of all the confrontations and fights I got into, I was never a bully. I always stuck up for the little guy, and I despised people who tried to take advantage of someone not willing to stick up for themselves.

Things got even better when baseball season started again, and Daniel, Dean, and I realized we had a gaggle of diehard female fans. A lot of them were girls from our classes. They came to every game and cheered us on. Having fans was another new experience for me, and as a bunch of freshman virgins, we ate it all up. I had gotten a lot of practice making out with random girls from my class, but I had never gone further than that. As freshman year drew to a close, I learned firsthand about the drama and emotions that come with dating and relationships.

That spring, I started going out on "dates," if you could call them that. They were usually a group of boys and girls who hung out on the weekend with the intention of making out. I remember one weekend in particular that taught me a valuable lesson on how not to date. That Friday night, I had planned a lovely evening for myself. I was going to hang out with four or five really cute girls, and one of them was a girl that I'd had my eye on for a while. We went to the movies, and I made sure to sit next to her. She was thick in all the right spots with a voluptuous body, tan olive skin, and a contagious smile. I could tell she thought I was hot, and all her friends were dropping hints to me for her because she was shy. We flirted back and forth until we got really comfortable, and then I swooped in and made my move. I started kissing her halfway through the movie, and we must have kissed for the rest of the film because the next thing I remember were the lights coming up as the end credits played. I decided that I really liked this girl, so I gave her my beeper number. Cell phones weren't a normal thing for teenagers to own back then. Only the rich kids and spoiled brats had cell phones freshman year, and I was neither. This girl was a bit of a princess, and clearly, she'd managed to talk her way into a little flip phone. We exchanged numbers, and we both left to go home. I went to sleep that night feeling like a million bucks.

Saturday night, I went out with an entirely different group of kids. My friend Katie had invited me and some of our honors classmates to hang out at a nearby park. Lily, my crush from math class, was going to be there, so I was excited, to say the least. This would be my first opportunity to spend time with her outside of school. Once we all arrived, we congregated near a large concrete pyramid structure at the edge of the park. We were all roughhousing and joking around. Most of us were smoking and having a few beers, but Lily was a good girl, and she didn't partake in anything. I liked that about her. She was smart, kind, and attractive. She had this ethereal, feminine beauty, and she mesmerized me when I looked at her. I think she liked me because I was a bit of a bad boy and a jock. I led the two of us a little bit away from the group, and I leaned over and kissed her. To my delight, she kissed me back, and we made out for the next couple hours. At the end of the night, I took her number and gave her mine, and then we parted ways. This night was even more incredible than the last. I was in utter bliss. All day Sunday, all I could think about was how lucky I was to have made out with not one but two beautiful girls.

My dreams weren't long lived, however. I returned to school on Monday morning to a rude awakening. Everything was cool until about midday when I saw Lily in the hall. She gave me the most evil glare I'd ever seen on her pretty face. If she could have shot lasers from her eyes and melted me where I stood, I'm sure she would have. I could tell there was a problem, but I didn't yet know what it was. Later that day, I learned that Lily and my date from Friday used to be good friends until they'd had a falling out. They had been trying to build bridges for a few months, but once they learned from their mutual friends that I had just two-timed both of them with each other, that was the end of their friendship. Now they hated each other, and I was officially an asshole player. They were fuming mad, and they both took their shots at me when I saw them. I was clueless. I had no idea what to do. The best strategy my fourteen-year-old brain could come up with was to choose the least mad of the two girls. That made Friday girl the winner. I cut ties with Lily, and math class was really awkward for the rest of the year.

As my first year of high school came to an end, I continued hanging out with many of my new friends, both my buddies from school and my friends who hung out at Keith's house. One friend in particular had a bachelor pad all to himself. He invited me to crash there when I needed a place to stay. He worked all afternoon and into the night, so he was rarely around. One evening, I came over to his place after going out with my girlfriend. Like usual, he wasn't there, so I made myself comfortable. I went into the bedroom, and that's when my eyes were drawn to the little safe on top of the dresser. I'd seen my friend grab a $10 or a $20 from there before when he'd ordered a pizza delivery. This night, I noticed that the door was unlocked. It sat temptingly ajar. I was a curious kid, so naturally I took a peek. I was shocked by what I saw. It wasn't the guns lying inside the safe that made my jaw drop, nor was it the bundles of $100 bills piled in neat stacks, although the money must have totaled over $100,000. No, it was something much worse and infinitely more enticing. There at the bottom of the safe was a brick of what I recognized to be cocaine. I gasped. Up until this point in my life, I had never tried anything stronger than weed. All I knew about cocaine was what I'd seen on TV. I was a stoner, not a coke head.

My mother used to call me "Curious George," after the little cartoon monkey who always got himself into mischief. Well, that night, curiosity got the better of me. I didn't pause to consider where this cocaine might have come from, or where it would be going. Obviously, my friend wasn't going to do all this himself. I didn't even stop to think about how many thousands of dollars this brick must have cost. I reached into the safe, picked up the brick, and brought it close to my nose. All of a sudden, my mouth went numb. I was getting a buzz from the cocaine without even snorting it. Something dark within me urged, "Go ahead, try it." I chipped off a little rock. Well, I thought it was a little rock. I didn't realize it was more than a fifty, but I didn't know any better back then. I crushed it up on the kitchen counter, and I cut it into two lines, just like I'd seen in the movies. I took a dollar bill out of my wallet, rolled it up, and snorted a line into each nostril, filling my nose with cocaine.

It was incredibly potent, even to the standard by which I would soon come to judge cocaine. With those two lines, I instantly fell in love with this new drug. I loved the seductive feeling of my whole face going numb and the ecstasy that followed, taking over my body and mind. The dopamine flooding my brain was like no other pleasure I had ever felt or even imagined. I didn't know it at the time, but this was the night I became an addict.

My thoughts felt like they were pinging back and forth like a pinball machine. I had the sudden urge to call my girlfriend. As soon as she picked up the phone, I felt a wave of desire flood over me. I opened up to her and spilled my heart. I was talking a million miles an hour and loving the sensation of the cold, tingly flames that ignited my brain into a thousand different fireworks. I don't remember much of what she said, but I felt intimately connected to her. Honestly, it felt like my whole body was exploding into a giant orgasm. She might have thought I sounded like a crazy person, but she stayed on the call with me for at least forty-five minutes.

Cocaine is the ultimate "gimme" drug. Once you start, you can never get enough. I did line after line that night until I literally couldn't do anymore because it was getting late and my friend would be back at any minute. However, before I closed the safe, I figured out how I was going to open it up again. It was a three-digit lock, and there was a sticker inside the safe listing the first two numbers of the combination. It would be easy to figure out the last number, and then I could have free cocaine whenever I wanted.

This sounded like a great idea while I was high as a kite. However, very rarely are good ideas formulated when you're high on cocaine. The person who was hatching this plan wasn't me, but somehow it also was. I was a good kid. I wasn't a thief. I'd never stolen anything from anybody, besides an occasional piece of candy from my parents' stash or bubble gum from the corner deli. To my credit, I never pinched so much as a dollar from the stacks of bills in my friend's safe. My brain still registered stealing money as wrong. I despised lying, thieving, and betrayal. Yet in this state of mind, I justified my actions by telling myself that my friend wouldn't miss these little bits of white powder. He clearly had lots of cash, so it wasn't like I was taking from someone who was poor. Besides, it's just drugs. It's not really stealing. My delusional logic took over and I dove headfirst into one of the most shameful periods of my life. I memorized the combination, closed the safe, and stumbled my way to the guest room. I lay down in bed, still buzzing from cocaine, and tried in vain to calm my heart as it threatened to pound its way out of my chest.

# CHAPTER 5

M y first hit of cocaine marked the beginning of my downward spiral. From that point on, I came to understand the depths to which an addict will crawl to satisfy the insatiable craving for that next high. I didn't use cocaine every day, but when I got the urge, there was nothing that would stop the pounding hunger except getting my hands on some of that magical powder. I would ride my bike over to my friend's place, checking to make sure he wasn't home, and I'd let myself in with the key he gave me. Each time I approached his front door, I knew there was a security camera watching me. He had installed it to keep track of everyone coming and going from his apartment, but I don't think he ever suspected that I was the one who was stealing from his stash. I'd give the camera a shameful glance, then I'd unlock the door and walk inside.

The shame I felt didn't last long. As soon as I crossed the threshold, all I could think of was the rush of pleasure I'd soon feel from doing that first line. Cocaine is overpoweringly seductive, and I had a one-track mind. I would hurry over to the safe, dial in the combination, and carefully take out the brick from the bottom shelf. Each time, I would chip off a little block—not even knowing how much I was taking—and crush it into a quarter baggie that I would normally use for weed. I would cut down a drinking straw, stick it directly into the bag, and inhale a huge hit into each nostril.

I never stayed at my friend's place for long. I would let the wave of ecstasy and endorphins wash over me for a few minutes, and then I'd stuff the bag of cocaine into my underwear—a place I figured that not even the cops would go—and I'd carefully put the brick back into the safe. I tried to cover my tracks as best as I could in my addled state. I felt like a genius for finding this free source of high-quality cocaine, and I didn't want anyone catching onto what I was doing. I hadn't thought far enough ahead to figure out what I'd do when this source of coke inevitably went away. Right now, I was locked in the perpetual present moment of addiction, living only for the next hit.

I left the way I came, walking out the front door, locking it behind me, and avoiding the perpetual gaze of the security camera. I wasn't sure how thoroughly my friend checked the footage, but I didn't want my eyes giving away the fact that each time I left his place, I was high as a kite with bloodshot eyes and a bag of cocaine shoved down my pants. I hopped on my bike and rode away, roaming the neighborhood, stoned out of my mind. Sometimes I would wind up at a friend's house or at a party. On these evenings, I would often take out my bag of cocaine to impress my buddies, and then I would share it frivolously until it ran short. At the end of the night, I'd return home and snort the rest, doing line after line until the sun came up. When it was all gone, I would lie down and try to rest, but sleep was elusive when I was that wired. I would spend the rest of the day strung out in a jittery haze, my eyes red and my mind racing, until I finally crashed and slept late into the next afternoon.

This cycle of cocaine use got worse and worse until it became a regular habit. I thought to myself, "I can stop this whenever I want to. I'm just choosing to do it because it's so much fun." I didn't want to admit it, but I was a full-blown addict now. I kept sliding further and further down the rabbit hole. Not long before, I had gotten my hands on a few VHS tapes of porn, and I felt the urge to watch them when I was high. I'd seen porn plenty of times before, but I figured that it would be even more of an intense pleasure rush after sniffing a few lines. That weekend, I snuck into my friend's house like usual, chipped off another block of cocaine into a quarter baggie, took two huge hits, and stuffed the bag into my underwear. I rode home as fast as I could, locked up my bike outside, and ran upstairs to grab the stash of porn that I'd hidden in my bedroom. I had a little TV-VCR setup in my room, so I plugged in a pair of headphones to conceal the noise, popped in one of the tapes, and took two more snorts of coke.

The dopamine from the drug mixed with the sexual pleasure from watching porn combined in my brain and gave me an experience that was more addictive and more damaging than either coke or porn alone. This quickly became my favorite activity. At the end of the night, I would jerk off to porn for hours until I had inhaled the last of my stash, and then I'd lie down wide awake in my bed, my entire body buzzing like a live wire. I would feel like absolute crap the next morning, depleted both mentally and physically. I didn't understand until years later how addictive porn can be, nor did I realize how emotionally damaging it can be for young people to watch it. I was just a clueless kid going through puberty, thinking I'd found a harmless source of pleasure. Instead, those cocaine-fueled nights marked more than a decade of porn addiction, a fixation that had an increasingly detrimental effect on my mental state, my health, and my relationships.

Those visits to my friend's bachelor pad went on for nearly two years. To this day, I have no idea where his supply of cocaine came from, nor do I know where he sold it. I was relieved that he never caught me, but I was also deeply ashamed of my actions. I hated stealing. I didn't want to define myself as a thief, and yet here I was, robbing from my friend week after week. I shudder to think of the trouble I could have put him in. He was no doubt doing business with shady characters who were far worse than the weed dealers I knew. I justified my actions by telling myself that I was really only hurting myself. What my friend didn't know wouldn't kill him, or at least that's what I wanted to believe. No matter how guilty I felt, it wasn't enough to stop me from making these stupid, impulsive decisions.

After several months, I think my friend might have finally noticed the little mousy nibbles that I was regularly chipping off the kilo-sized brick in his safe. One day, I showed up to his place, and there was a new safe sitting on top of his bedroom dresser. He didn't ask me about it, so I don't know if he suspected it was me. I wasn't the only person who came and went from his apartment, but if he had watched the security footage closely enough, he probably could have put two and two together. Before cocaine, the sudden appearance of this new safe would probably have stopped me dead in my tracks. It might have even been enough to shock me into changing course, but now the inner addict in me persisted and found a way around this roadblock. The new safe used a key lock instead of a combination, so I would either have to pick the lock or figure out where he had hidden the key. After about an hour of searching through his apartment, I saw a water jug in his bedroom that he had filled halfway up with change. Sitting there among the coins was a little silver key with a black top that looked like it might be the right size to fit the lock. Once I saw it, I started devising a way to lift the key out of the jug without making it obvious. I got a wire coat hanger from his bedroom closet and unwound it, turning it into a hook. I gently eased this makeshift claw into the jug and fished out the key by the little ring that was threaded through the head. Key in hand, I rushed over to the safe, my heart pounding in my chest. If this didn't work, I would have to go out and buy some bobby pins, and I was not looking forward to learning how to pick a lock with hands that were trembling from jonesing. I felt a wave of relief as the key turned smoothly in the lock and the door to the safe popped open. Sitting inside as if it were waiting for me was the brick of cocaine. I could almost hear a choir of angels singing, I was so happy. I chipped off my regular little block, ground it up, and rewarded my ingenuity by packing my nose full of coke. I dropped the key back into the jug, put the coat hanger in my bag for next time, and rode away on my bike, feeling both proud and ashamed that it had been so easy for me to outsmart my friend.

Looking back now, I can see how pitiful it was to stoop to such depths, but my craving for that amphetamine high was so powerful that it took over all reasoning. I did some of my most shameful acts in this period, and I'll always feel guilty for those times of desperation. I fell in love with the rush of euphoria and pleasure that exploded through my body and flooded my brain with dopamine "happy feelings." The high was short lived, and it was always followed by a long depressive period of anxiety, paranoia, and jonesing. I'll never understand how I could convince myself that it was a good idea to take that next hit of cocaine. The higher I soared, the further I would crash, and I knew that I would end up feeling disgusting, strung out, and miserable.

That summer flew by in a drug fueled haze, and suddenly sophomore year was upon me. I was somehow still in honors classes despite being a stoner. I never did homework and often cut class, but I still managed to maintain a B average by acing my tests. I had also become one of the top dealers at my school. Everyone knew that if you wanted weed, I was the kid that you talked to.

I was now using whatever substances I could get my hands on. Weed had opened the door for me, coke had led me through, and I was open to anything that could give me the next blissful high. That was how I was introduced to ecstasy. A few of the kids from my neighborhood had started doing E, and they gave Tim and me some to try. Ecstasy was more intense than anything I'd taken so far. It gave me an even bigger rush than cocaine. It came in a little pill, but despite its small size, it packed a mighty wallop. Within an hour of taking that first hit, my body started to tingle from head to toe. I felt a profound sense of connectedness to everyone and everything. It was like experiencing the world for the first time.

There was a group of about fifteen of us who were all tripping that night. I walked around the neighborhood with these kids that I barely knew, having heart-to-heart conversations and feeling like it was the most meaningful connection I'd ever had. One of the guys in the group cracked open a jug of orange juice and passed it around to make the high last longer. I don't know whether it was placebo or not, but what I can say is that the OJ tasted like pure ambrosia. He also gave us some straws to chew on. This came in handy because my jaw had started chomping and swinging back and forth. Ecstasy has some strange effects. All I knew was that I wanted this high to last as long as possible. I took a pack of Newports out of my pocket and smoked them until every last cigarette was burned down to the filter. Then I took out some blunts I had on me and smoked them one after another. The cigarettes and weed combined to make the effects of the ecstasy even stronger. I don't think I had ever been so stoned.

Our group walked along for hours until we found ourselves at the beach. Ecstasy is the ultimate party drug. It brings everyone together. I remember having the most intimate conversations with some of these kids. It felt like we could read each other's thoughts. It was a chilly fall night, and we didn't have any place to stay, so we all cuddled up together on a park bench along the pier, hugging each other to keep warm.

When morning hit, I felt like death. I had barely slept all night, and my mouth tasted like dried blood from biting my tongue and cheeks. My body was freezing, sore, and depleted of nutrients. This is the thing with uppers. What goes up must come down. However high you get, you get twice as low when you crash.

As the sun rose, we stumbled back to our respective houses. When Tim and I returned home, I remember getting in so much trouble because we had told our parents that we would be staying at a friend's house that night, but they had figured out that we weren't there. I was terrified that my parents would guess what I'd been doing. My pupils had grown so large they were nearly the size of my irises. I have light blue eyes, but all you could see was a slight bluish ring surrounding bottomless black holes. I certainly looked like I was on drugs. My parents still considered me to be a good kid, however, and they never suspected that I was doing something as dangerous as ecstasy. They punished us with some chores and a warning not to lie to them about our whereabouts, and they let us go to our rooms.

The next two days were a swirling abyss of depression. The come down from ecstasy was devastating, and I instantly regretted that night of partying. My body was an out-of-whack bundle of aches and pains. I felt like a live wire. Ecstasy floods your brain with so much dopamine and other happy molecules that it burns out the natural production of these chemicals. I wish I had known how slippery a slope this was. I thought I was in control of my drug use, and I still considered myself a casual user. I wasn't able to admit that the drugs were now in control of me. If I had gotten even a glimpse of the horrors that were to come, I'd like to think that I never would have continued down that path. Hindsight, however, is 20/20, and I wouldn't be the person I am today without those experiences.

I might have been losing control of my life, but I was the last to know it. For the most part, I was still a happy go lucky kid. School was great. My best friend Daniel was demoted from the math and science institute to the honors class, so I got to hang out with him all day. I was friends with everyone in my year, and to top it all off, I now had a beautiful girlfriend. Lily and I had gotten back together after the drama from the previous year had died down, and for the most part, she kept my head on straight. She wasn't able to keep me out of trouble, however. I was still selling weed every day in school. I made sure to sit at a desk at the back of the classroom next to the door so I could service my customers as they shuffled into class. In fact, in some of my classes, I would push my desk halfway behind the lockers that lined the hallway wall. I would lean my chair back into the open door and sell pot to the kids that walked past. I wasn't afraid of the teachers catching on since they never paid me much negative attention. I was more concerned that my financial transactions would be picked up by the security cameras that were installed in the hallways. However, so long as I was doing business in the doorway, no one had to be any the wiser.

I sure had a real racket going on. Many of the teachers liked me because I was a friendly kid and very charming. I was a class clown and a bit of a wiseass, but I wasn't a bully. I was never cruel or malicious to anyone. I was one of the stars of the baseball team, and the faculty knew that I came from a good family. Although the security guards and the teachers rarely bothered me, they would occasionally do a hall sweep where they would punish any kids they caught cutting. I sometimes ran errands for the assistant principal, so I had a valid excuse to cut class. I got my hands on a green hall pass from the assistant principal's office, and I kept it in my book bag at all times. The teachers rarely stopped me to question why I was out of class, but if they did, I would pull out my hall pass, and they would let me go on my way. It seems inconceivable to me now, but throughout that year, I never got into trouble for dealing drugs. High school was a big game, and I was becoming a master player.

After school, I would usually go to Lily's house and chill out. We would watch movies and fool around all afternoon until her parents got home. She had this awesome finished basement with a big screen TV, a wraparound couch, and a pantry with all the food I could eat. It was absolute heaven. I would arrive at her house with the munchies from smoking all day, and we would eat and make out with the latest blockbuster playing in the background. Lily was the first girl that I ever deeply cared about, though I don't think I was in love with her. I've been lucky enough in my life to love and be loved in return, but I was far too young at that time to know what it meant to love a woman. Still, she taught me a lot about myself and about relationships, and I'll always be grateful for the lessons that I learned from her.

Around my fifteenth birthday, we took our relationship to the next level, and we lost our virginity to one another. To this day, I think she had sex with me as part of my birthday gift. Girls did things like that in my high school. This was an important rite of passage for me, and I finally started to feel like I was transforming from a boy into a young man. I wasn't just any young man, however. I was also an addict, and that first sexual encounter hooked me on a new source of pleasure. Sex became yet another habit that I would do anything to satisfy.

It's funny, when you first have sex, you have no idea what you are doing, but you feel like the man. The sound of a woman moaning and panting in my ear felt like a drug, and I couldn't get enough. I would do whatever it took to get that rush. Looking back at it now, I realize how comically bad I must have been in bed. I don't think I ever gave my first girlfriend an orgasm. I looked for tips and strategies in all the wrong places. My only sources of information were pornography and the wildly inaccurate suggestions of friends who were just as clueless as I was. These were probably the worst places to get advice, but it was all I had at the time.

Between my thriving business, my newfound popularity, and my first steady girlfriend, I was living on cloud nine. I was high as a kite, both literally and figuratively. I was smoking so much weed that I had become a full-blown stoner. Marijuana became part of my identity. If I wasn't smoking, I was thinking about smoking or figuring out the next time I would be able to smoke. It took up most of my free time and all of my social life. I no longer played with my friends or did any other social activities. The only reason we hung out together was to get high. I think we'd forgotten how to do anything else. I would smoke in school, out of school, before school, after school, and then I would look forward to smoking even more on the weekends. I was a regular Cheech and Chong, and so were my friends. What made it even worse was that my flourishing business afforded me an unlimited supply of weed. Looking back from the viewpoint of the businessman that I have become, I realize that smoking from my own supply cost me a lot of profit, but I didn't see it that way at the time. I just saw selling weed as a way to smoke as much as I wanted and afford all the munchies I could eat.

My habit had become a serious problem, but unfortunately, I had no motivation to stop. As a teenager in the early 2000s, being a student was my only real responsibility, and I was still able to pass all my classes with a B average because of my test taking ability. My addiction to weed had dried up any aspirations I had to excel at anything. It gave me just enough drive to get through life, but not enough to actually live it. Growth and success are achieved by stepping out of your comfort zone and taking on the challenges that the world throws at you. I never asked much of myself while I was growing up because I was content with the cool little pothead life I had designed. I thought I was on top of the world. What a fool I was. I was throwing away all the opportunities that life was giving me while wearing a big, dumb smile on my face. I thought I was the smartest person in the room. I hadn't yet learned that you never get away with cheating, lying, or cutting corners. Eventually, you have to pay the piper and deal with the consequences of your actions. However, try telling that to a fifteen-year-old, know-it-all kid. Try telling him that he should apply himself and stop being a lazy bum. He will laugh you out of existence. At that age, I thought I had it all figured out. I was sure that everyone else was a blithering idiot for not seeing my righteous truth.

In recent years, I've heard more and more arguments in favor of the legalization of weed. People say that it isn't addicting and that it should be available to everyone. I'm not here to argue against medical marijuana. It is a medicinal plant that alleviates pain and improves people's quality of life. I think it has proven its use in treating cancer and other severe conditions. However, the statement that weed isn't addictive is a joke. It is highly addictive. The reason you don't see people robbing homes or selling their bodies to get more of it is because it doesn't cause extreme withdrawal. However, just because it isn't as potent as heroin doesn't mean you don't jones for it. You will experience uncomfortable withdrawal symptoms if you quit smoking weed cold turkey. Try to get a good night's sleep if you quit abruptly after you've smoked every day for years. Try to enjoy a nice meal after you've gotten used to the ravenous pleasure of the munchies. Try to stay calm and relaxed when your coworkers talk shit about you behind your back or the guy in front of you cuts you off in traffic. Then tell me if you can just quit anytime you want with no problems or consequences.

No matter the side effects associated with marijuana, it looks like its widespread legalization is all but inevitable. Regardless how culturally acceptable weed may become, we should never sell our youth short by making it accessible to people who are underage. It might not be as physically destructive as coke, heroin, or meth, but it does destroy the will and the drive to succeed. When people start smoking as kids, they risk never finding their passion, never discovering their purpose, and never working to their fullest potential.

I remember one Thursday at the end of sophomore year, I got particularly stoned before I went to chemistry. We had a new teacher in that class who wasn't very good at her job. At the beginning of the week, she had begun teaching us a new formula, and I remember it was very confusing. A few of us tried to ask her to explain it more clearly, but she was dismissive and kept teaching it the same way. Eventually, we just went along with her. It was easier to tune her out than to try and fight her. Unbeknownst to us, she had been teaching us the wrong formula all week. On that Thursday afternoon, she admitted her mistake. Then she announced that there would be a test the next day that would quiz us on the correct formula. She tried to make it up to us by launching into a lecture about the correct formula, but it was too little too late. The class erupted into chaos. I became absolutely irate. Doing well on tests was my bread and butter in school, considering I did no other work out of pure stoner laziness. I started screaming at the teacher and arguing that we all needed an extension because of her mistake. She did not take this well, and it quickly escalated. I wound up cursing her out, and she called security to kick me out of class. The security guard who escorted me out was a buddy of mine, so I left without any resistance and laughed about it with him as we walked to the principal's office.

I didn't know it at the time, but this event marked the end of my honors education and the beginning of my slide into deeper addiction. The teacher argued her case to the principal. She said that I was lazy and unruly, which of course, I was. She explained that the honors class could not afford to have me distracting the rest of the students with my funny anecdotes and wiseass remarks. She claimed that I only came to class for laughs and attention. Also true. I had managed to maintain a low B average that year, but this would soon take a nosedive. The administration decided that for my junior year, I would be demoted into a lower academic class. I would no longer benefit from even the meager amount of accountability that I had experienced in my honors classes. As I would come to find out, this new class was filled with a motley crew of misfits and troublemakers who would hasten my slide into substance abuse and failure.

# CHAPTER 6

⌇

J unior year rolled around, and my life began to fall apart. It was like I was driving a car full speed ahead one moment, and the next moment the roadway beneath me crumbled and I found myself careening off a cliff. My altercation with my sophomore chemistry teacher was the last straw for the school administration, who until then had largely tolerated my antics. The school kicked me out of all of my honors classes and placed me in a program called College Now, which was the opposite of its lofty sounding name. It was essentially the second lowest academic class that the high school had to offer, right above the special education program. Its ranks were filled with the jocks, the wannabe gangsters, and the misfits that the school had given up on. It certainly wasn't an environment conducive to learning.

I was pissed off that the administration had thrown me into this classroom. I was a troublemaker, to be sure, but I didn't think I was a bad kid, and the challenge of the honors program had kept me engaged enough to pass my classes. Now that it was clear that my school didn't care about me, I lost any interest in caring about school. Within those first few weeks of junior year, my grades plummeted, and I started dabbling even more with harder drugs. The kids I was hanging out with were more than happy to finance my lifestyle so long as I supplied their daily marijuana habit. I was becoming a regular gangster, but that's not who I was on the inside.

I missed my buddies and the fun times that we had together. My school was big enough that I didn't cross paths with many of my good friends during the day. I still got to see them outside of the classroom, but it wasn't the same. As much as I had rebelled against my honors classes, I found myself hungering for the structure that they had provided. I needed an outlet for all of the pent-up anger and frustration I was feeling, so I decided that I was going to join the football team.

At my school, the way you got to be on the team was by attending football camp the prior summer. I knew this, but I didn't care. I showed up at practice, walked over to the coach, and told him, "I want to be on the team. I'm great at sports, and I think you should let me play." The coach probably saw this as hubris. He told me, "No way, Parker. Everyone else here is in football shape. You wouldn't be able to keep up. Go to camp this summer and come back next year. If you do that and show me you're a good player, I'll let you on the team." I wasn't expecting this answer, although looking back, I can understand his reasoning. Even though I was a star athlete in baseball, I had no organized football experience. Nevertheless, I decided I wasn't going to take no for an answer. "Coach, there's no way I'm waiting until I'm a senior to play football. I'll see you tomorrow."

He waved me off as a joker, and I'm sure he never expected to see me at practice again, but the next day, I showed up and did the warmup on my own off the field. While the players practiced, I ran around the track, and when I was done, I sat in the bleachers until practice was over. Day after day, I showed up and busted my ass on that field. Even when the coach told me to go home, I didn't budge. I was determined. I wanted to show him that I was dedicated and that I really wanted to play. I felt like I needed to prove that I was someone who never gives up.

After about a month of practices, the coach came over to me and said, "Parker, what the hell are you still doing here?" I replied, "I told you, coach, I want to be on the team." He looked at me incredulously. "Get outta here, Parker, go home." I shook my head, "Nah, I'm staying. I want to play." The coach waved dismissively and walked away. The next day, however, when I showed up to practice, the coach came over to me again. "All right, all right, you can be on the team. But you're not gonna play in any games. You're not ready." I had broken him down. I smiled and said, "Thanks, coach." Then I jogged off to join my teammates. I think a few of his players had put in a good word for me. Afterall, I was their dealer. I got most of them their pot, and I took really good care of them.

A few weeks after the coach let me officially join the team, he relented on his promise to keep me from playing in high school games. He didn't put me on every time we competed, but when he did, I was expected to carry my weight. While I was good at tackle football with my friends, I soon learned that it became a completely different animal when you added refs and rules. I had no football form, no knowledge of the game, and I was 5'10" and 150 pounds soaking wet. I looked like a stick figure with huge shoulder pads that were far too big for my frame. It was almost comical. However, what I lacked in knowledge and skill, I made up for in heart and unchained ferocity. I was a maniac when I put on those pads. I had no fear and would run full speed into the biggest, baddest player in the league with no concern for my own well-being.

I developed a reputation for being completely unhinged, and the team soon realized that if they let me play, they stood a better chance of beating our competition. Before each game, I would sit alone in a corner with my Walkman blaring while I chewed on my lip until I drew blood. The taste of my own blood always put me in the zone and got my adrenaline pumping. This became a ritual before every game for the next two years. I didn't get much playing time the first year, but it was still a great outlet. Running full force and ramming my body into an opponent helped me release the rage and frustration that I had been bottling up for so long. It was incredibly cathartic.

The other benefit I got from being on the team was the camaraderie with the other guys. It almost felt like being in army boot camp training.

I thrived on that experience of brotherhood and being part of something bigger than myself. The sweat, the pain, and the torture of football were like nothing else that I had experienced before. It was a far more intense sport than baseball. Our workouts were grueling, but we were in it together. We would push each other to the absolute limit and get every ounce of will out of one another, and when it was over, we would be that much closer. Playing a football game on a team of brothers is like going to war together. You depend on the guy next to you with your life and vice versa. The kinship I felt for everyone on the team was one of the few things that kept me from spiraling completely out of control. I was profoundly unhappy in high school. At times, I was nearly suicidal, but no one realized it. I didn't want anyone else to know.

My grades were still plummeting that fall, but for the moment, I had a reason to avoid flunking out entirely. I had to maintain a high enough GPA to stay on the football team. As fall turned into winter, however, I started to slip again. I never fully recovered from being taken out of my honors class. Like they say, you are who your friends are. I was used to socializing with smart kids who did their homework and showed up every day. I never made close friends in my new classroom. Instead, my buddies were high school dropouts and twenty-something-year-old drug dealers that I would hang out with in the streets. Seeing these guys enjoying their freedom, I was tempted to drop out, as well, but if I wanted to keep playing football and selling weed to my classmates, I couldn't leave school. I recognize now that it was my responsibility to rise above and make the most of this new situation, but at the time, my brain was so addled by drug addiction that all I could feel was anger and self-pity.

I was by no means the only kid in my high school whose life was turned upside down by drug addiction. My best friend Daniel all but stopped going to class in junior year and bombed out of school. He was a smart kid, but like me he had gotten into marijuana, cocaine, and ecstasy, and it led him down a dark path. Daniel had been one of the star players on the baseball team, but once his grades took a nosedive, he wasn't allowed to play anymore. I was teetering toward the same fate as him. If I slipped just a few grade points lower, I would be kicked off the team. I loved baseball more than just about anything in my life, and of course I wanted to keep playing, but my addiction didn't care about what was important to me. The only thing that mattered anymore was finding the next high.

These days, I was still going on sporadic cocaine sprees. These binges weren't every week, but they were intense, and they always ended the same way. I would wind up barricading myself in my room, smoking cigarette after cigarette in a state of strung-out paranoia. All night long, I would stare at the bottom crack of my door, imagining shadows and noises that weren't there. I was so afraid of getting caught doing cocaine that I wouldn't even leave my room to use the bathroom. Instead, I would urinate in large water bottles and hold onto them until I could dump them out in the morning. I remember one time, I left a bottle at the top of the stairs, and my stepfather picked it up, thinking it was apple juice. When he opened it and smelled the obvious stench of urine, he was furious. I got a good tongue lashing for that ordeal.

As much as I was drawn to the seductive feeling of cocaine, it wasn't my go-to. My favorite drug back then was ecstasy. I would take a couple pills and hang out in the neighborhood with all my friends, or at least the people who claimed to be my friends. In reality, most of them were scheming scumbags with no real loyalty. It was pretty much an "every man for himself" environment, but when we were on E, we would tap into our higher selves and become sensitive, thoughtful human beings. It was amazing to me how the hardest gangster could turn into an emotional mess, telling me about their greatest hopes, dreams, and fears in life after just one hit.

One night, I was hanging with a group of about twenty people, all of us bugging on ecstasy in the handball court at the park. We were busy drinking orange juice, smoking blunts, chewing on straws, and smoking cigarettes when a couple of police cars rolled up. I was always told that if you get caught with one pill of ecstasy, it carries the same jail time as manslaughter, and each additional pill multiplies that sentence. I panicked because I had three hits in my jacket in a crumpled-up cellophane cigarette wrapper. With three manslaughters in my pocket, I thought for sure I would be going away to jail for the foreseeable future.

There were at least one hundred hits on all of us, though they were mostly with the girls. The cops got out of their cars and told us to stand up against the fence so they could search us. We were starting to freak out when the cops decided to let the girls go, since they weren't allowed to search them without a female officer present. Most of the guys breathed a sigh of relief, but not me. I was still panicking. One of the cops walked over to me and spun me around. He asked me why I was here in this park, drinking orange juice and chewing on a straw in the middle of the night. I mumbled, "I don't know, I like orange juice," and I lowered my head. The cop grabbed his flashlight and shone the bright blue light into my eyes. He let out a huge belly laugh. "Hey, look at this kid's fucking pupils! Come over here, guys." He signaled to the other detectives. Now all four of them were laughing and making fun of how I looked. One of them asked me, "What the hell is wrong with you, kid?" I tried to think fast, but the only excuse that came to mind was blaming it on my girlfriend's mother. My girlfriend Lily was Italian, so I said, "I wasn't feeling very good today, so my girlfriend's mom gave me some weird Italian remedy. It tasted awful, but it did the trick." He wasn't buying it. He proceeded to search me, asking me if I had anything on me that I shouldn't have. I knew damn well I did, but I was always told when dealing with cops to keep your mouth shut and say as little as possible. He checked all my pockets, stuck his hand down my pants, told me to take off my shoes, and finally he reached inside my jacket and found the pocket where I had hidden my stash. In one fell swoop, he pulled out the cellophane wrapper with the three hits inside, as well as my red beeper. I could see the hits in his hand, and now I was sure I would be going to jail for a triple manslaughter charge. I almost put my hands up and told him to slap the cuffs on me because I knew it was all over. He shouted, "Aha!" Then he directed his flashlight beam onto the items in his hand. I thought he was looking at the hits, but instead he was looking at my beeper and all the different numbers that had called me. He said, "What, are you some kind of drug dealer? Who are all these numbers?" I replied no over and over, and eventually he gave up asking. By nothing short of a miracle, the detective completely missed the three hits of ecstasy that were sitting there in his palm. It was as though some divine force had put an invisibility cloak over the drugs. I felt like the luckiest kid in the world. All the stars and planets had aligned to give me the perfect escape. The cops couldn't find anything on us, so they told us to get out of the park, and they drove off. That night could have been the end of my childhood, but God had other plans for me. That wasn't how He was going to teach me my lesson.

I started to feel invincible. In school, I developed a real name for myself as a drug dealing, smooth-talking, tough guy that was not to be messed with. I began to believe my own hype. I would survey my territory with Eminem blasting in my headphones. Songs like "I'm a Soldier" and "Till I Collapse" were my personal soundtrack as I walked the halls with a bookbag full of drugs and two pockets full of money. I wholeheartedly felt like a savage little badass soldier who wasn't afraid of anybody. My confidence permeated my entire persona. I never backed down from anyone, I stuck up for any kids that I saw being bullied, and I pushed the limits of life in every situation. I was an extremist. I loved adrenaline. It was by far my favorite drug. I enjoyed running from truancy officers, fighting with other gangsters, and doing anything I wasn't supposed to do.

I started taking ecstasy so often that I developed an entirely different persona while I was on it. My name on E was Steve Staletti, and I was out of my mind. I was an intense, mile-a-minute, impulsive gangster, and I did the most bizarre things just because I felt like it. Some days, I would take ecstasy before I went to school and show up as Steve Staletti. What an experience that was. I would be tripping balls, swaggering through the hallways, talking to anyone who would listen. I would leave in the middle of class to smoke cigarettes in the bathroom, the stairwells, or wherever I pleased. My friends enjoyed my alter ego. I would show up to school and announce, "I'm Steve Staletti, bro," and my friends would laugh and slap me on the back. They would exclaim, "You're crazy, Parker!" I ate up their attention. I thought, "Fuck yeah, I am crazy!" Looking back at this time with an adult's understanding, I realize that this was merely a coping mechanism. I was overcompensating to make up for the feelings of inadequacy that had plagued me since childhood. I had lived so many years feeling helpless and weak, and this behavior was the means that I had found to take back my power. In hindsight, I wish I hadn't gone to such extremes, but I am glad that I was starting to overcome the victimhood mentality that had defined me as a child. I believe that taking stupid action is better than taking no action at all, and these actions allowed me to step into a more dominant role in my own life. No matter how much pain I went through, I am forever grateful for the powerful life lessons that I learned.

When I was on ecstasy, I felt like a superhuman. Not only did I imagine that it made me feel a hundred times better, but I also believed that it improved my abilities a hundredfold. It felt like combining a genius pill with the holy grail of performance enhancers, where I could figure out all of life's mysteries and accomplish impossible feats of physical prowess. I decided to test my theory by taking a hit before a baseball game. It was probably just the drug talking, but I did feel like I performed better while I was high. I experienced a kind of laser focus, and I played with unlimited intensity, sportsmanship, and love for the game. We won that day, and I was the MVP. I went 3-5 with two doubles, one homerun, and 5 RBIs. Was this a coincidence? My drug-addled mind didn't think so.

I tried everything while on ecstasy. My favorite activity was sex. I would have sex with my girlfriend for two or three hours at a time, which felt incredible to me, although looking back it must have been disturbing for her. I don't know how she didn't know I was using. I had a gallon of water by the bed, and I drank the entire thing without needing to stop to use the bathroom. That was how profusely I was sweating. My girlfriend must have thought I was an animal. I had no idea what I was doing in bed, but I still thought I was hot shit. I wasn't really conscious of anyone other than me during this selfish time of my life.

The sole reason I didn't take ecstasy every day of my life was because of the comedown. As amazing as everything felt while I was high, the crash was twice as intense. In the days that followed each binge, I would be unable to sleep, dehydrated, fatigued, and riddled with body aches. During that time, I looked like a zombie. My mouth, lips, and tongue would be chapped and bloody from the involuntary jaw movements that would cause me to bite myself. Sometimes I would be a mess for days afterwards, depending on how hard I partied. Ecstasy also caused me to become super depressed after each trip, and those effects can be permanent. During the euphoric state, the drug floods your brain with so much serotonin, dopamine, and norepinephrine that it depletes your natural reservoir, and you become deficient in those happy chemicals for a long period afterwards. Back then, I had no idea what I was doing to myself. All I knew was that when I took this magic pill, I felt happier than I had ever felt before in my life, so I took it as often as my body would allow.

This was the beginning of a depressive cloud that would follow me for nearly ten years. I was never satisfied with anything. It was as though I had burned through all of my life's joy in those first few years of high school. I had finally found happiness, confidence, and a social life, and within a matter of months, I had lost all gratitude for it. I was constantly trying to fill an empty void in my heart and soul, but to no end.

I was in a dark place, but no one ever knew it. I was good at hiding my feelings. My unhappiness would manifest as one bad experience after another. I felt like I had the worst luck in the world, and it was creating a snowball effect in my life. I remember one day, a girl in my class told me that there were four kids who were planning to jump me after school. She liked me, so she decided to risk giving me a warning. I looked over and noticed four guys at the back of the room, all staring at me. I glared right back at them. I didn't know what to do, but I didn't want to wait until the end of the day to get jumped, so I had to come up with a plan. I walked up to the teacher's desk, grabbed a stapler, and then strutted back to where the four guys were sitting. As I stared them straight in the eyes, I gripped the stapler and jammed four staples right into my face. I didn't blink or break eye contact. Needless to say, they chickened out about jumping me.

I developed some unhealthy coping mechanisms for dealing with the increasing social stress of high school. I was paranoid and hurting, and I ended quite a few relationships during this time just to punish and self-sabotage my life. I was the king of cutting off my nose to spite my face. My relationship with my girlfriend began to suffer, and I turned increasingly to porn to fill the void. Those few seconds of short-lived pleasure were sometimes all I had to look forward to in a day. I would snort cocaine and jerk off to porn until the sun came up, and in the morning, I would be flooded with intense feelings of regret and shame. I would start the day with giant bags under my eyes, covered in clammy sweat, dehydrated, and exhausted. Some mornings I would have uncontrollable hallucinations of pornographic scenes that would flash before my eyes. It was like living in a surrealist nightmare. I felt like a perverted troll. I almost didn't put this in the book because I'm so ashamed of that time in my life, but I want to bring awareness to the severity of this issue, especially for younger generations. So many people struggle with porn addiction, especially with internet porn being so easy to access. I want teens and young adults to understand just how debilitating porn addiction can become, and I want them to know that it is okay to reach out for help when they need it.

One night, I picked up an eight ball of cocaine and started doing it with a few friends until I got paranoid and biked home to hibernate in my house for safety. I barricaded myself in my room and wound up watching porn and smoking cigarettes until it was light outside. If that wasn't bad enough, I had a baseball tournament in the morning, and I didn't want to disappoint my stepfather or the rest of the team. There was no way of getting out of this. I had to play.

I hadn't slept a wink all night, and I was exhausted and dehydrated. I could barely see straight as I dragged myself out of bed and pulled on my clothes. I still had some cocaine left, so I decided to bring it with me to help me get through the game. There was a little porta-potty next to the field, so as soon as I arrived, I did some lines to keep me awake and alert. As I walked back to the baseball diamond, my heart was racing a million miles an hour. I was sweating and my jaw was swinging back and forth. I don't know how I didn't get pulled off the field before we started practicing.

I was the backup catcher on the team and one of my best friends, Louie, was the starter. We would do warmup practice before every game and hit ground balls and flies to the other players. I stood at home plate for the practice. Louie usually warmed up the pitcher on the sideline, but not today. He was messing around, standing behind me and signaling one of the players to throw it to him. So, when I was expecting the ball to be thrown to me, it would instead soar way over my head, or far left or right, and I had to jump all over the place to try and catch it. This was making me look like an idiot, and it really started to piss me off. I told Louie to cut it out, but he thought it was hilarious. After a few more balls flew over my head, my blood started to boil. I was getting furious. A red haze clouded my vision, and then I blacked out.

I don't remember what happened next. I only know what people on the team told me later, after everything went down. I caught the next baseball that Louie threw, but instead of holding it and flipping it to the coach, I wound up to throw the ball, and then it dribbled out of my hand. My teammates knew that something was wrong. I tensed up, and then spasms started to shake my body. I was having a seizure. My stepdad and Louie grabbed me up and corralled me to the fence. Even though I was seizing, I somehow mustered the strength to fight them off, and then I fell unconscious on the ground. They got on top of me to make sure I wouldn't swallow my tongue.

Suddenly I woke up, and I realized that there were a bunch of people on top of me, pinning me down. Unaware of what was going on or how I got there, I started to freak out. I don't know how I gathered the superhuman strength, but I tossed them off me like I was the Hulk. Then I staggered to my feet and tried to run away. Not realizing that I had no balance or sense of direction, I ran full speed into the backstop fence and landed flat on my back. I lay there until I heard the wail of an ambulance siren and felt rough hands grab me and slide me onto a stretcher. My stepbrother Tim jumped in the ambulance with me, and we headed to the hospital to get me evaluated by a doctor.

This was a traumatic event for everyone on my team, but instead of demoralizing them, it fueled them up, and they rallied behind me to win the entire tournament. One of my friends on the team actually had the game of his life that day and was scouted by a college coach who happened to be in the stands. He received an offer that afternoon, and the next fall, he got to go to college on a baseball scholarship. At least some good came out of my near-death drug experience.

At the hospital, the nurses asked me what had happened, and I blamed the incident on fume exposure from painting my friend's house the day before. They clearly didn't believe my story, so they drug tested me and ran my blood. I realized with horror that I still had a little bag of coke in my sock, so when no one was looking, I grabbed it and threw it on the floor, hoping I wouldn't get caught with it. Somehow, none of the nurses saw the bag lying there. The doctors knew it was an overdose, but with good old doctor-patient privilege, they couldn't tell my parents. I breathed a sigh of relief. I thought I had gotten away scot-free. It didn't occur to me that there were worse things that could happen than my parents finding out about my cocaine habit.

When I returned to baseball practice a few days after the seizure, I realized that something was wrong. I had played baseball for most of my life, and up to that point, I had enjoyed pinpoint accuracy when pitching a ball. Now all of a sudden, I couldn't throw the ball straight to save my life. I would be looking at a target twenty feet away, and no matter how hard I tried, I couldn't get the ball anywhere near it. It felt as though my skills had been sucked out of my body by the aliens from *Space Jam.* Somehow, the seizure had permanently affected my hand-eye coordination.

My friends on the team now hated warming up with me before a game because they would have to chase the ball over the fence or into the outfield every other throw. It got to the point where I would have to take an entire bucket of balls with me whenever I practiced with someone because my throws would be so erratic. Most of my mechanics were normal, but I couldn't seem to let go of the ball at the proper time. From being an all-star player for most of my life, it was extremely embarrassing that all I could do now was lob grapefruits. My teammates wrote it off as Chuck Knoblauch syndrome. He was an all-star second baseman for the Yankees who had an amazing defensive glove, but one day he forgot how to throw the ball to first base. He racked up dozens of errors by throwing the ball wild, and eventually he was cut because he couldn't hack it anymore. I went along with this explanation because it was easier than admitting what was really happening. Deep down, however, I knew that my drug addiction was starting to cause me irreversible damage. I was terrified, but I didn't know how to stop.

# CHAPTER 7

---

For many people, senior year in high school is the pinnacle of childhood. You're at the top of the food chain. Your school schedule gets easier, and you have more free time to spend with your friends. In my senior year, I managed to whittle my schedule down to four or five classes, which was about half of my normal course load. I thought this was great. I wanted my high school days to be over with as little work as possible so I could hurry up and get to adulthood. I didn't have many plans for my direction in life once I graduated, other than to make as much money selling weed as my budding businessman self could muster. Like most teenagers with too much money and too little responsibility, I spent my cash on random crap, like drugs, video games, and porn. Even though I was making more money each month than most of the adults in my community, I didn't have a single clue about saving or growing my financial resources.

I got a real taste of reality and where my priorities lay when I went to football camp in the late summer before my final school year began. This was a week-long sleepaway camp where we trained every day from morning to evening to get into "football shape." It was a chance to bond with our teammates in the woods and form the bonds that would allow us to win as a team. All the other players prepared for the camping trip by packing heavy. They brought food, bed sheets, pillows, plenty of clothes, things to do, and all the amenities of decent living. Not me, though. I brought a book bag with seven pairs of socks and underwear, four sweatpants and shirts, and all the weed and cigarettes I could smoke. I also slipped in a few Vicodin pills for good measure, figuring that I would need them for pain. I didn't even bring a toothbrush, a pillow, or a towel. I was in for a week of hell. The first few days, I slept on a plastic mattress in the middle of the late summer heat while mosquitos gorged on my sweaty body. I brushed my teeth with my finger, and I air dried after each shower, standing naked in a bunk of twenty boys, feeling like an idiot. Eventually, one of the other guys gave me some bed sheets and a towel, but it was still gross. I wore the same sweats and filthy clothes every day and night to practice. I must have stunk like a farm animal, but I didn't care. I had enough weed to last the week, and that was all that mattered.

Most of the time, I didn't even bother to leave the cabin to light up. I would climb up into the rafters and try to blow the smoke up, as if that would make the odor disappear. When the coaches were around, I would hide above the showers and look down at them as they searched for the source of the smell. No one ratted me out because I was the guy who got them their weed. They also knew that I was a crazy motherfucker, and I would kill them if they snitched. That fear of what I might do to them was enough to ensure that they would leave me alone to continue my slow spiral of self-destruction.

That summer I discovered that there's nothing like the bonding that goes on in football camp. I was the new guy on the team, so I had to go through a little hazing to prove myself. There was a kid in one of the other bunks that called me out. He wouldn't stop giving me a hard time, so I decided to go into his bunk by myself and face the music. As soon as I entered, he and several of his buddies jumped me. They beat me up, but it wasn't anything crazy. Afterwards, they respected me and knew that I wasn't some punk kid they could pull rank on. This trial by fire was just part of the initiation onto the team.

I dished out the blows just as much as the other guys did. One day, a few of us were horsing around, and in the ensuing struggle, I grabbed a fire extinguisher and accidentally cut open my friend's arm. I felt bad, so I decided to even out the score by slamming myself in the head with the steel cylinder, like some stunt from the movie *Jackass*. I was high as a kite at the time, so I misjudged the amount of force I used, and I ended up knocking myself out cold. I woke up with a roaring headache and a huge lump on my temple. My forehead was so swollen that day that I couldn't even pull on my helmet. Looking back, I think I may have given myself a concussion because I could barely see. The coach didn't ask too many questions. He just rolled his eyes and let me sit out for the rest of the day and ice my head.

I was always a glutton for punishment, and I knew how to punish myself worse than anyone else could ever do. It was yet another unhealthy coping mechanism that I had developed as a kid. Looking back on those days, I sometimes don't know how I made it out alive. As I recall my experience at football camp, it sounds tortuous and barbaric, yet I can assure you that those were some of the best days of my life. I got to prove to myself and every other person on that team that I was a warrior. I demonstrated with my own blood and sweat that I could get through any challenge that came my way. My teammates and I battled like soldiers every day that week. We would wake up at the crack of dawn together and go running for miles through woods as the humid morning turned into a stifling afternoon. When we returned to the camp, we would do three practices throughout the day, living off of fumes in the sweltering summer heat. It was a battle of might and will, and we developed a mutual respect for everyone who made it through without giving up. I was now initiated into a brotherhood of young men who would sacrifice their bodies to protect the team. I truly miss those days, those experiences, and the hard lessons I learned. I wouldn't trade all of that pain and torture for the world.

Football was the greatest outlet I could have ever asked for as a traumatized, angry teen. It allowed me to release all the feelings of rage, depression, and helplessness that I'd bottled up inside me. It wore me out physically and pushed me to my absolute limits. It gave me a positive, sanctioned way to channel the violence going on inside my head. I loved making brutal physical contact with the other players. I would run full speed into the other guys and either lay them out or get knocked on my ass. No matter the outcome, the jolt of pure adrenaline from the impact was better than any drug.

Even though I had been training hard since junior year, I was still one of the smallest players on the team. I didn't let this hinder me, however. Instead, I used my size to my advantage because no one expected a guy weighing 155 pounds to be a savage beast. I decided exclusively to pursue defense because I loved dishing out pain and stopping my opponents in their tracks. I had the heart of a middle linebacker in the body of a safety, and I became one of the best tacklers on the team. I was fearless on the field, and my intensity would rub off on my teammates. By now, my lips were bruised and tattered from chewing on them. There was something about the taste of my own blood that would get my adrenaline racing and drive me to make plays that were each crazier and more reckless than the last. I tackled some of the best players in the league, not with strength or form, but with sheer force of will.

I'll never forget the time I decided to take ecstasy during a game. I still considered E to be the mother of all performance enhancers, and I wasn't expecting it to lead to one of the worst decisions I made on the field. I was running down on the kickoff because I was the gunner. My job was to sprint down the field before anyone else, so that's what I did. I ran full speed ahead with laser focus, intending to crush the player receiving the ball. Unfortunately, I was so tunnel-visioned that I didn't see the 275-pound blocker who stepped in front of me right before I could make the tackle. He hit me with his helmet right under my chin, and the contact lifted me off my feet and threw me at least three feet into the air. It was the hit heard around the world. Everyone in the crowd let out a loud "Ooooh!" I saw stars and nearly blacked out. I most likely received another concussion. I couldn't see straight, and I had to be taken out for a large portion of the game because the hit to my head had affected my inner ear. My balance was off, and every time I tried to run, I wound up stumbling full speed off to the left. Ecstasy ruined what could have been the winning play for my team. In the grand scheme of things, however, that was the least of the destruction that this drug would cause in my life.

One of the perks of being an upperclassman in high school was having friends who had their own car. At the beginning of our senior year, my girlfriend got her first pair of wheels. She would drive to school every day, and most mornings she would pick me up from home. She had a little red Trans-Am GT sports car, and I got it into my mind that I wanted to take it for a spin. One rainy morning, she was in a rush to get to class, so she parked the car and left me the keys so I could hang out in the school parking lot. I told her that I would come to her classroom later and bring her the keys. To this day, I don't know why she trusted me, but she left the keys in the ignition, got out of the car, and walked into the school building. I climbed into the driver's seat. I couldn't believe my good luck. I had the car all to myself. I lit up a joint, and like the ballsy kid that I was, I decided to go for a little joy ride. I didn't have class first period, so there was nowhere I had to be. I drove around the oval shaped parking lot, testing out the handling. The little car was fast and fun, and before I knew it, I was speeding away from the school grounds.

As I was zipping along the school's driveway, I saw my friend Brooke trudging to school. I slammed on the brakes and called out to her, "Dude! Get in the car!" She ran over and slid into the passenger seat, flashing me a wicked grin. She was always down for an adventure. I zoomed back to the parking lot, flooring the accelerator and then pumping the brakes to try and corner like they do in NASCAR. I was doing about thirty miles per hour down the length of the parking lot when I hit a patch of wet leaves. I tried to compensate for the skid, but the more I tried to swerve, the more the car spun out of control, and I ended up crashing nose-first into a tree.

The impact ripped the bumper clean off the car and bent the front axle. I sat there in a state of shock, thinking how the hell am I going to fix this? Brooke chose this moment to bail. She hopped out of the car without a word or a backwards glance and trotted off in the direction of the school. This was my mess to deal with. Unfortunately, I had no idea how to clean it up. I opened my door and climbed outside, staring at the bumper lying there on the ground. Still in shock, I tried to reattach it, but it was too misshapen to fit back onto the car. I dropped the bumper and it landed with a thud onto the wet ground. I shook my head, still not quite believing this was really happening. What was I going to tell my girlfriend? Excuses rushed through my brain. Maybe I could make up a story that someone had hit the car as I was driving it. I paced back and forth, breathing heavily. Eventually, I sobered up enough to realize that there was no way around this. I was going to have to grow a pair and tell my girl that I had crashed her car. I walked over to the school building, went into her classroom, and bent down to whisper the bad news into her ear. She stared at me for a few moments, an expression of horror and betrayal contorting her face. Then she started to cry. She cursed me out loudly, causing more than a few heads to turn at the sound of fresh drama. She jumped up from her seat, stormed out of the classroom, and rushed over to her car to see the damage with her own eyes.

It was the beginning of the end of our relationship. Her dad absolutely hated me after that. I told my father what had happened. He was angry at me, but he didn't want my girlfriend's dad coming for me. He probably could have gotten me expelled. My father loaned me $4,000 in cash to pay for the damages, with the understanding that I would give it to my girlfriend and then repay his loan with my own money. I was earning decent wages at the time, but I was used to spending it as fast as I made it, so I told myself that I would have to tighten my belt a little until I paid my father back. I gave my now ex-girlfriend the cash to fix her car, and then I started saving up my own money to repay my debt. After a month or so, I had finally squirrelled away enough of the profits from my weed business to equal the $4,000 I owed. I kept the money in my safe, and I planned to give it to my father when I saw him the following weekend.

One day that week, I happened to mention the loan money in passing to my stepbrother, Tim. Tim was deep in cocaine addiction at that time, and his mind and will were no longer his own. I came out of the bathroom later that evening, and Tim rushed up to me and gave me the biggest hug. He said, "I love you so much. You are the best brother ever." This seemed out of character, and I wondered what was going on. Tim left the house to score some cocaine, and suddenly it hit me like a baseball bat to the forehead. I ran to my safe, and all the money was gone.

I stormed into the kitchen in a screaming rage and grabbed the biggest butcher knife that I could find. I knew that Tim would go to his girlfriend's place once he had paid for their drugs with my money, so I took a shortcut across a huge grassy field and made my way to the other side of the neighborhood. I arrived at his girlfriend's house about twenty minutes later. I held the butcher knife in one hand behind my back and yanked open the unlocked front door with the other, looking for all intents and purposes like a deranged serial killer. In my addled state, the plan I had come up with was to wait in the doorway until Tim came down and then stab him in the chest. I had clearly not thought things through. I yelled for Tim, but his girlfriend and her father came first to see who was at their door. Tim showed up, too, but he hung back, no doubt guessing why I was there looking for him. Suddenly, I realized how ridiculous this plan was. I yelled through the doorway, "Tim, where's my money?" He shook his head. "What money? I don't know what you're talking about. I didn't take your money." I was seething with rage, but I knew that if I lost control here and now with this knife in my hand, it would not be good. I gritted my teeth, turned around, and walked back home.

When I got back to the house, I told my mother what had happened. I hadn't ratted Tim out since we were kids, but this was different than him punching me or stealing my toys. My mother drove immediately to his girlfriend's house and started screaming at him, "You didn't take that money from Kevin—you took that money from his father. So, if the money's not back in twenty minutes, I'll tell his dad what you did. He'll be looking for you along with his brothers, and you don't want that." Tim must have been scared because within twenty minutes the money was at my father's bar, minus $25 that he must have already spent on cocaine and cigarettes.

That incident was just another example of the power that drugs can wield over people. They can make you do things that you wouldn't dream of doing in a million years. They can also tear apart families. My relationship with my stepbrother was forever changed after that night. We drifted apart, and I barely spoke to him. We said hi and bye, but that was sadly the extent of our interactions.

The anger I felt toward Tim was more about his betrayal than about the money itself. For a long time, I didn't know the value of money because I made it so easily and didn't work very hard for it. I feel that it is essential for kids to get the experience of earning money through hard work, or else they won't learn its worth. I was an impulsive teenager, and I would piss my money away on anything that I wanted. I rarely counted my earnings. I would just throw it into the safe in my room and take out a wad of it when I wanted to buy something. That was until one day, when I looked in my safe and realized that something was wrong. Even my careless disregard for my finances could not hide the fact that there was a lot of money missing from my stash. I had been making an obscene amount over the last few months, but I could tell that it was not stacking up in the way that it should have been. I had a suspicion that Tim had been periodically breaking into my safe and skimming off the top. He had recently been introduced to crack, and he careened headfirst into full blown addiction. This was the turning point that stole his promising future as a professional baseball player. He was kicked off the team, and he more or less stopped going to high school. I didn't associate with him much at this point, but I knew that he hung out with the crackheads near the beach. I only knew this because some of those same guys were my clients. I would supply them with their ecstasy and weed. Apparently, Tim had learned how to pick locks from his new social circle, and he was using his newfound skill to crack open the padlock on my safe.

I was angry that Tim was stealing from me again, but mostly I felt sad. No addict wants to be addicted. None of us want to lie, cheat, and steal to get a substance just so that we can avoid feeling like death. We want the highs, yes, but mostly we want to take our minds off of trauma and pain. Addiction is a trauma response, so when an addict can't get their drug, they aren't just dealing with the physical and mental effects of withdrawal. They are also struggling with the agony of the underlying emotional wounds that are still festering under the surface. When kids discover that they can numb their pain with narcotics, it's much harder for them to develop healthy coping mechanisms as they get older, and it makes their addiction that much more entrenched. Tim wasn't a bad guy. He wasn't evil. He was hurting, and drugs were the only thing he had found that would make that pain go away.

One day, I took out all the money from my lockbox and hid it in a spot where Tim wouldn't find it. I left a single $1 bill in the safe, and on it I jotted Tim a note. I wrote, "Tim, I know you've been stealing my money every single day. If you needed money, you could have just asked me. Here's the last dollar I will ever give you because you're dead to me. I know you need it more than me, so I know you're going to take this."

I signed the bill and I placed it in the middle of the safe where I knew Tim would see it. I put the key on top of the safe so he wouldn't even need to pick the lock, and I used a pen to draw a little dot in the middle of the keyhole so I would know if it had been moved. I left my bedroom, closed my door, and went downstairs. Sure enough, when I returned fifteen minutes later, the key had been moved and the dollar bill was gone.

I shook my head. This incident held a mirror up to my face. I didn't want to acknowledge it, but I realized that this was exactly what I had been doing when I had stolen the cocaine, chip by chip, from my friend's safe. Tim reminded me how all-consuming addiction can be. Your dependence becomes greater than anything else in your life. It doesn't matter how much you love someone or how guilty you feel for hurting them, you will steal from them without a second thought if it means satisfying your cravings and staving off the pain of withdrawal. This was a blatant, desperate move. Any logical, sober person would have read that note and quickly closed the safe out of shame and embarrassment. It scored Tim only $1, and for what? His actions had potentially ended a family relationship. I felt like I lost a brother that day, and it took me many years before I could forgive him. From that point on, I made sure I had as little contact with Tim as possible, even though we still lived under the same roof. I vowed right then and there never to smoke crack, as if that was the problem. I still thought that I was so much better than Tim because I was just sniffing cocaine. I told myself that I would never stoop as low as him. Little did I know the depths to which I would have to sink before I realized that I wasn't better than any other person on this planet.

Senior year flew by, and soon senior prom and graduation were upon us. My friend Daniel was one of the more popular kids in high school, and even though he had all but dropped out by that point, he was still voted to be the prom king of our graduating class. He didn't even graduate with the rest of us. Toward the end of the year, the principal told him that he had missed too much school to get his diploma that year. A group of my friends and I petitioned the school on Daniel's behalf, and for a little while, it seemed like we had struck up a deal. If Daniel could show up for every class on his schedule the last week of school, he would be allowed to graduate. The principal was cynical, though, and I think he knew that Daniel wouldn't be able to complete this task. Indeed, Daniel showed up for every class that last week except for gym, and the principal used that as the reason to flunk him. Somehow, the school still allowed him to come to senior prom. I don't know how that decision was made, but whatever the school's reasoning, I'm glad that Daniel got to be there. We all had a great time and partied the night away. The venue was a beautiful place in Brooklyn with an outdoor patio where all the couples could dance. Daniel and I snuck up the stairs of the fire escape so we could smoke some blunts and take ecstasy. We sat together in silence, looking down at our classmates dancing below, and realized somewhere deep inside that this was the end of an era.

The summer after my senior year was a disjointed time. Many of my friends scattered as they got ready for freshman year of college. Some of them were going to local colleges, some were going out of state, and it was a dissolution of our little close-knit band. Things would never be the same after that. Upon graduation, I not only lost my friend group, but perhaps even worse, I played my final games of baseball and football. The structure and outlet that these sports provided me were essential to my mental health, and without them, I began to descend even further into drug use.

That fall, I started my freshman year at the College of Staten Island, or CSI. It is a public college that is part of the City University of New York system. I found CSI to be like an extension of high school. I was still living at home, and I had no goals for my future other than selling drugs. The only difference was that the classes were harder. Based on my experience in college, I believe that it is essential to attend university with a clear plan for what you want to accomplish and a timeline for how you will achieve it. Gone are the days of using your college years to party and find yourself. College is hugely expensive these days, and if you're not strategic about your goals, it can be a waste of time and money. When I was at college, I felt like I was in limbo. I was failing my classes, selling drugs on campus, and partying as much as I could to distract myself from the way that my life was falling to pieces.

I was selling a lot of ecstasy at that time, and one of the best places to find buyers was in the clubs. The only problem was that even with my fake ID, the bouncers were suspicious of me, and I didn't want them catching me with hits of E in my pockets and calling the cops. That's when I recruited my posse. Within the first few months of freshman year, I made friends with a group of beautiful girls who would help me smuggle drugs into the clubs. It was a perfect ruse. No bouncer was going to stick his hands down a woman's dress. No matter how much he might have suspected her of carrying in narcotics, he would never give her a strip search. I was a different story. The bouncers suspected that I was responsible for the drugs that were showing up in the clubs, but they could never figure out how I was doing it. On more than one occasion, they took me into a back room to strip search me, but I was always clean. I didn't have so much as a cigarette on my person.

My method was simple. Every weekend, I would pick up the girls in my car and give them about fifty hits each, which they would put into their underwear. I jokingly called it their safe box. I gave them money to get into the club and buy drinks, and while I watched from the corner of the room, they would grind up on guys on the dance floor and sell hit after hit of ecstasy until they had run through their stash. After closing, they would bring me the money they had made, and I would give them each a cut. We would all hang out afterwards and party until it was daylight. I gave them weed, coke, molly, whatever they wanted. I considered myself a real pimp back then. I had never made such easy money. I raked in thousands and thousands of dollars every weekend. I thought I was living the high life. The girls loved to party, and they in turn were able to get me into some exclusive, wild events. They showed me that beauty can open doors. Without them vouching for me, I would have been just another college kid. With their endorsement, however, I was their friend Kevin, the drug dealer.

I was now a regular gangster. I had five different guys working for me selling weed. Some weeks, I was making upwards of $1,500 a day. I was eighteen years old. I wasn't a little kid anymore. My mom couldn't tell me what to do. I had more money, drugs, and insane life experiences than I knew what to do with. There were five or six different social circles that I was part of, and all of them loved to party. I would bounce back and forth between these different groups of friends and drink, smoke weed, do coke, take ecstasy, and do whatever other drugs were available. I didn't much care what I took so long as it fucked me up.

All this time, it was insane how much money I was making just to piss it away on drugs and other frivolous things. I really wish that I had thought to put some of what I was making into savings, but back then, I lived for the moment. I developed some really stupid money habits. If I saw that a $20 bill had a tear in it, I would throw it in the garbage and get another. Some days, I would roll a $50 blunt, and before I was done smoking it, I would throw it out and roll another. I would go to strip clubs with my friends, even though that environment made me feel gross and uncomfortable, and I would blow hundreds of dollars on the dancers. I was irresponsible with my resources, and I was obsessed with my image. I wanted people to see me as this larger-than-life big spender. I was still an extension of the person I had become in high school, only now I had no rules holding me back, and I was free to destroy my life on a heroic scale.

About six months into my freshman year, my experience with addiction took a disastrous turn for the worse. I was driving down Hylan Boulevard, the main drag in my Staten Island neighborhood. I had committed to a left-hand turn and was waiting in the middle of the intersection for a break in the oncoming traffic. While I was waiting, the light turned yellow and then red. My plan was to quickly complete my left-hand turn now that the oncoming traffic had stopped and get out of the way before the cross traffic got their green light. I had a boatload of drugs in my car, and the last thing I needed was to get hit while committing gridlock. Just as I was turning, a city bus coming from the opposite direction ran the red light and barreled toward my car. I swerved right to try and avoid him, but at the same moment, he swerved left and smashed into the front driver's side corner of my car. I went from ten miles an hour forward to twenty miles an hour backward in a split second. My truck was completely destroyed, and now I was sitting in a demolished vehicle with my airbags deployed, blocking traffic.

To make matters infinitely worse, I used to keep all my drugs in the panel of my car door. I had a pound of mushrooms, dozens of baggies of weed, and a bag with hundreds of hits of ecstasy in it. When the bus made impact, it busted up the whole front end of my truck. My driver's side door exploded, and my drugs went everywhere, spilling all over the seat and onto the floor.

I looked up and saw the bus driver kicking everybody off the bus, probably so there would be no witnesses. He ran over and hollered at me, "This is your fault! You did this!" I was like, come at me bro, because I knew I hadn't done anything wrong. He was the one freaking out on me. So, I leaned back against my seat and kicked my car door clean off the hinges. I must have looked like the Incredible Hulk or something. When I did that, the driver's eyes popped open in pure fear. He started backing up and put his hands in front of him like I was going to attack him. Of course, I wouldn't have. I was just so frustrated because he was screaming at me. I yelled back at him, "What the hell are you talking about? You ran that red light!" There was even a witness that stayed at the scene and vouched for me that the bus driver had been at fault. But now I had a much bigger problem. I had drugs all over my car, and the cops would be here any minute. I thought to myself, "Shit, after all this, I'm going to get arrested today."

By the grace of God, at that very moment, my good friend Katie happened to drive by the accident. She saw my car splattered all over the street, and she pulled up to see what was going on. I grabbed her and said, "Katie, you gotta help me. Take this! Bring it to your house and get it out of here. I'll come get it later." I stuffed her coat pockets with bags of weed, mushrooms, and ecstasy. She booked it with all my stuff and got back in her car. Just as she was driving away, the cops pulled up. I thanked God for not completely destroying my life that day. Little did I know that He had a longer plan for me.

I stood there, all banged up, as I made my report to the cops and waited for the tow truck to arrive. I really didn't know what was going on or how I was feeling. Mostly, I felt numb. An ambulance came and I decided to get in and go to the hospital. It really was a bad accident, and I figured that I should get myself checked out by a doctor. I didn't think I was hurting at the time, but that was just because I was in shock. By the next day, I wasn't able to move my neck or my back. I knew that I had really messed myself up. Eventually, I went to the doctor and got MRIs. They found out that I had a herniated disc in my lumbar spine; I had sciatic nerve damage from trauma to my L5 and S1 vertebrae; I had military neck, scoliosis, and whiplash; and all of this had happened as a result of the accident. I was in so much pain already, and when I got this diagnosis, it became ten times worse. I thought to myself, "Now I know I'm broken."

My family told me, "Don't worry, we're going to get a good lawyer. We're going to sue the shit out of the city. The bus driver was at fault for running the red light." My doctor sent me to a chiropractor, but it didn't help. All it did was make me feel uncomfortable, and it didn't alleviate any of the pain. I decided that I didn't want to keep going back. My lawyer found out that I had stopped going to the sessions and told me, "You have to keep going to treatment. You have a huge, million-dollar lawsuit right now. If you stop getting treatment, the judge is going to think that you're faking your injuries, and you won't be able to recoup any money." I didn't like the treatments that I was receiving, but I kept following the lawyer's advice. That was when someone told me that if the chiropractor wasn't helping, I should try a pain management doctor. They would prescribe me painkillers and make the pain go away. I had done Vicodin and Percocet on occasion before, but I had never had access to a prescription. I knew that I had an addictive personality. I told myself that I would have to be very careful with this medication, but I had no idea how addictive opioids could be. I was clueless. This might seem naive today, but my accident was back in 2005. It was years before the opioid crisis had become an epidemic that was plastered across newspaper headlines and broadcast every day as part of the 24-hour news cycle.

I knew from taking Vicodin on the street that I didn't like the way it made me feel, so the pain management doctor gave me a prescription for 5 milligrams of Percocet. I started taking those pills, and that was the beginning of the end. That little bottle started a period of turmoil in my life that culminated in my demise.

The Percocet completely consumed me, and before I knew what was happening, I was addicted. It was messed up because it didn't just take away my pain like it was supposed to. Whenever I would take a pill, I would feel as strong, tough, and energetic as Superman. During the few hours of each high, it was like I became invincible. I would go to the gym and work out until I was completely exhausted. I thought to myself, these pills aren't downers, these are uppers! And I love uppers. Before I knew it, I was combining the Percocet with cigarettes, and it intensified the high. It got to the point where I needed to take the Percocet first thing in the morning just to wake up, and if I ran out of my daily allotment, I would feel sick by the evening. I talked to the doctor, and he raised the dose from 5 to 7.5 milligrams. Soon after that,

I got him to give me 10 milligrams and then 15. It sounds insane today, but this is how they would prescribe opioids back then. They handed them out like candy, and they would just keep raising the dose higher and higher. There were very few restrictions or guidelines. The only warning the doctor gave me was, "These are narcotics, so be careful."

After a couple of months on Percocet, I started to lose any remaining focus I had for my college studies. Even though I was taking pain killers, I still felt like I was in pain all the time. That's what opioid drugs do to you. They numb you, but when you're not taking them, you feel in worse pain than before because your natural pain tolerance has been diminished. As soon as the dose wears off and the real pain kicks in, your body will actually start experiencing additional sources of pain that have no physical basis. I always felt like my body was breaking in half. It got so bad that I couldn't concentrate for long enough to sit in class anymore. The swings between numb detachment and writhing agony were getting bigger and bigger, and I felt like I was about to crawl out of my skin. Midway through my third semester, I dropped out of college and started freefalling into oblivion. Rock bottom, it would seem, was still a long way down.

# CHAPTER 8

My slide into opioid addiction didn't only affect me, of course. My parents became understandably disturbed by my increasingly erratic behavior, and my mom asked me to leave the house. Looking back at it now, I realize that I was an adult, and it was my responsibility to behave like a grownup. It was my privilege to stay at my parents' house, not my right. At the time, however, I was pissed off, and I left my childhood home in a huff. I asked my stepmother Debbie if I could stay with her and my brother, Sean. She said yes and allowed me to sleep on the couch. The problem with this arrangement was that I didn't have my own room. Debbie's house was small, and my brother Sean and I were too big to share bunk beds like we had when we were children. My drugs weren't going to hide themselves, so I had to find a place to stash them. I tucked my mushrooms deep into Debbie's closet, and I buried my weed in a cubbyhole in Sean's bedroom wall. I decided that I would sneak into their rooms as necessary when I had buyers. Those days, I was either high as a kite or jonesing, so I didn't have the presence of mind to come up with a plan B for when they inevitably found my stash.

I must have mentioned to my friend Daniel that I had hid my weed in my brother's room, so rather than beg me for a bag, he called up my brother and pestered him, instead. Daniel must have given Sean one hell of a sob story because Sean finally caved and agreed to bring him some weed. Daniel showed up at Debbie's house at 10:00 at night, and Sean snuck out to meet him. Sean put a bag of weed inside a CD case and pretended that he was giving Daniel some music. Debbie had a nose for sniffing out trouble. She was intuitive like nobody's business, and she knew that something was up. She called total bullshit and asked Sean why this kid was hanging around her house. She didn't believe for a minute that Sean was giving Daniel a CD. She searched his room and found two little bags of weed sitting just inside the cubbyhole. Then she ripped open the wall and found the motherload. Debbie was furious, and Sean got in a ton of trouble. She dragged him upstairs to her bedroom and screamed at him for a good half hour. My brother glared at me afterwards as if to say, "You motherfucker, I got chewed out because of your annoying-ass friend who wouldn't leave me alone about your drugs." Regardless of how furious he might have been at me, Sean took Debbie's dressing-down in stride. He held his tongue and didn't snitch on me. I am eternally grateful for the loyalty my brother has shown me throughout the years. He has always been there for me, no matter how destructive my life decisions have been.

After this incident, Debbie asked me to leave her home. It was clear to both of us that the dynamic wasn't working, and I'm sure she was able to figure out that I was the source of drugs in her house. I had a moment of panic, wondering who else I could stay with, and that's when I thought of my cousin, Dana. Dana and I had always been close. She was my cousin Jimmy's little sister, and the two of them were like my siblings growing up. I asked her if I could crash at her house, and she told me that I could stay as long as I wanted. It was a lot of fun being at her place. She would party on the weekends and have a great time. Looking back, that environment wasn't the best for me as an addict, but at the time, it felt like a welcome respite from the constraints of both of my parents' homes.

Those days, I was doing odd jobs here and there to make legitimate wages, but mostly I was selling drugs. I was making stupid amounts of money. I bought a car, and I would drive around all day with three hot girls in my backseat, smoking joints and delivering weed, ecstasy, and shrooms. I had a beeper and a phone, and I created a sort of fast-food menu that my customers would use to request my wares. Depending on the number they messaged me, I would deliver their drug of choice: #1 was for weed, #2 was shrooms, #3 was ecstasy, and #4 was coke. I was expanding fast. I had a bunch of people working for me, running product to increase my sales. I was serving both New York and Pennsylvania back then thanks to connections I had made on my trips to visit my cousins. I thought of myself as an international businessman, but really, I was just an addict with a lot of drugs in my car.

Dana's place was a one-bedroom duplex, but it had a full, unfurnished basement that was perfect for my lifestyle. She shared the basement with her neighbor, so I threw out the stuff that was on her side, and I hired one of my druggie friends to come frame out a little room for me. No matter how high I might have been, I didn't want to sleep on a filthy, concrete floor. My friend built this box with two-by-fours, plywood, and sheetrock. The basement ceiling was just seven feet high, so the room could only be a short six feet tall with the floor installed. The flooring was made of wooden slats covered with outdoor pool carpeting. I didn't have a bed frame or box spring, so I put my twin-sized mattress directly on the floor. The sheetrock didn't keep out the bugs, so I shared my basement room with spiders and roaches. I paid my friend in weed to build this shithole for me. At the end of each day of work, I would give him a quarter ounce of weed to smoke. I had cash on hand, but it was easier to pay him out of my stash. You know that you are an addict when you will pass up making money to get free pot.

I lived in this little room for a year. I was doing large quantities of cocaine at the time in addition to my prescribed Percocet. During these cocaine binges, I would become so paranoid that I would barricade myself in the basement. I was terrified that people were coming to get me. Whenever I would hear a creak upstairs, I would shove pieces of wood and random debris under the door so that no one could get in. Unfortunately, this also prevented me from leaving the basement. I remember one of these cocaine-fueled nights in particular. That evening, I was ashing a cigarette through a big hole that I had torn in the sheetrock. Over the months, I had thrown cigarette butts and other junk through this hole, which had collected on the basement floor outside. Suddenly, I started to smell smoke. When I looked through the hole in the sheetrock, I saw embers sparking into little flames. My cigarette ash must have lit some of the debris on fire. I was high as a kite and wasn't thinking clearly, so I didn't even consider unblocking the door and getting water from upstairs. I looked around, but other than a few cans of soda, I didn't have any liquid in my room. That's when I got the bright idea to pee on the fire. I had to go to the bathroom anyway, so I walked over to the hole in the wall and urinated through it onto the fire. Luckily, the flames were low enough that my urine was sufficient to extinguish them. The problem was that there was no ventilation, so the intermingled smell of piss and smoke lingered in the basement for the remainder of the time that I lived there.

As bad as things were, they were about to get much worse. A few months into my stay at Dana's house, I found out that my friend Nathan, one of the guys who was dealing for me, had gotten arrested. When he was released, I talked to him and asked him if he had ratted me out to the cops. He said no, and I trusted him. I gave him an ounce of weed as a freebie to help him get back on his feet. I tried to do the right thing by him. I thought there was loyalty amongst thieves, but apparently, I was wrong. About a month later, I went to drop off Nathan's regular package of weed. I picked him up in my car, and he climbed in the back seat. As soon as we got on the road, a cop car drove up behind me and pulled me over. I shrugged it off, thinking that it wouldn't be too bad because my drugs were carefully hidden. I was confident that the detectives wouldn't be able to find them. I just had a lot of cash on me, which I believed I could explain away. I rolled down my window and asked the officer why he and his buddy had pulled me over. He said, "You're being pulled over for tinted windows." I told him, "But officer, these are stock tints. My back window isn't even tinted." He replied, "Oh, so you're going to be a smartass? Get out of the car." I thought, oh great, here we go. I got out and turned to face the officers. Out of the corner of my eye, I saw Nathan throw open his door and run as fast as he could around the corner. One of the cops chased after him. The other cop grabbed me by the head and smashed my face against the windshield. He wrenched my arm behind my back, dug his elbow into my neck, and screamed, "Don't you fucking move! You stay right here!" I flinched, and he smacked me in the head. I was sprawled there, trying to keep calm. I felt relieved that at least my friend had gotten away. I hadn't given him the weed yet, so he had nothing on him. I thought to myself, at least we're not going to get arrested for the transaction. The cop yelled at me, "Do you have anything in the car?" I said, "No, officer." Then he opened my trunk, which was illegal because I had not given him my permission. He went straight to the speakers inside my trunk, took off the screens, and proceeded to extract two pounds of weed, half a pound of mushrooms, and a baggie filled with ecstasy. I thought to myself, how the hell did this cop know to look there? He also opened up my glove compartment and took $1,500 in cash that I had hidden there. The officers arrested me and put me in jail. They didn't apprehend Nathan, so he got off scot-free that time.

I was shocked and furious that I'd been caught in this way. I realized that I would now have to spend money on legal representation. As soon as I could, I hired a lawyer, which cost me $5,000. At the time, I was already in debt to my dealer, a guy named Nick, because I had lost $5,000 worth of his product when the cops raided my trunk. Between the lawyer's fee and the money that I owed Nick, I was suddenly $10,000 in the hole. I knew I was responsible for my debt, so I hustled to try and pay Nick back as quickly as I could.

About two months later, while the case against me was still ongoing, I picked Nathan up to give him his next delivery of weed to sell. Once again, as soon as we started driving, a police car pulled us over. When the officers got out of their vehicle, my jaw dropped. They were the same exact cops that had confiscated my drugs and arrested me the first time. In that moment, I knew that I was well and truly screwed. I asked them why they had pulled me over this time, and they told me it was for tints. I said, "So you want to do this again? You know my tints are stock. What is really going on?" They yelled, "Get out of the car!" This time, my "friend" didn't run. He stayed with the car. They asked me if they could look inside my vehicle, to which I said no. They opened my driver's side door anyway, and this time, they looked down on the floor and saw two hits of ecstasy. I know for sure that I didn't have any E on me that day, but my "friend" Nathan did. At first, I thought he must have dropped it; then it slowly dawned on me that he had probably planted it on the floor for the cops to find. I never left drugs out loose in my car. My hiding location at that time was inside my dashboard vent. I hid my wares very carefully, and the only way you would know where to find them was if someone told you. The cops didn't waste any time. They pulled out their flashlights, ripped off the dashboard vent, and grabbed several bags of weed and mushrooms. They arrested me, and they let Nathan take my car. That was reckless of them because the guy didn't even have a license, but it was becoming clear that this was all a setup.

They hauled me off to jail, and I sat in my cell fuming. I realized that Nathan had ratted me out. After everything I had done for him, he snitched on me, no doubt for an immunity of his own. I was angry at

Nathan, but I was just as pissed off at myself. I had once made a pact with myself that I would stop dealing if I got arrested, but after I got arrested that first time, I kept going. I doubled down, and here I was back in jail in an even worse position than before. I was one judge's ruling away from going to prison for more than a decade. I was filled with regret and shame for the shitty choices I had made that had led me to this jail cell. I knew I was screwed because they got me for ecstasy. At the time, E carried a sentence of two years for each pill, and I'd been in possession of twenty hits during my first arrest, not including the two that Nathan had planted on me the second time. That was in addition to the bags of mushrooms and weed that the cops had pulled from my car both times. I figured that I would be lucky to get only ten or fifteen years. I was terrified as I contemplated my future.

When I got out of jail again, I called Nathan to ask him about what had happened. He didn't answer my call, so I texted him. His only reply was to tell me that he had returned my car and put my keys under the mat in the front seat. When I got to my car, I opened the glove compartment, and I saw that all my money was gone. I texted Nathan again and asked him, "Dude, you got my money?" He texted back, "No, I gave it to them. I told them it was yours." I asked him, "What the fuck do you mean you gave it to them?" No reply. I was fuming. I texted him, "You had $700 in your pocket. Where is that?" After a minute, he wrote, "I told them it was yours and they took it." The money in Nathan's pocket was the cash he was going to pay me for my weed. At this point, I knew without a doubt that this was an informant situation. If I didn't get a top-notch lawyer, I would be going away for the foreseeable future. I was completely screwed.

I was never one to stop digging once I had started to shovel myself into a hole, so I decided to confront Nathan. I went to his neighborhood park where I knew he would be, and I saw him hanging out with a bunch of gangsters. I called to him through the fence, "Hey! C'mere, I want to talk to you." He said, "Why? What's up?" I said, "Come over the fence." He shook his head, "Nah, I'm good over here." I was done with this pretense. I yelled, "Motherfucker, you ratted me out!" I was so pissed off that I lunged at him and tried to grab him through the fence. He backed up, and I started to climb over. That's when a few of the other guys reached for their guns. That stopped me in my tracks. No matter how angry I was at Nathan, I knew that I didn't want to get shot over this. So, I jumped down off the fence and gave him the most withering look of disgust and disappointment that I could muster. I had been so good to this kid. I had made him somebody, and this was how he repaid me, by disrespecting me and ratting me out to the cops. Looking back now from the vantagepoint of adulthood and sobriety, I can empathize with the guy. He was just a teenager who'd had the shit scared out of him by the police, and he had decided to save his own skin by giving them my name. The bottom line is that loyalty only goes so far; there aren't many people who will choose to save your hide over their own if they get into a bind.

As I sulked away, I had the dawning realization that I was in the wrong line of work. I wasn't cut out to be a gangster. The success I had enjoyed in my life as a dealer had come more from luck than from mafioso toughness. I was riddled with anxiety because I now owed my guy Nick around $10,000, and I still needed to shell out some serious cash to afford legal representation that was good enough to beat the cops. I hired one of the best lawyers in Staten Island. He cost me another $10,000 that I didn't have, but to his credit, he understood that mine was a deceptively simple case. When I went to court, my lawyer told me, "You're going to get up there and plead guilty to the charges." I was horrified. "What the fuck do you mean, plead guilty? I'm paying you 10-grand, so I don't have to plead guilty." He said, "Just trust me, kid. Plead guilty." So, I went up to the judge and pleaded guilty to a traffic infraction for having tinted windows. The cops had pulled me over for tints, and that was all they were going to get from me. They couldn't get me for possession because they had conducted an illegal search and seizure. I paid a ticket for tints that I didn't even own, and I left the courthouse a free man without having to serve so much as an hour in prison.

I was ecstatic to get off so easily. For months, I had been mentally preparing myself for a lengthy prison sentence. I was sure I was going to have multiple felonies, yet I got through the most serious legal issue of my life without even a misdemeanor on my record. It was amazing that the police had bungled things that badly. At first, I thought they were just incompetent, like keystone cops. Then it dawned on me that they were probably crooked cops. When they arrested me, I had drug money in my car, and they were supposed to confiscate it, report it, and submit it as evidence. Instead, it simply vanished, and my hunch is that they probably pocketed it. There was no record of the money in their police reports, and it didn't show up in their evidence against me. They got $1,500 when they arrested me the first time, and they got another $1,700 from me and Nathan when they arrested me the second time. They did two illegal search and seizures, and they got a $3,200 bonus from it.

I want to be clear that I'm not saying that all cops are crooked. There are a lot of amazing police officers out there risking their lives for us every day. However, cops are not paid well relative to the work they do and the risks they take. This drives some of them to get extra money by skimming off of the dealers they arrest or simply becoming dealers themselves. The cops who arrested me knew that I wouldn't bring up the money in court because it would incriminate me as a drug dealer, so they got to keep my $3,200, putting me in an even more precarious position with Nick.

After that debacle was over, I went to talk to Nick. I tried to explain to him why I couldn't work for him anymore. The police don't like losing a case, and when I escaped prison time because of their corruption and incompetence, they came after me hard. No matter where I was or what I was doing, they were always on my tail. They pulled me over for the simplest things, like getting fuel at the gas station. I couldn't even walk outside without cops following behind me in a cruiser. I had made them look stupid, and they were searching for any reason to arrest me. The next time they wouldn't be so careless, and they would make sure that I went to prison. I knew I would have to lay low and stop selling drugs for a while.

Nick listened to me with a stony expression on his face. When I had finished, he said, "I don't know what to tell you. You owe me 10-grand, and you gotta pay me back." I thought of reminding him that I had made him more than 100-grand over the three years that I had worked for him, but I held my tongue, figuring that this would just make things worse.

I felt stuck, and that drove me to seek out the wrong people to try and fix the problem. As was my wont, when I found myself in a bad situation, I wouldn't stop or change course; instead, I would keep digging in the hopes that I would tunnel my way through to the other side. Unfortunately, all that this did was drag me in deeper. I talked to one of my druggie friends about the problems I was having with Nick, and he introduced me to a man named Enzo. Enzo was an old Italian guy, and he looked every bit like an evil Al Pacino. My friend told me that Enzo was a gangster in the Mafia. He reassured me that this guy could help me out with my predicament, since I was still wet behind the ears. I decided to ask Enzo for his assistance, since he seemed to be a big-time guy. I was really gullible back then. I later learned that while Enzo might have known some wise guys, he was really just an old street punk. Regardless, he played the part. He pretended to walk the walk and talk the talk, and he looked like one of the guys from Goodfellas. Whatever his gangster status might have been, he did seem to know the streets, so I told him about my situation. I explained that I needed protection from my dealer and his associates. I owed this guy 10-grand that I couldn't repay, and I didn't know what to do. I was genuinely terrified that Nick was going to kill me. My anxiety was going through the roof, and I was taking a lot of drugs to try and manage it, which was causing me to freak out even more. Enzo gave me a long look and said, "Listen kid, you're with me. Nobody's gonna touch you. They're gonna have to talk with me first. Let's go have a sit-down with this guy and tell him what's going on."

Enzo arranged for the three of us to sit down at a table. At this meeting, Enzo strong-armed Nick. He said, "This kid is with me, and you can't touch him. If you need anything, you can call through me." What I didn't realize was that Enzo's M.O. was extortion. After the meeting, he told me, "You want protection from this guy, so here's what you're gonna do. You're gonna pay me for that protection." At the time, I was just thankful to have someone on my side. I trusted that Enzo would be able to keep me alive. I had $2,000 in my pocket, so I gave Enzo half of it. I said, "Here's $1,000. Thank you so much for doing that. That was really nice of you." Enzo squinted at me. It was clear to him that I didn't have a clue how these arrangements normally went. He said, "Yeah, sure kid." As he was putting the money in his pocket, he said, "I will look out for you, kid, but you gotta give me $200 a week. Or you could sell ounces of weed for me." The price that he quoted for weed was unreasonable for the market; it was nearly double the price that I would normally pay working for Nick. I shook my head, "Listen, I don't have a job, so I can't afford $200 a week, and I don't want to sell anymore. I want to get out of this game. I've learned my lesson, and I'm done with it." Enzo was essentially extorting me to leave Nick and come deal drugs for him at a higher cost. I told him, "I appreciate the offer. Thank you, but no thank you. My $1,000 is yours. Thanks for everything that you did today." His tone started to get menacing, "You know, kid, you can't just walk away like that. I did you a favor protecting you." Now I was doubly stressed out. I said, "I really don't know what to tell you, bro. I was told that you might be able to help me, and you did. I gave you money for your help, and that's it. That's all that I got." He stared at me like I was stupid. He said, "Listen, kid, that's not the way this works." I pushed back, "Well, that's how it works for me because I'm not doing this. I'm not going to pay you every single week. What am I, a fucking schmuck?" Enzo's tone got suddenly quiet, almost friendly, "Alright, alright, listen. I'll figure something out. But if I need a favor, you'll help me out?" I didn't fully comprehend the implication of this question. I reassured him, "Yeah, sure, no problem. I'll help you out."

Two weeks later, he called me up. He said, "Listen, kid, I need five pounds of weed for some friends of mine." I said, "Okay, no problem. I can introduce you to somebody." The guy I decided to "introduce" him to was Nick, my old dealer, the same guy that Enzo was protecting me from. In my mind, I had a brilliant plan. I was going to kill two birds with one stone. I could make Nick some extra money with this deal because I hadn't made a payment toward my debt in a while. I could also do Enzo a favor by officially introducing him to Nick as a business connection. I was clinging to a sliver of hope that I would be able to balance everything out and walk away clean from this mess that I had created. Deep down, however, I knew that I was being dangerously naive.

Enzo's friends wanted five pounds of weed, and he arranged for one of his buddies to pay me $6,000 for it. I told Nick that Enzo had associates who wanted to buy from him, so Nick got the weed from his boss and prepared to make the deal. On the day that everything was scheduled to go down, Nick and his boss drove Enzo and me into Brooklyn to the agreed upon spot. We pulled up behind a car that was filled with Enzo's friends. As soon as we were parked, Enzo said, "Give me the weed. I'll go to the car and give it to them, and then I'll come back with your money." Nick said, "No, that's not going to work. Go get me the money. After that, I'll give you the weed, and then you can go." Enzo shook his head. He said, "They're not going to do that. They're gonna want to see the weed first." Nick turned around and stared at Enzo and me in the backseat, his voice rising to a shout, "What the fuck is going on here? Are we going to do this or not?" I broke out into a cold sweat. I was growing more anxious by the minute. Here I was, sitting in Nick's car, sandwiched between three drug dealers, realizing that something was terribly wrong. I could sense it. I knew in my heart of hearts that this was a scam. To make matters worse, I was the middleman who had brokered this deal. Once everything played out, I knew this would not be a good situation for me to be in. I was frozen in my seat while Enzo, Nick, and Nick's boss argued back and forth for what felt like ten minutes.

"Give me the money!"

"No, give me the weed first!"

Finally, Nick said, "Why the fuck do I need you? How about I take the weed over to them and collect the money myself?" Enzo shook his head, "Listen, this is not going to happen unless you let me go over there with the weed. These are big time guys, and they are not going to want to meet you. Either I'm going to do it, or nobody's going to do it." Nick turned to me and looked me dead in the eyes. He asked, "Do you vouch for this guy?" I said, "Yeah, I mean, he's alright, he's a cool guy." Nick stared at me for a few seconds. Then he said, "Okay," and he handed Enzo the five pounds of weed. Enzo took the package, got out of the car, and walked over to the car in front of us. After that, everything happened so quickly. Enzo opened the back door and got inside. As soon as he slammed the door shut, the car sped off at breakneck speed and never came back. I couldn't quite believe what I had just witnessed. There was a moment of stunned silence. None of us moved. Then Nick and his boss both turned around from the front of the car and glared at me. The realization hit the three of us at the same time. Enzo and his buddies had just stolen $6,000 worth of product from us. I didn't know what to do, so I called up Enzo on my cell phone. He picked up and yelled loud enough for everyone in Nick's car to hear, "Don't you ever fucking call this number again or I'll kill you!" Then he hung up. There was no way forward after that. Nick told me in a somber voice, "Kevin, you're responsible for that $6,000. You vouched for that guy, and he just stole from us." I told them, "Listen, I'm really sorry, but I don't have any money." Nick's boss looked at me coldly and said, "Well, then you're dead."

Nick's boss announced that we were all going to go see his boss, a guy even further up the food chain from the two of them. Nick started the car, and we drove wordlessly back to Staten Island. I thought to myself, "Fuck it, I'm going to be killed today." I was trapped in the back of Nick's car. I had nowhere to go. Plus, I was at fault. I told myself that I deserved this. By all rights, I should have been crying, but I was in such a state of shock that I just sat there in an emotionless daze. Everything felt unreal. I texted my friend Taylor and told her, "I think I'm going to die today. Shit went down with Nick. I want you to know, in case shit happens to me." Finally, they pulled up to their boss' house. They walked me inside and explained the situation. Several of the boss' goons pulled guns on me. I pleaded for my life. The boss kept asking me, "Why should I trust you? Why should I let you leave here today? Why the fuck should I let you live?" I whimpered, "I'll get you the money. I didn't mean for all this to happen. I'm so sorry. I swear, I've been doing good business up until now. I've just been in a bad situation for a few months."

Miraculously, the big guy let me go. He tried to scare me, but he wasn't Mafia tough. Even though I got away without injury, being threatened with death ramped up my anxiety even more. It didn't matter that Nick and these guys above him were street thugs and not made men. When money is involved, regular thugs can be just as deadly as the Mob. I returned home to my basement with the realization that I now owed Nick $16,000, and I had no way to pay him back. I started to have a mental breakdown. It wasn't smart of me, but I needed to do something to snap me out of this tailspin, so I did more cocaine.

I was all kinds of fucked up in the head when my cousin Dana came down the basement stairs and warned me, "Hey Kevin, your father is coming here to see you right now. He says he needs to talk to you about something." I said, "Right now? Fuckit, I'm in big trouble." I had been doing lines of coke and my heart was racing, so I popped a Xanax to try and calm down. A little while later, my dad showed up at Dana's house. He didn't say anything to anybody. He just walked down into the basement, looked me in the eye, and said, "Are you okay, Kev?" I broke his gaze and tried to muster some casual nonchalance as I replied, "Yeah, dad, yeah. I'm fine, why?" He came closer and said, "No really, you okay?" I repeated, "Yeah, why?" That's when my own father punched me as hard as he could right in the chest. Boom. He's a big guy, and he blasted me. I staggered three feet back. I had never been hit in the chest that hard in my life. I smashed into the sheetrock and almost broke through. My father approached me again and tried to smack my face, but this time I blocked it.

That was the first time my dad hit me as an adult, and he never hit me that hard before or since. He felt bad afterwards because he had punched me with such extreme force. After I blocked his second blow, I put my hands down. I didn't want to get into a physical altercation with my father. I respected him too much to do that. He grabbed me by my shirt, yelling, "What the fuck is wrong with you?" Apparently, my stepmother Debbie had found the mushrooms that I had left in her closet back when I was sleeping on her couch. My father let me go, and then he pulled me into an enormous hug. He said, "I love you. You just drive me crazy sometimes. You can't go leaving drugs in your stepmother's house." I swore up and down, "Dad, that's been there for a year. I just forgot that it was there." He and Debbie thought that I had recently snuck into her house without telling her and stashed my drugs there.

My life was crumbling apart piece by piece. My dad punching me highlighted how far down I had fallen. A few weeks after that incident, I was doing cocaine with some druggie friends in my basement room. I had bought a hundred hits of ecstasy, and I brought it out to share. As

I opened the bag, it fell to the floor, and at least half of the pills spilled out and fell in between the wooden slats of my makeshift floorboards. Around a grand worth of ecstasy that I had paid for with my dwindling cash was now scattered somewhere on the dirty basement floor below. I remember falling onto my knees and screaming, "My life is fucking ruined!" All my money was gone, and all my good friends had left me. I was so enthralled and caught up in my addiction that it took me months to realize that my friends from high school and college had started to distance themselves from me. They didn't know what they could do to help me, but they knew they couldn't stand by and watch me destroy myself. They scattered away from me, just like those little hits of ecstasy.

At the time, I was angry at my friends for abandoning me, but I don't fault them now. Here's the hard truth. You have only two options when you are the friend or family member of an addict. You can either stay with them and enable them to destroy themselves, or you can distance yourself and show them that you do not support their actions. The best and often most gut-wrenching way to handle the situation is to demonstrate that you will not be part of their addiction by leaving them alone. It is human nature to want to help someone in pain; however, the addict needs to know that if they are going to go down that dead-end road, they are going to travel it without you.

All these decisions led me step by step to my decline. It was never one big choice. It was lots of little pieces that added up, like bricks laid end to end along a path to hell. I went from weed to cocaine to ecstasy to opiates, and nearly every drug in between. It is horrible to think about, but I consumed every ounce of kindness that my family and friends gave me and used it to feed my addiction. I now understand that the only way for my loved ones to help me back then was to let me hit rock bottom as fast as I could. I needed to reach that low point so I could start digging my way out.

Instead of trying to reconnect with my friends, I started hanging out with this guy named Ira at his squalid home. Ira was an obese, forty-year-old cocaine dealer who liked to try to make it with young girls. He would give me cocaine if I brought chicks over, so I would convince seventeen and eighteen-year-old girls to come and hang out with me at his place. I didn't want to acknowledge how wrong this was at the time, but when I look back at it, I recognize that this guy was a pedophile who was feeding cocaine to underage girls in exchange for sex. This was the company I was now keeping. I would knock on Ira's window whenever I needed coke, and he would let me in. It was an awful experience being at his place. His house was a dirty, murky hoarder's den. I would be there all night long, snorting line after line until I was a jittery mess.

One day, I reached a breaking point. I knew I had to ask for help. I went to my father's bar and had a nervous breakdown in front of him. I was overwhelmed by the situation I was in with Nick, and I finally came clean to my father about everything that had happened. I confessed about my drug dealing, and I explained the reasons why I owed this guy money. My dad listened to me, and then said, "Kevin, I want you to tell this guy to meet me at my bar." I grabbed my phone and texted Nick that I wanted to meet with him. I told him when and where to show up, and I explained that we were going to have a sit-down with my father to settle up the money that I owed him.

My father was a highly respected man in Staten Island. A lot of people would come to him for advice, and it was well known that he had the support of some real tough guys in the city. I remember a time when I was playing baseball in middle school. I was catching, and a kid from the other team got up to bat, so I started talking smack to him. I was just trying to get in the kid's head so he would miss the ball, but his father took it more seriously than I had intended. He was staring daggers at me from behind the backstop, and when I didn't take the hint, he started screaming at me, "Who the fuck do you think you are, kid? You leave my son alone!" This of course embarrassed the hell out of his son, but he just kept yelling at me. It almost seemed like the father wanted to fight me. He yelled, "What's your name, kid?" I called out to him, "I'm Kevin Parker." That name caused a sudden shift in the guy's demeanor. It was like he had gotten a cold drink thrown in his face. He stopped yelling and asked me, "Wait, what? Are you Kevin Parker Sr.'s son?" I called back, "Yeah, that's me." He looked horrified for a moment and then said, "Hey kid, I'm so sorry. I'm so sorry, I really didn't know." Later on that day, he came over and handed me a $100 bill. He said, "Listen, I'm really sorry. I didn't mean to disrespect you. I didn't know who you were. Just tell your father I did the right thing by you." That experience really left an impression on me. I thought, who the hell is my dad that some guy is giving me a hundred bucks for disrespecting me? This guy wasn't a nobody, either. He was the family member of a high-ranking guy in the Gambino family. So, my dad had connections, and a lot of powerful men respected him.

At the sit-down, my father was there with a few of his tough guys. Nick walked into the bar and took a seat. My father said, "So, Nick, I hear that my son was dealing for you?"

Nick said, "Yeah, that's right."

"So, how much did he owe you?"

"Sixteen-grand."

My dad looked at Nick for a moment and then said, "Hmm, $16,000. So, he was dealing for you over a long period of time, I guess?"

"Yeah, about three years."

"I see, I see. Okay, let me ask you a question. Let's say you go to Atlantic City. You put a dollar in a machine, and you win a thousand bucks, but then you don't walk away. After you win, you choose to stay at that machine because you want more money. You decide to play again and again, and each time you lose. You spend every penny of that $1,000, and now you're stressed out because you lost all the money that you had initially won. So, now you take $1,000 of your own money, and you put it on the table. You start gambling, and you are losing more and more. You go through that $1,000 that you took out of your own pocket, and then you decide to gamble another $1,000. You keep putting your own money on the table and losing it. Whose fault is that?"

Nick didn't say a word. He tried to keep his expression blank, but it was clear he was getting nervous. My father continued, "My son came to you and said that he didn't want to sell for you when he was only $5,000 behind. You should have walked away then. He was arrested, he went to jail, and he decided that he wanted to stop dealing. He asked you if he could quit, but you told him that he couldn't stop until he paid you the rest of your money. So, you took a chance. You put more money into that machine when he clearly told you to walk away. So, my son is not paying you a single fucking dollar. If you ever have any problems, you come to me."

Nick nodded vaguely and left my father's bar without a word or a backward glance. A few weeks later, I heard that he had attempted to put a hit out on me. He was on the other side of town, and he tried to get somebody to collect the money, but no one would take the tab. Then he tried to hire someone to kill me, but his guys told him that he didn't have the authority to do that because of my father. I heard this through one of my father's associates who dealt with the situation. From that point on, Nick left me alone. He stopped harassing me about the money that I owed him. I finally knew that I was protected and that I didn't have to worry for my life at the hands of another person. My own hands, of course, were a different matter.

Once my father realized how bad things had gotten for me, he gave me every opportunity to make an honest living. He first got me a job as an electrician. I learned electrical work in a non-union setting. I was only making $12 an hour, but it was a two-year apprenticeship that would eventually allow me to join the union and earn a good salary of at least $150,000 per year. Unfortunately, I turned my nose up at the job because I was an addict, and I wanted to make big money right away. I was still heavy into drugs, so I would often play hooky or show up to work stoned. I was caught in a seemingly never-ending spiral of addiction and failure. My boss didn't like me, but he was hesitant to fire me because I was my father's son. Eventually, he couldn't take it anymore, and he laid me off. After I lost my job, my father looked into my housing situation. He saw that living with my cousin Dana was making it too easy for me to have access to drugs, so he moved me back in with my stepmother, Debbie. She and my brother Sean created a bedroom out of part of the dining room so I could have some privacy. I stayed with Debbie and Sean for about a year. Looking back, I really do cherish the time that I got to spend with them.

My father tried again to help me, and in doing so, he made my life both better and worse in equal measure. He pulled some strings and got me into the concrete laborers' union. It was the Local 20, and the job was being a professional slave. We worked on buildings all over Manhattan, and our job was to do whatever labor the tradesmen required. Our responsibilities included moving materials up and down scaffolding, pouring and grading concrete, and any other backbreaking work that was needed. It was our job to lug, move, clean, and do all the dirtiest, grimiest tasks that you can imagine.

My comrades and I did hard labor forty stories up in the air, and we worked out in the elements no matter the weather. It could be pouring down rain or gusting snow, it didn't matter; we had to do our jobs. The good news was that I made $34 an hour, which was decent money. The bad news was that the arduous nature of the job was exacerbating my existing spinal injuries and causing me to increase my already extreme dose of Percocet. The choice to take the route of quickest gain was a mistake that I would make over and over until my addiction finally forced me to fight slowly and methodically to stay alive.

# CHAPTER 9

W hen I turned twenty-one, I spent my birthday alone because I didn't have any real friends left. My birthday that year was on a Tuesday, so I had a drink with my father at his bar, and then I went home early so I could wake up for work the next morning. I found it sadly ironic that on the one birthday where I got to celebrate my right to drink, I didn't have any friends who cared about that milestone. All my "friends" were addicts, and twenty-one didn't mean anything to them. It wasn't a celebration for them because they had been getting drunk and high since they were fifteen.

I surrounded myself with people who did drugs, could get drugs, or wanted drugs. I noticed my changing social circle, but I didn't want to acknowledge it. I tried to get over the fact that my old friends didn't want to hang out with me anymore, but it still hurt. I had an on-again off-again girlfriend at the time, and as my drug use got worse, we started having serious relationship issues. During her junior year of college, she went to Australia to study abroad for six months. I saw her before she left and told her that I loved her and that I would miss her. Two months into her program, she called me up and told me, "I just want to tell you that I can never speak to you again. This is over." Then she hung up the phone. She never told me the reason why, but I am almost positive it was because of my addiction. She had been my girlfriend for five years, and then she was gone in an instant. I was devastated. I tried to move on, but I ended up numbing the pain with more pills.

I left my stepmother Debbie's house shortly after I started my job at the concrete laborers' union. She and I had a big blowout fight, which was usually how things went with my addiction. I would get into an argument over my drug use, and then I would storm out of the house and move somewhere else. This time, I moved back in with my mother and my stepdad.

I still saw my father every week. His bar had a full kitchen, and I could drink and eat there for free, so I would hang out after work. My father was one of the coolest guys I knew. He was always well respected by the tough guys in the neighborhood, so people at the bar treated me with deference as his son. I knew that if I showed up for a beer and a burger, I would be sure to find people who would give me the recognition and respect that I craved.

I needed that recognition more than ever those days. I was working twelve-hour shifts under grueling conditions as a concrete laborer, five or six days a week. As my workload grew, my pill use increased to match. I was already getting fifteen milligrams of Percocet, so when I asked my doctor for a higher dose, he labeled me as a drug seeker and cut me off of my prescription. Unfortunately, I didn't have the time or energy to look for a more permissive pain management doctor. I was exhausted from the backbreaking labor I was doing every day, so it was much easier to buy opiates on the street.

It was a vicious cycle. I needed to work to get my pills, but I needed my pills to go to work. Most of the money I was making was going toward Percocet, cocaine, weed, and any other drugs I could get my hands on. I felt like I was a slave to my pain and my addiction. Even though I was learning a great trade and was quickly becoming skilled at it, I knew deep down that I was just treading water. Many of my cousins were in the trade, and some of them were my bosses. They knew how cutthroat this business was, and they wanted me to succeed, so they gave me lots of chances to get involved. They worked me hard and encouraged me to take on even more hours. This would have been a great opportunity if I hadn't been high as a kite every day. On several occasions, I nearly fell off the building where I was working, which was now more than forty stories in the air. I didn't want to acknowledge how unsafe I was becoming on the job site. I would hurt myself every day in a combination of drugged out clumsiness and self-destruction. I remember this one time when I jumped onto a four-inch nail and drove it straight through my foot. Another time, I smashed my hand with a hammer. I would find new and creative ways of injuring myself, and then I would take more pills to dull the pain. I had turned an excellent career opportunity into a really cruddy life for myself.

Even without my addiction, the combination of having a bad back and a manual labor job was not a good mix. After a few months, my crew got the contract to work on the new Yankee Stadium. It was a humbling experience. Unless you were somebody important, you were a nobody. I was just a grunt compared to the workers who had seniority, so I was treated like shit. I had to do whatever I was told to do, whenever I was told to do it. I hated how small and unimportant I felt when I was instructed to jump into the mud pile that would someday be Yankee Stadium and shovel shit for twelve hours. My life as a dealer had given me an inflated sense of significance, and this job was the absolute antithesis of that.

Concrete burns you. It heats up during the curing process, and if you get it on you, it will blister your skin. When concrete hardens, you have to chip away at it, and the dust gets into your lungs, no matter what protection you wear. My skin was always raw, and I was coughing up grey sludge every day. I got the dirtiest jobs because I was the newbie, and I got crapped on by everybody else that had been there for ten or fifteen years. They worked me like a dog, and I learned how miserable it can be to make an honest living. I was sometimes tempted to return to dealing, but the threat of a bullet in my brain always stopped me. Nick and I had an uneasy truce, and I didn't want to push my luck.

At the same time, I loved the camaraderie of being one of the guys and working together to complete such a seemingly impossible task. It was gratifying to see our collective labor start to take the shape of the enormous stadium. I felt a sense of pride to be working on a project of this scale. I knew that not many other people would be able to handle the kind of work that I was doing. It was physically and psychologically exhausting, but I persevered, and it was a great feeling at the end of the day to sip an ice-cold beer with the boys while we rode the Ferry home to Staten Island.

In the meantime, I had an ongoing lawsuit against the city for the bus accident that had damaged my back and neck. My lawyer kept telling me that it was going to be a million-dollar lawsuit. I would be rich if I just kept following his advice. This went on for several years, until one day my lawyer called me up and said, "Listen, we've got to settle." I told him, "What the hell do you mean, we've got to settle? I thought we were going for the gold. I'm in a lot of pain, and I need that money." My lawyer replied, "Well, they are offering you $12,000, and I recommend that you take it." I was shocked. "What the hell? I don't want $12,000!" He said, "Alright, alright, let me see if I can get more." He went back to the negotiating table and returned to me with an offer of $15,000. He tried to convince me, "Listen, that's the best you're going to get. You really should take it."

I was an addict, and I didn't have a lot of money. I was spending it as fast as it came in to pay for my pills. $15,000 sounded like a lot of cash at the time. I tried to rationalize it with myself. I told myself that the lawyer must know what he was doing; after all, he was supposed to be one of the best in the city. He was certainly one of the most expensive. I don't know why the lawyer didn't throw out that initial offer from the city. We had a witness, it was a city bus, and everything was in our favor. I should have told the lawyer to go fuck himself, to keep going back to the city until they agreed to pay me at least $500,000. Instead, my addiction told me to grab the cash that was offered and run with it. As had become my pattern, I took the easy, short-term route. My mindset was attuned to quick gratification. Get it now because you don't know if you'll get it later. I accepted the $15,000 settlement. I started spending it as soon as I received it, and within about three months, I blew through it to feed my habit.

That was a real low point. I felt hopeless. I was in so much pain from the accident, pain that still affects me to this day. I had counted on receiving a huge settlement that would allow me to quit my job and get some respite from the daily grind that was exacerbating my injuries. For a long time, I despised myself for blowing my chance to receive this payout, all because my drug-addled brain lacked the focus to search for a better attorney. To be fair, $15,000 is still a lot of money. It is the down payment on a house or the price tag on a car. It is the cost of a high quality thirty-day rehab facility. To my addict brain, however, it was just a few handfuls of pills.

Looking back at it now, I recognize that it was a blessing that I didn't get the full settlement. If I had hired a new lawyer, fought tooth and nail with the city, and finally gotten the money I was owed, I would most likely have gone on a massive bender and overdosed. Receiving only $15,000 limited the amount of damage I could do to my body. Wayne Dyer said it best: "If you change the way you look at things, the things you look at change." I used to berate myself for letting such a huge fortune slip through my fingers. I carried all that regret, guilt, and shame in my heart. It wasn't healthy, and it kept me from healing. Now that I can see the big picture, I believe that God had a plan for me not to get that money. I received enough cash to hasten my slide down to rock bottom, but not enough to end my life. Robin Williams once said, "Cocaine is God's way of telling you you're making too much money." If I had been able to buy $500,000 of cocaine, ecstasy, and opiates, I would probably be dead today.

Along with my addiction to substances, I was also dealing with an unhealthy addiction to sex. I would go on sprees of sleeping with one woman after another in quick succession. My father's bar was five blocks from my house, and it was a great place to pick up chicks. I drank on the bar's tab, so I didn't have to worry about spending money on alcohol. I was a young man that got a lot of respect because of my father, and that made me believe that I was some kind of boss. Whenever a new girl came into the bar, I would act like a bigshot and try to get her into bed.

That went on until I met a woman named Gina. She was an important part of my journey to hell and back. Gina was nine years older than me, and she was emotionally and developmentally my superior. By all rights, we should never have been together, but I'll always value our friendship and the things that I learned from her. She radiated a whole-hearted authenticity, and I know that she genuinely cared for me. I loved her to the capacity that I could, and I still love her as a friend to this day, but I was not capable of being a loving companion to anyone at that time. I was a full-blown addict, and I was in love with my drugs.

Gina was good to me, but I lied to her from the first day that we met. I knew that she was older than me, so I told her that I was twenty-six to narrow our age gap. She was attracted to me, and I think that was enough to keep her from digging too deeply into my fabrications. Eventually, one of her cousins found out what was going on and told Gina my age. She was shocked and somewhat embarrassed at how young I was. How could she have fallen for this kid? Somehow, I got her to come back to me, and we started dating in earnest. I initially just wanted a casual fling with her, but our relationship soon became deeper.

Gina became my mentor, almost like my conscience. She was a successful businesswoman, and she showed me that I could be an inspiring, positive force for other people. At that time in my life, I was in such a negative place. I was cheating death every day with the amount of drugs that I was taking, and I had no discipline or structure in my life. Gina was a nurturing mama bear who took care of me and tried to keep me focused on my future. It was the first relationship where I felt genuinely cared for. She lifted me up and motivated me to be better.

It was healing to have her feminine energy in my life. She helped me discover the masculine, assertive man that I am. Like everyone, I have a feminine side, but I am by nature a very masculine person. I learned polarity and relationship dynamics from her. The saying "opposites attract" refers to this unique balance of masculine and feminine energy that makes two people compatible with each other.

When I was with Gina, I tried to be a good person. I didn't do cocaine or ecstasy in her presence. I didn't even smoke weed around her. I took my pain killers so I could continue going to work, but I kept the dosages reasonable. When she wasn't around, however, I would go on cocaine benders. Sometimes, she would call me up while I was doing lines of coke. I would put all her calls to voicemail and hide in my room. She would get concerned and upset, and I wouldn't have the balls to tell her that I was high in my room sniffing coke. I didn't want her to see me because I knew it would break her heart. I let her down over and over. I behaved this way with all of my girlfriends. Every relationship I'd ever had ended because I was doing drugs. This was the first time, however, that I felt truly ashamed and guilty for being an addict.

I didn't want to lose Gina's friendship, so I manipulated her into enabling me. Instead of admitting to her that I had a problem, I convinced her to help me get more painkillers. As I twisted her tighter around my finger, I saw first-hand that turning a loved one into an enabler is as toxic for that person as it is for the addict. I felt terrible that I was exploiting her to get drugs that were killing me. It was selfish of me to coerce her into being part of my addiction. I took her away from her friends and exposed her to a world of darkness and depravity that she didn't deserve to experience.

It slowly dawned on me that I was ruining Gina's life. As much as I cared for her, I also knew that she was nine years older than me, and she wanted a man who would marry her and settle down to raise a family. I knew I couldn't give that to her, and it would be selfish of me to string her along and take away those years of her life. She should be free to go find her own happiness. I tried to end things, but she asked me not to break up with her. She said that she wanted to stay with me. I told her to think about it, and a week later, she came to me and said, "You know what? You're right. We really do need to break up." We stopped dating one another, but luckily our friendship was strong enough to survive. I am blessed that she is still one of my good friends to this day. Any time I'm feeling down or lost, she is there with excellent advice to guide me. She always knows the right words of wisdom to help me keep going.

At that point in my life, Gina was pretty much the best thing that had ever happened to me. It required all my willpower to break up with her. I used my last ounce of self-respect and dignity to let her go and give her the freedom to live the life that she deserved. I was in such a volatile, disordered state that I could have easily destroyed her, and that would have been a tragedy. I would have lived with that on my conscience for the rest of my days. Instead, I went on with my shitty existence, doing drugs and drinking at my father's bar every night.

One evening, my father came over to me while I was knocking back my fourth or fifth beer. He pulled me into the back room and said, "Hey Kevin, I want to show you something. Take a look at the tab you've been running up." He put a piece of paper in my hands. It was an itemized list of all the alcohol and food that I had consumed at the bar's expense over the past month. I realized with a shock that it was more than $3,500. He told me, "That's just the stuff that the waiters have been keeping track of. There's even more stuff that they've been giving you without recording it. That right there is triple my monthly rent. You're gonna put me out of business drinking like this." The truth was staring back at me from that little slip of paper. I had become a freeloading alcoholic. I wasn't just an addict, I was a mooch, and I hated myself for that.

My bar tab was one of the first concrete pieces of evidence that showed that I had a problem. Of course, if my father had gone through my cell phone, he would have realized that my social circle consisted of junkies and crackheads. Those were the only people who could stand to be around me anymore. I surrounded myself with the most toxic addicts that I could find, and I lived from one urgent drama to the next. Whenever I would hang out with these guys, we would get involved in robberies or other illegal activities. We were always getting into huge brawls. I knew that I was in a bad place, but I didn't know how to get out. This went on for several years. My life became a chaotic jumble of substance abuse and sexual addiction. After breaking up with Gina, I didn't try to find another girlfriend. I just slept with whoever would have me, and I watched porn on the days when I couldn't manage to get a woman into my bed. My only source of happiness was the fleeting experience of sexual stimulus.

Despite receiving constant help from family and friends, I wasn't getting anywhere in life. My cousins Jimmy, Jason, and Andrew, as well as my friend Dylan, were all my superiors in the concrete laborers' union. They wanted me to succeed, and they tried time and again to help me get good paying jobs to work on. I repaid their care and concern by blowing them off. I would often show up late to work, and some days, I wouldn't show up at all. I made up outlandish excuses for my absences, and I didn't care if any of them believed me.

This went on until one day, I was on a job site where I didn't have one of my cousins or friends there to cover for me. I had gotten the job directly from the union, and I worked on it for about a month. I learned a new trade while I was on this job, which was how to build a deck. When you are constructing a deck, the carpenters will put up "legs," which are four-by-four pieces of wood that represent the height of the floor. It was our job as laborers to use the crane to place a load of three-by-fours into a spiderweb pattern, perpendicular to the four-by-fours. We would then walk along these loose lengths of wood and guide the crane as it lowered down pieces of plywood, which we would place on top of the three-by-fours. When we were done, the carpenters would come in and nail everything down. This created a deck that was strong enough to support tens of thousands of pounds of concrete. It was a dangerous, scary job. We were working thirty stories in the air and building forms for the next floor. Since we were at the top of the building, there was nothing to latch onto. If we fell off the side of the building, we would die. The sheets of plywood were like the sails of a ship—they were at the mercy of the wind. If we were moving a piece of plywood and a gust of wind came along, we could be blown off the roof to our death. We had to learn how to maneuver the plywood so that the force of the wind would push the boards down and toward the center of the roof. The guys on the job site tried to teach me how to move the plywood safely along the deck, but I was tripping on painkillers, and I didn't think I needed to listen. When I guided the boards, I would let the wind carry me along. It gave me an adrenaline rush, and that kind of thrill was all I had to live for anymore. I remember one time, the wind dragged me all the way to the edge of the building, and I nearly flew off. At the last minute, I let go of the piece of plywood, and it fell thirty stories to the street below. This was a huge safety violation. The whole job site got shut down, and I got in a load of trouble.

I'm grateful that the union didn't fire me after that, even though they probably should have. I was never lazy on the job, but I was always high, and on my paydays, I would often go on massive benders. I would be wasted the next morning, and I would usually call out of work. Some days, I would even do coke on the job. I could always find guys who were selling drugs on the side to make some extra money. They could all tell that I was an addict, so I didn't even have to seek them out. They would come to me. I thought it was great because I didn't have to bring drugs with me—I could get what I needed at work.

Finally, my boss had had enough. That morning, I arrived several hours late after missing work the previous day. My boss came up to me and said, "Listen, Parker, if you miss another day, don't bother coming in— you're fired." I didn't know what to do. I didn't want to lose my job, but I was also a slave to my addiction. That night, I stayed up doing coke, and I slept through the next workday. I showed up the following day and made up an elaborate story that my stepmother had a stroke and almost died. I remember looking at my boss as I spoke this lie and seeing a look of disgust come over his face. He could tell that I was completely full of shit. I felt so much shame for lying about something as serious as a medical emergency. I would never wish that upon my family in a million years, and yet here I was, claiming that my stepmother was on death's door. That was the best excuse that my drug addict mind could come up with. I didn't want to lose my job because then I would have no income to pay for my habit. My boss shook his head at me and walked away. He said, "How fucking dare you say that?" At the end of the day, he gave me my check, which is what happens when you get laid off. I found out later that my boss knew my stepmother. That was why he was so angry that I had lied about Debbie having a stroke. I felt guilty for dragging my stepmom into my mess. What a fool I was.

Somehow, I managed to get another job with the union after that. I'm sure that my family pulled some more strings for me. Once again, I was high as a kite at work. For this job, I was working by myself in a basement laying concrete. In the corner, I noticed that there was a gas-powered generator sitting next to a large pile of wood. I don't know what the hell I was thinking, but I wanted to see if a spark from the generator would light gasoline on fire and burn the wood. There was a gas tank nearby, so I poured some gasoline onto the floor space between the generator and the woodpile. I waited for a minute or so, but nothing happened. I was disappointed, so I struck a match and threw it onto the gasoline. The floor erupted in a fireball, and I called for help. The boss came running down and put out the fire. He screamed at me, "What the fuck are you doing? Are you out of your fucking mind?" He physically kicked me in the ass and told me to get off the job site. As I was leaving, he told me, "Don't you come back here ever again! You could have killed us all!"

I remember how illogical I was when I was using, and how I would rationalize the craziest things. My thinking patterns were so obscure and completely jumbled. I was literally out of my mind. When I look back at this time in my life, I am reminded of the U.S. Government's early experiments with LSD. They gave acid to spiders and watched what happened. When they were dosed, these arachnids built insane, disordered webs. When I look at the photos of those webs, they seem as incoherent as my brain was when I was high. I felt like I was thinking straight, but I was really an irrational mess.

I realize now how dumb I was when I was on drugs. I couldn't hold a job to save my life, no matter how hard I worked. I bounced around these kinds of jobs for a while. I would work a job for a month or two, get fired, and then collect unemployment for a little while. That was how I survived for several years. Even when I was out of work, I would get odds-and-ends jobs so that I could afford my addiction.

I worked for my uncle for a little while. He was a general home improvement guy, but he mostly worked as a roofer. He was doing a roofing job in the middle of summer, and he asked me to help him out. It was sweltering hot, and I was high on painkillers. One afternoon, he told me to go get us lunch, so I went to a Burger King. As I was standing in line to order our burgers, I fell down and had a seizure.

My uncle waited for me for a half an hour. He had no idea where I was. I think he assumed I had skipped out on work because it was so hot. He went to search for me, and he finally found me lying on the floor of the Burger King, disoriented and incoherent. I had no idea where I was or even who I was. The workers were trying to figure out what was going on because I didn't have any ID on me. They kept asking me who I was and where I was from, but I couldn't answer them. All I knew was that my name was Kevin. I had no other recollection of my identity. It's probably lucky that the employees didn't call 911 right away because I would have been a John Doe. Finally, my uncle tracked me down to the restaurant and rushed me to the hospital. The doctors found out that I'd had a seizure from a combination of painkillers and cocaine. By now, I'd had multiple seizures from drug use, and this one wouldn't be my last.

After that, my family got me back in the union. I worked sixteen-hour shifts for this guy named Fred who was one of the meanest slave drivers I have ever known. He had also been my boss when I was working on Yankee Stadium, so I knew what to expect. Fred was the kind of guy who seemed to get off on pushing people to their breaking point. He would scream at us and work us to the bone until we started to go insane. We're good friends now, but at the time, I couldn't stand him. If you ask him, he'll admit that he loves being an asshole and yelling orders at people. While I was working for Fred, I was trying to get off of painkillers because of the seizure, so I decided to switch to ketamine instead. I don't know what I was thinking because ketamine is a tranquilizer. When you take it, you can't even walk. It's like you're in moon shoes. I was taking high enough doses of K that I could taper back on opiates, but this limited the amount of work I could do. It felt like my body and brain were trapped inside molasses. The guys would yell at me, "Parker! What are you doing?" I couldn't answer them because I couldn't move. That's how I would start my day.

I was a good worker, and Fred and the other guys liked me, but I was all kinds of fucked up on the job. After one too many times spacing out on K, I realized that I would have to change what I was taking. I started using suboxone instead, but one day I took too much, and I had a seizure on the job site. After this seizure, I realized that as much as I wanted to work, I couldn't go back to the union. The physical nature of those jobs was breaking my body apart, and the only pain management solution I had come up with was taking more drugs.

I went to see another doctor, but instead of helping me manage the pain, he tried to diagnose me with epilepsy. That was his best guess based on my seizures. I didn't tell him about my extensive history of drug abuse. He prescribed me gabapentin as an anti-seizure medication, but I didn't like the way it made me feel. I was caught between a rock and a hard place. The drugs that had once made it possible for me to do manual labor were now making it impossible to do my job. I didn't want to admit it, but I was running out of options. A doomsday clock had begun ticking, and each second brought me closer to the end of my life.

# CHAPTER 10

———— ❦ ————

At this time, my life with my mother and stepdad was becoming more chaotic by the day. I was constantly arguing and fighting with them. I thought I was this rebel kid that was too cool to live under their rules. I wanted to get out of their house, but I didn't have anywhere else to go. I talked to my brother Sean, and he told me that he was looking to move out of my stepmother Debbie's house. He called me up one day and told me that he wanted to get an apartment. We started looking for places that were within our budget, and before long, one of my father's friends came through to help us out. He had just opened up a new bar, and above the establishment was a two-bedroom apartment that he was willing to rent to us for $900 per month. He kept the price low as a favor to my father. That was crazy cheap for Staten Island, and my brother and I jumped at the opportunity. We didn't have any money, but we knew we couldn't live at home any longer.

We showed up at the apartment, and there was no furniture, so we moved the contents of our rooms into the two bedrooms. We painted the living room, but that was the only real decorating that we did. We left the other walls bare. It was like a frat house. My brother had just turned twenty-one, I was around twenty-four, and we were finally free to live as we pleased. I was still heavy into drugs. Even though I was trying to reduce my dosage of opiates, I was still doing cocaine, along with anything else I could get my hands on.

I was working lots of odds-and-ends jobs, and my brother was a carpenter in the union. He was young and irresponsible, so he would sleep in most days and continually show up to work late. Like me, he had family connections that helped him keep jobs that anyone else would have been fired from. If I were reasonably sober, I would wake him up in the morning and get him to go to work, but most of the time, I was too stoned to show up to work on time myself. At that time, I was mostly getting week-long or half-week jobs in the union. At the end of each job, I would get paid, and then I would go on unemployment until my next job.

Both Sean and I were spending our money as fast as we earned it, but between the two of us, we managed to scrounge enough to furnish our apartment. We bought a big screen TV and a second-hand couch. Our apartment became a party spot. The bar was three or four months away from opening, so we had the place all to ourselves. My brother Sean was a popular guy, and he would invite thirty to forty people into the apartment every weekend. We would set up beer pong tables and supply dozens of cases of beer for people to drink. There was no smoking allowed in the building, but we didn't care because there was nobody there to tell us to stop. We would smoke cigarettes and blunts all night long. We had wild, crazy, fraternity-style extravaganzas. We would invite women over, get them drunk, and encourage them to strip naked. It was an insane atmosphere to live in, and it was the worst thing I could have done for my addiction.

I came from a strict household, so I was reasonably responsible as far as cleaning was concerned, but my brother was a slob. I would clean the place spic and span, leave to go to work, and by the time I came back, the apartment would be a mess again. Some mornings, I would have to wake up at 5:00 a.m. to go to work, and I would walk into the living room to find twenty people passed out on the floor from the previous night's house party. There were cigarette burns in the rug, chicken nuggets on the couch, and canned spaghetti all over the floor. Some days, it was like living in a pigsty. My brother and I would frequently butt heads over whose turn it was to clean. I wasn't any better than him, of course. I would lock myself in my room and do cocaine all night long.

To make matters worse, I was introduced to crack during my time at the apartment. One night, I wasn't able to get any cocaine, and somebody told me that they could get me crack instead. I had never tried crack before. I knew that it was supposed to feel good, and I was already high, so I decided to try it. I figured, why not, what was the worst that could happen? I got some, and I wound up smoking it all night. I wasn't a huge fan of crack because I was used to cocaine, but I still smoked it on numerous occasions. When I would smoke it, I would open my window and blow it outside to keep my brother from smelling it. I tried to delude myself into believing that he wasn't aware of what I was doing, but of course, he knew everything that was going on. Still, he respected my privacy and made sure not to disturb me when I was using.

My brother wasn't a drug addict at my level, but he was an alcoholic. He would go out drinking every night, and during the day, he would go through bottles of Southern Comfort. It got so bad that he would get the shakes if he didn't drink. One night, we even got into a fistfight, and my brother and I rarely fight. He came home at 2:00 a.m. completely wasted. He was stomping up and down the stairs, screaming. I tried to get him to calm down, and he started cursing me out. I told him that if he didn't shut up, he would be sleeping on the stairs. I slammed the door to the apartment and left him on the staircase. He started pounding at the door, screaming, "Let me in! Let me in!" I screamed at him to calm down, and he kicked the door right off the hinges. I yelled, "Are you out of your fucking mind? What are you, crazy?" He picked up a garbage bag filled with glass whisky bottles, and he swung the bag at me. One of the bottles cracked and split open my foot. I howled and punched him two times in the face. Boom! Boom! He yelled, "I can't believe you just hit me!" We were even at that point. I told him to sleep it off, and I tried to get some rest before work the next day. That was one of the few times in our adult lives that we had a knock-down-drag-out fight. Most of the time, we were rowdy but not violent, at least not with each other.

There were so many people coming and going that to this day, I meet strangers who come up to me and say, "Hey Kevin, remember that party we had at your apartment?" It was the place to be. There were burns in the carpet and massive holes in the walls. After a while, we didn't even try to fix them. When our landlord would come by each month, he would freak out, screaming, "You can't smoke in here! Put that out! Give me my rent!" He would never speak to my brother like that, only to me. Unfortunately, Sean and I had gotten in the habit of spending our rent money before it was due. We would often come up short when our landlord showed up to collect. Every few months, our electricity would get shut off due to non-payment. Whenever this happened, we would light candles and try not to burn the place down. We were terrible, and looking back, I really feel sorry for our landlord. He was doing a favor for our father, and he didn't deserve to be treated that badly.

My brother was a wild child. I will never forget the time that my brother and I went out with my friend Daniel to this neighborhood club. We went to party and have a few drinks, but little did we know that it was a private, Brooklyn party for a bunch of juicehead kids. They were juiced up on steroids with their shirts off and their muscles out, and they were doing dance battles against each other, looking like a bunch of weirdos. There were some cute girls there, so we stuck around. We didn't realize that everybody else knew each other, and we were crashing their party. My brother knew the bouncer, and he had let us in.

My friend Daniel knew how tough my brother and I were, and he kept trying to reassure us, "I'm telling you man, if anything goes down tonight, I got your back. I can handle it. You know what I'm saying? It's gonna be crazy. You know you can trust me. I got you." Sean and I kept rolling our eyes like, "Yeah, yeah, sure. There's not gonna be any fighting tonight, so don't worry." But sure enough, while I was dancing with a girl, these two kids got into a fight right in front of me. As they were hitting each other, one of them bounced into me, and I staggered back and bumped into another kid. This guy looked at me and punched me right in the face. I punched him back and knocked him out cold. As he sprawled out on the floor, someone turned the lights on.

Most of the kids scattered, but two of them grabbed me and dragged me out of the club. They had me pinned between a fence, the stairs, and their car. I was stuck, and then three other kids showed up. I knew that I was going to get my ass kicked that night. I wondered, where's Daniel? Where's my backup? As I was standing there, one kid swung at me, but I ducked and hit him instead, laying him out on the ground. A second kid hit me, and I punched him back, knocking him out clean. A third kid had his fist cocked back, ready to knock my lights out. I saw this and prepared to get the beating of my life. Suddenly, out of nowhere, my brother ran over like Bruce Lee, jumped onto the hood of the car, and drop-kicked this kid right in the face. It was nothing short of a miracle. He and I were fighting back-to-back, like in a Jackie Chan movie. We were in the wrong place at the wrong time because there were now about fifteen kids who wanted us dead. They rushed in and tried to beat us up. They were taking their turns coming after us, and we were ducking and weaving and hitting. We knocked out so many kids that they were lying on top of each other like dominoes. As we were fighting, we kept tripping over guys who were collapsed in a heap on the ground. The adrenaline was pumping through our bodies, and my brother kept screaming, "Alright, who's next? Who's next? Who wants to get some of this?"

At one point, there was a guy who managed to get between my brother and me. We both saw him and spun around at the same time, clocking him on either side of his head. His entire face exploded. There was blood everywhere, and I could tell we had done some damage. My brother and I looked at each other like, "Oh my God, did we just kill this kid?" We realized we needed to get out of there fast. We climbed out of the little area where the guys had tried to trap us, and one of our friends pulled up in his car. Sean must have called him while I was fighting off the juiceheads. Our friend yelled, "Get in!" We both dove into his car through the windows, screaming, "Go! Go! Go!" We sped off, and sure enough, my friend Daniel was sitting on the corner waiting for his mom to pick him up. That put the length of our fight into perspective. We must have been beating up those kids for five minutes straight, and five minutes of fighting is a long time. Daniel had enough time to call his mother and stand there while she drove over. My brother and I leaned out the window and yelled, "Hey Daniel, thanks for having our backs!" That fight was a real bonding experience for my brother and me. We lived on the edge and we made the best of everything that we had. We are thick as thieves to this day because of adventures like that.

When the bar opened up downstairs, our landlord lived upstairs in the apartment next to us. The speakers were loud, and he had to wake up early for work, so the bar would shut off the speakers underneath his floor at night. To compensate, they would crank up the speakers that were under our floor. Our apartment would be vibrating all night long, and I would still have to wake up at 5:00 a.m. to go to work. After a week of this, I'd had enough. I put on my robe and my slippers, and I walked down to the bar, rubbing sleep out of my eyes. I decided that if I had to listen to music all night, I might as well get to choose the songs. I would put money in the jukebox and select the playlist that I wanted to hear. Sometimes I would pick slow, sappy love songs just so that I would be able to fall asleep. The bar patrons got to know me. As soon as they saw me coming, they would look at each other like, "Damn it, he's coming down here to mess with the music again."

At some point during all this partying and craziness, my father caught me paying for pills. I had my guy come up the stairs, give me the pills, and then leave. Most likely, our landlord saw this on the security camera footage and informed my father. My father came over unannounced and said, "Hey Kevin, who was that kid who came up here the other day? What did he give you?" I had to think fast. I lied and told him, "He just wanted to borrow a DVD." My father knew I was full of shit. He said, "You're fucking lying to me again. Get that kid over here right now. I want to talk to him." I refused, saying, "I'm not bringing him over here for you to yell at. I'm not gonna do that to him." My father pivoted in his approach. He took all the money out of the apartment. He confiscated my credit card, my debit card, and my ID. He took possession of anything I could possibly use to buy a substance. At the end, he said, "Kevin, you're going to stay in this apartment, and you're going to sweat this out. If you need anything that will help you get through this, just call me, and I'll get it for you. I will bring you all the Ensure, Pedialyte, and bottled water that you need. I will be there for you if you need any kind of emotional support. But you are forbidden to leave these walls. Your brother is going to watch you, and the landlord will be watching the cameras in the hall. Stay here, or you will be in a shitload of trouble." I never wanted to disobey a direct order from my father. I respected him too much to do that. I said, "Yes, sir," and he locked me in the apartment.

My parents had tried sending me to a detox facility once before, but it didn't work out well for me. I still had bad memories of that experience in rehab. At the time, I was staying with my stepmother at her house, and I was dope-sick from all the pills that I was taking. I still believed that I could somehow self-medicate myself into sobriety. My stepmother Debbie was assertive when it came to taking care of my brother Sean and me. As things once again spiraled out of control with my addiction, I was backed into a corner until I really didn't have a choice. That time, my stepmother took the initiative and arranged for me to go to a detox facility. Somehow her insistence broke through my hardheadedness, and I finally agreed to get help.

My stepmother drove me to the detox facility, and that's when I found out that the only time they take you in immediately is if you have an alcohol or Xanax problem and you're actively using. Those two substances cause physical withdrawal, and you can die if you detox without supervision. I played along and told them that I drank a ton and popped lots of Xanax. I gave them that white lie, and I didn't reveal that my main problem was opioids. They admitted me on the spot. It was 5:00 a.m. when I checked in, before the crack of dawn, because the facility had told my stepmother that if we arrived any later, I might not get a bed that day.

Almost immediately, I realized that coming here was a mistake. I hated the facility. A lot of people were court mandated, so they were there against their own will, and they didn't want to get clean. Some of them were there for their tenth, fifteenth, or twentieth time, and they were doing it just to have regular meals and a place to sleep that wasn't on the street.

I was pretty spoiled back then. I was used to sleeping in a comfortable bed and eating lots of good food. I was expecting that the staff would take away all my medication. What I didn't expect was for them to make me sleep on an awful, medical cot with no back support. My back and neck were in excruciating pain, both from the withdrawal and from my old injury. I couldn't even find comfort in eating. The food was trash. It tasted like cardboard. Shit on a shingle was the special each night.

To make matters worse, they gave me a little bit of methadone on the first day, but on the second day, they cut me off. They told me, "You don't get any more of this. You just gotta sweat it out." Using addict logic, I replied, "Well, why the hell do I have to be here if you're not going to give me any medication or do anything for me? My bed is like concrete, the food is terrible, and I don't like it here. I can just do the rest of it at my house."

I was there for only about four days. On the fourth day, I was jonesing and feeling sick, so I went to the counselor and said, "Listen, I'm signing myself out. I don't want to be here anymore." The counselor gave me a skeptical look, so I changed tactics and declared, "I'm cured! I don't need any more treatment." The counselor shook her head and warned me, "Kevin, you know you're not cured." I replied, "Yes, I am. I'm good. I'm done. I just want to be in my own bed. I'm not detoxing anymore. I want to do this my way." I wasn't required to be there by law, so against the advice of my counselor, I signed myself out and left the facility.

I called my stepmother and told her that they had released me. I told her that I was cured. She had no experience with my degree of addiction, so she assumed that I was done with treatment. She came right away and drove me home. We returned to her house that afternoon, and three hours later when she left for work, I called somebody up and ordered some pills to get out of withdrawal. I got away with it for a little while, but eventually my stepmother caught on that I had never stopped using.

Looking back at it now, I realize that this facility was an incredibly counterproductive environment. I felt like I was set up to fail. Like many people, I had started using opioids because of an injury, and yet I was given a mattress that exacerbated my back pain. I also had an easy means of escape. I could check myself out at any time and go back to my comfortable bed and my drugs. There was no rock or hard place trapping me, giving me no option but to get clean. The pain of not using was still greater than the pain of using, and I wasn't ready to stop. I hadn't reached rock bottom yet.

When you force somebody's hand like that, you need to have an action plan in place because if you give an addict any way out, they will take it to stay in their addiction. The rehab facility should have given my stepmother a timeline for how long it normally takes an addict to get sober, and they should have given her a backup plan, like a thirty-day program to help me remain drug-free. They could have at least provided my stepmother with information about trained counselors that I could speak to. Addicts need guidance and structure. You can't take away someone's addiction and then put them back into their drug infested environment without any guidance or supervision.

Detox is not a cure, and families need to understand that it is only the first step in a long process. The addict has just enough sobriety to gain some mental clarity. They are still vulnerable and impressionable. If they are not pushed in the right direction, they can just as easily turn back around and go twice as hard into their addiction.

When my father locked me in my apartment, it was the first time that I had tried detoxing on my own. It was brutal. I was shivering, sweating, vomiting, and having bouts of diarrhea. It felt like there were bugs crawling all over my legs. My head split open in a massive migraine, and my bones felt like they were breaking. It was like having pneumonia, the flu, and the worst stomach bug all at once. It was a torturous experience. I felt like I was dying. Sleep was out of the question. Any time I tried to doze off, my legs would jerk out of control, and anything I ate or drank gushed violently out of both ends. Withdrawal from opiates is no joke. It is the worst pain that you will ever experience. You feel like you are going to die, but the thing is, opiate withdrawal won't kill you. Opiate use, on the other hand, can and will.

I went through hell for about six days, and after that, I was able to get out of bed and walk around the apartment without excruciating pain. After ten days, I was able to do a bit of exercise. After two weeks, I felt almost normal. My issue was that I had chronic neck and back pain, and I still carried the limiting belief that my pain could only be treated with painkillers. I went about thirty days clean without taking pills. I was still smoking weed and drinking, which impaired my judgment. At the end of the month, I told myself that I could take one pill. Then I waited two days and took two pills. I waited another day and took three pills. Before I knew it, I was taking pills every day again. My father believed me when I told him that I was clean. He didn't realize that I had gone right back to my old habit.

I knew that I had to stop taking these pills somehow, so I started using Xanax. I thought if I took enough Xanax, I could put myself in a coma while I was detoxing from painkillers. My friend got me a bag with a hundred Xanax in it, and I started taking half of a two-milligram tablet at a time. That was enough to knock me out at first, but not for long. I soon graduated to one pill, then two, and before I knew it, I was taking five Xanax at a time on top of the Percocet. I would take a little handful of them and throw them into my mouth. I was an extremist. That's how I lived my life. I thought I was smarter than everybody, and I thought I could self-prescribe. It got to the point where I was taking Xanax and painkillers together to get high, and I had forgotten that I had started using the Xanax to help me detox.

I was having trouble getting jobs in the union because I had burned all my bridges from not showing up, being high on the job, and pulling dangerous stunts. Still, I was a hard worker. I got a job with a guy who did home improvements. I was pretty handy, so this seemed like a good opportunity. One day, I was installing crown molding in a house. I was using a nail gun to affix the molding to the top of the wall. The gun jammed, and I pressed the button to unstick it. Unfortunately, I was so high that I pressed the business end of the gun against my palm when I freed the nail. Like an idiot, I shot the nail straight into my hand. I froze. I sat there at the top of the ladder in a state of shock, staring at the nail jutting into my palm. I couldn't quite believe that I had just shot myself. The owner of the company started freaking out because he thought he would get sued. I told him, "Chill out and bring me a pair of pliers." I grabbed the pliers, clamped them onto the nail, and yanked the nail out through the back of my hand. That was another potentially catastrophic decision. You should never treat a puncture wound yourself—always let a medical professional do it. When I pulled the nail out, the wound started bleeding profusely, and I wrapped my hand with some rags. I tried to blow it off. I said, "I'm okay. Just give me a band-aid, and I'll get back to work." My boss realized that I was a danger to myself and everyone else on the job site. He sent me home and told me to get medical help. As with every other job I had held, my boss fired me because of problems relating to my drug use.

At this point, I knew that I was one more fuckup away from death's door. My addiction was becoming truly uncontrollable. I was smoking crack, sniffing cocaine, and taking pills every day. I finally began to admit to myself that I was an addict. Unfortunately, I wasn't yet ready to acknowledge that I needed outside help. I still believed that I could self-medicate myself off of painkillers. I tried many different ways to do this. I cooked ketamine in my microwave and used it for days on end until I was trapped in a tranquilized state where nothing seemed real. When I came down off of K, I would pop more Xanax. I wanted to recover from addiction all on my own. I hadn't yet come to the realization that even if I were the most self-sufficient man on earth, I would still need help because my addiction was greater than one person could manage. I would never defeat this monster by myself.

My brother and I found out that we were about to lose the apartment. We hadn't paid the electricity in over a month, and it was about to get shut off again. Our landlord was furious with us because we hadn't paid the rent in about four months. He asked our father to help him get us out of there. He promised that he wouldn't sue because of his personal connection to our family, but he was at his wits end with us. We had trashed the apartment so badly that it would take thousands of dollars to get it back into rentable condition. We were disrespectful, we had taken advantage of his generosity, and we had created a wedge between him and our father. We were bad news.

Eventually, my father moved my brother and me into his home. He had a three-bedroom apartment, and he was by himself. My girlfriend at the time came along with me and stayed in my bedroom. My best cousin Jimmy was always looking out for me, and he tried again to get me a job. There was a union position that had opened up for renovating Madison Square Garden. I took the job and went back to working twelve-hour days. Jimmy was my boss, so I had a nice in. However, as with everything in my life, I set myself up for failure. I lied on my tax forms and pretended that I had nine dependents. This allowed me to raise my income from $1,200 to $2,400 per week. I am amazed to this day that I didn't get audited. I was making a ton of money and spending it on drugs. Even though I knew my father would kill me if he found out, I started doing drugs in his home.

My father soon caught on to what was happening. He found me nodding out on my bed a few times. I was doped out on pills. I would sneak out at night to meet up with my dealers. I tried to pretend that I was just tired from work, but he didn't buy it. He said, "Kevin, you're not tired, you're an addict." One day, he marched me over to the full-length mirror in my room and said, "Look at your face and tell me you're not an addict!" I tried to deny it, but it was becoming more and more exhausting to lie.

Things were bad enough that even my cousin Jimmy couldn't keep making excuses for me. He had to fire me from my job. I was a hard worker, but I was dangerous, and he was right to let me go. I was numbed from all the painkillers, and I would do crazy stunts like hanging off the end of the building without being properly tied into my harness. Jimmy understood that I was a liability. He knew that if I kept going down this path, I was going to die someday soon, and it would be a huge lawsuit if it happened at work. When Jimmy fired me, I made a big fuss about it. I argued that I was the hardest worker on the team, and I tried to get a bunch of the guys to back me up. I did a whole poor-me routine, and I embarrassed the shit out of my cousin because I wasn't supposed to know that I was getting laid off that day. Jimmy had done me a kindness by telling me in advance, and I threw it in his face.

When I got fired from that job, I had no money, and for the last few months that I was with my father, I needed to find a way to pay for my drugs. My father had a huge urn filled with quarters, dimes, and nickels. It was probably ten thousand dollars in change that he had collected over the years. I would tip the jar over and scoop out a hundred dollars here, a hundred dollars there. I told myself that he'd had this cash for years and hadn't spent it, so I might as well use it. That was how I justified stealing from my father. I would scoop out handfuls of change, hide it in my coat pockets, and walk over to the ShopRite's Coinstar machine to exchange it for cash.

I was also getting money from my girlfriend. She was working at the strip club, and she would give me some of her earnings each week. It made me feel uncomfortable, almost like I was her pimp, but I didn't have enough dignity left to refuse money that was given to me. At the time, I had started taking Lyrica for pain. It is a fibromyalgia drug, and it is also used to treat seizures. It isn't a narcotic, but it is a controlled substance. Once again, I decided to be my own unlicensed doctor and try to wean myself off of painkillers using another substance.

One day, my father came to my room and said, "Kevin, what's going on with my spare change jar?" I must have stolen $1,500 by that point, and my father was starting to notice. I came up with a lame excuse about needing money because I had been laid off, and I told him that I would repay every last dollar, a promise that I had no intention of keeping. One time, I put twenty dollars in quarters into the jar to show him that I wasn't trying to rob him, but it was really just a half-assed attempt at making myself feel better.

I had finally burned enough bridges that everyone in my life realized that I was an addict. No one trusted me anymore. My father didn't know what to do with me. He talked with my stepmother Debbie, my mother, and my stepdad Gene to try and figure out ways to reach me. After a few conversations, they decided that tough love was the best approach to use, and they all agreed to get together to stage an intervention. It was a good idea, and it came from a loving place; however, they made a mistake in choosing to orchestrate the intervention themselves instead of hiring a professional to lead the process.

Interventions are powerful tools for getting through to an addict, but they have to be led by a trained interventionist who has years of experience observing and leading the procedure. The leader must be a neutral party. They cannot be affiliated or related to the addict, otherwise the addict will assume that they have an agenda and fight back. My parents didn't know this. They had good intentions and love in their hearts, but their attempt unfortunately backfired. Years later, the negative experience that I had during my intervention lit a fire under me to become a professional interventionist. My parents' actions ultimately guided me toward a successful career path. But I am getting ahead of myself.

My parents and stepparents tried to duplicate the interventions that they had seen on TV. My stepmother Debbie barricaded me in my room at around 9:00 a.m. At 10:00 a.m., she woke me up from a dead sleep. My girlfriend was in bed with me, so I was already hostile toward my stepmother for bursting into my room. Debbie shouted, "Get up! Get out of bed! Get up right now!" I slowly complied. I didn't know what was going on, but whatever it was, I was pissed off that she was embarrassing me in front of my girl. I dragged myself out of bed and followed Debbie to the kitchen. My girlfriend followed behind me. When I walked into the room, I saw all of my parents there, staring at me with serious expressions on their faces.

My father, my mother, and my stepdad Gene were sitting at the kitchen table. Debbie was standing in front of me. She told me, "Kevin, we know that you have a drug problem!" My father stood up and made me walk to my room and open my safe. He grabbed the bag of Lyrica that he found inside. He told me, "Kevin, you've got to get rid of this now. Flush it down the toilet." I didn't want to disobey my father, so I walked to the bathroom and flushed the little bag of pills. I decided it wasn't a good time to argue with him or say that going cold turkey might be a bad idea. I think my father assumed that taking away the Lyrica would be just like when he had made me give up opiates. He had no idea that sudden withdrawal from Lyrica can have life-threatening side effects, including grand mal seizures. It wouldn't have been as bad if I had been using it appropriately, but I was taking four times the prescribed dosage in my misguided attempt to replace the painkillers. In a bitterly ironic twist, the high dose of Lyrica put my body in an even more precarious position than the opiates ever had.

Debbie led me back to the kitchen. "Kevin, you have to go to rehab right now!" I was barely awake. I told them, "Listen, I know. I know I have a problem. I'm sorry. I know I need to get help. I just don't think I can do it right now." I was at the point where I could admit that I needed to be in rehab, but I wasn't ready to go that morning. However, that was the ultimatum that my parents gave me. Debbie shook her head. "You have to go right now. Get your shit, we're going. We can bring you more of your things when you're there, but you have to be in rehab for at least a year." I was shocked. Most rehabs are a month or two, not a full year. I told her, "I'm not leaving my girlfriend and my life for a whole fucking year." My parents must have told my girlfriend what was happening because she chimed in, "I'm going to break up with you if you don't go today." I said, "Whatever. Fuck you too. I don't need you. I'm not leaving for rehab this minute. Give me some time, let me get my shit together, and then maybe I'll go." Debbie kept pressing. She said, "No, the way this works is you're going away for a year or maybe eighteen months, and you're leaving right now. If you don't go to rehab this morning, you are no longer welcome in this house. You have a choice. You can either go to a facility or get out of the house." Unfortunately, Debbie had cornered me like a wild animal while also giving me an escape route. I told her, "Fuck you! You don't get to tell me what to do. I'm outta here. I don't need this. You're gonna tell me that I either gotta go away for eighteen months or leave the house and never come back? Fuck you. I don't need you. If I'm gonna get better, I'll do it on my own. I'm leaving."

I walked out of the kitchen, cursing at the people who had raised me, loved me, and cared for me my whole life. They didn't try to stop me. They were angry and shocked, and they didn't know what to do next. I went to my room and put on my jeans, my shirt, and a pair of sneakers. I opened my bookbag and threw in a spare set of clothes and a few pairs of socks and underwear. I threw my bookbag on my back, I lifted my fifty-pound safe onto my shoulder, and I stormed out of the house. I slammed the door on my way out. I was so pissed off. I couldn't believe that they had given me such a terrible ultimatum. I walked along the side of the road with my backpack and my safe, cursing and moaning at my parents. Anybody passing me by must have thought I was some psycho who had just robbed a house. I walked a half a mile to my friend Daniel's house, and I banged on the door. Daniel's mother greeted me with a smile that turned to a look of concern when she saw my bedraggled state. She was a sweet woman, and I was very close to her. I had unfortunately also manipulated her into being one of my enablers. She used to give me pain pills out of her own prescription when I ran out. She loved me like a son, and I used that to my full advantage. Her son Daniel was even worse off than me. He was always high on dope or Xanax, which made him paranoid and belligerent. He didn't work, and if his mother didn't give him pills, he would go into a rage. When Daniel got out of hand, his mom would often call me to straighten him out, which I usually agreed to do.

When I arrived at her doorstep with my sob story, she welcomed me in with open arms. I told her that my parents hated me and that they had kicked me out of the house. In true addict fashion, I remained blameless in my narrative, and I didn't tell her the real reason why I had left home. She said, "Kevin, you're like a son to me. You can stay here as long as you want." I put down my backpack and my safe, and I decided that I was going to get high now that I was no longer under my parents' thumb. I called up some of my druggie friends, and I asked for cocaine, heroin, crack, whatever they had. I distinctly remember, however, that none of my friends showed up with anything that day. I was pissed off because I had no money to buy anything, and I was jonesing.

Daniel's mom cooked me a big dinner of macaroni and cheese that night, and then she said, "Why don't you go lay down. It's been a long day." I went to bed in the guest room and passed out from exhaustion. To this day, I don't think I took anything before I went to sleep. Daniel's mom said that I never left the house. I even checked my phone, but there isn't any correspondence indicating that anyone came over to bring me drugs.

That should have been the last night of my life. That macaroni and cheese should have been my last meal. Daniel's mom wishing me goodnight should have been the last thing that I ever heard. In my sleep, I had another seizure and choked on my own vomit. Daniel's little sister found me in the morning, face first in puke, completely unresponsive. My heart had stopped, and I was turning blue. She knew exactly what had happened because the same thing had happened to Daniel a few years prior. She called the ambulance, and while she was on the phone, Daniel came into the room. This is one of the saddest parts of that whole episode in my life, and it shows you how low down addiction can drag you. Daniel's sister later told me that when I was dying on the floor, Daniel bent down and went through my pockets. Instead of mourning me, his best friend in the whole world, he riffled through my jeans. He didn't find any drugs, but he did take the last few dollars that I had to my name. His addiction told him to take whatever he got his hands on because it was a waste of money on a corpse. It took me a long time to forgive Daniel for doing that. Now that I have worked for years as a coach and have helped many people overcome addiction, I have a better perspective on Daniel's actions. I'm sure he was also sad about me dying, but an addict's mind doesn't think in terms of relationships—it only thinks in terms of resources.

When the ambulance arrived at Daniel's house, I was clinically dead. My heart had stopped, and I was unresponsive. The EMTs did CPR and zapped me with the defibrillator, and finally my heartbeat started again on the ride to the hospital. The EMTs worked on me and got me to critical but stable condition by the time I entered the ER. After they brought me back to life, they hooked me up on all sorts of machines; however, they didn't realize that the oxygen tank they were using was empty, so I almost died again. Thankfully, they soon realized their mistake. They put me on a ventilator and rushed me to the ICU.

I spent the next three weeks in a coma, hovering in a plane of existence between life and death. As tenaciously as I clung to life, my body was shutting down in a systemic cascade, and I nearly died several more times before I started to emerge on the other side of that hellscape. I have very little memory from this time, other than the nightmare of the strange island paradise that remains as vivid as any waking memory I possess. My mother and father, however, were there through it all. They saw the worst of my struggle, and I want to let them narrate the next chapter of my story.

# CHAPTER 11

───────────── ～ ─────────────

## My Mother's Story

Let me start from the morning when we found out that Kevin had been hospitalized. I actually kept a notebook because his hospitalization was so complicated and so involved. There were so many different surgeries and so many things that went wrong during that hospital stay. Thank God in Heaven, there were even more things that went right.

On the morning that Kevin overdosed, I had gone to the dentist. It was the morning after the intervention that we attempted. I think it's important for people to be aware that you don't always realize when things are going wrong with your loved ones, especially when you are dealing with an adult. We knew that Kevin was having problems, but we weren't exactly sure what was going on. My husband Gene and I knew that he had changed, but as a mother, you love your kids, and you don't want to accept certain things. You go into denial. His father and his stepmother had seen changes, too. We all started talking with each other about what was going on, and we decided that we needed to confront Kevin. It turned out to be a disaster because we didn't know how to stage an intervention. There were five of us there that morning—myself, my husband, Kevin's father, his stepmother, and his girlfriend. We caught Kevin off guard, and not in a good way. He was on Lyrica at the time, and Kevin's father made him throw his Lyrica down the toilet so that he could go cold turkey. That was the first time

I had ever heard of Lyrica. I just thought Kevin was taking too many opioid medications, which he had started because of his bad back.

I was told all my life that tough love would prevail, and that's what we tried to do. We told Kevin that he had to go to rehab, and he fought with us over that and stormed out. He was living at his father's house at the time because he had gotten evicted from his apartment. That night, I went home after the intervention and cried myself to sleep. I kept thinking to myself, "How did this get away from me?" I just wanted to go scoop him up, but I had done that too many times. I was really trying to be tough this time, so I let it go, hoping that Kevin would come to his senses.

Fast forward to the next day. I left in the morning to go to the dentist because I was scheduled to have a tooth pulled that day. I went up the hill to the dentist's office, and on my way, I started to get panicky because nobody had heard from Kevin. Nobody knew where he had gone after he had stormed out of his father's house. So, all these emotions were going through me, and I called my ex-husband, Kevin's father. We have a pretty decent relationship as far as raising him. As soon as he picked up, I said, "We've got to find Kevin. Have you heard from him?" He told me, "We're doing tough love, remember? You and his stepmother both hounded me about that. That's what you wanted to do, so that's the plan. Now's not the time to change your mind. I'll check a couple of places that I know he goes. He's probably at his friend's house. But Barbara, everybody told me to do this, and now I'm getting a little annoyed that you're telling me that I've got to go find him."

I got home from the dentist, and still I hadn't heard any news about Kevin. I tried to put it out of my mind and give it a couple of hours. My husband had gotten home from work a little while earlier. He was a firefighter, and he'd had a shift at the firehouse overnight. He had done some research on Lyrica that night, and when I walked in the door, he said, "Barbara, I've been reading about Lyrica, and you can't just stop taking it. You have to wean yourself off, or you'll have seizures." We had no idea. Now I felt even more panicked. I had a kind of intuition that something was terribly wrong. I remember walking up the stairs to my room, and that's when I got a call from Kevin's father. He said, "Barbara, get to Staten Island University Hospital. Kevin overdosed." The whole world stopped. My stomach fell. I can't bear to think about that day.

My husband Gene and I rushed to the hospital. It was less than five minutes away. We got to the emergency room, and my child was lying there. My big, strong, cement worker, union man of a son who I was so proud of, he was unconscious with tubes going into his face. He was unresponsive, and his eyes were half open. It was an awful sight. His father and stepmother were already there. He was being attended to by a young doctor who told us that the next hours and days would be touch and go. He told us that Kevin was found unconscious on the floor of his friend's guest room, lying in his own vomit.

From that moment forward, our lives changed. Everything was upside down. They took him up to the ICU where they worked on him. They gave him medications called "pressers." Pressers push your blood toward your core. They prioritize your internal organs so that you stay alive, like when you get frostbite. The pressers took all of his blood flow from his extremities and routed it toward his heart, lungs, kidneys, and liver. I was signing all sorts of papers, and I didn't know what was going on. I was devastated and overwhelmed and confused, but obviously I couldn't just let him die—I had to do something. He was lying in the ICU, hooked up to all these machines. Finally, they got him stabilized, but he was still unresponsive.

My memories from this time are awful. They are shaky and unclear. My husband and I were crying and holding each other. One doctor came out and said, "I want you to start preparing yourself. People who have been here in this state often don't come back." Kevin had 10% oxygen at that time. I remember looking at the machine and wondering what must be going on with his brain. The doctor told us that once someone gets to an oxygen level that low, there is a real possibility of brain damage.

We lived in that ICU for four months. We had special chairs that we slept in, and the four of us took six-hour shifts being with Kevin. It was devastating because we thought every day that we were going to lose him. I was stubborn, though. I kept saying to the doctor, "No, he's not going to die. Absolutely not." Some of the doctors thought I was delusional. I watched Kevin deteriorate and shrink down to nothing. He had fevers that were so high that they could not move him without risking his life. He had aspirated vomit into his lungs. Vomit is caustic, so when he breathed all that in, it caused an infection that led to high fevers. At times, his fever got up to 108 degrees. He started to get septic. His hands and feet were all swollen up. When he went into the coma, his eyes were half open, and they stayed that way the whole time. His eyes dried out, and he had bad corneal damage after that. There were so many complications. The fever would come down, but then it would spike again, and they couldn't isolate the source of infection. We were there every day—day and night—just praying.

I used to sing and whistle to Kevin. I would go into his room, close the door, and whistle for him. I have a loud, strong whistle, so I tried to entertain him with that. I would sing to him, even though I can't sing to save my life. I remember I used to sing this song from an old movie called *Oh, God*. It starred George Burns, and in it, he played God. At the beginning of the movie, he sang a song to a little boy dying in a bed. It was a song from the musical *Guys and Dolls* that went: "I got the horse right here, the name is Paul Revere, and here's a guy that says if the weather's clear, can do, can do, this guy says the horse can do." I sang it over and over again. The funny thing was, when they asked Kevin what he remembered from being in the coma, he said, "I don't know, I don't remember much, it was like a slip and slide, but I do remember something to do with Paul Revere." It was really touching.

I was at the hospital day and night. I wanted to make sure that Kevin knew that I was there for him. Our joint families even had Thanksgiving dinner together in the hospital ICU. I encouraged Kevin's friends to come visit him too, and they came out in force. There were a lot of people who cared about him. We had about fifteen people at all times there to see Kevin. He was a wonderful person, and he had a lot of friends. He was such a good kid. I used to look at him and say, "He never hurt a soul. Why is this happening?"

For most of the time Kevin was in the ICU, he was so sick that they thought he was going to pass any day. I was young when I had Kevin, and he had never been baptized. When we really thought he was going to die, we decided that we wanted him to be baptized at his bedside. There was a priest on call at the hospital, and one night, things got really bad. His fever was 108 degrees, and he wasn't responding. We requested that the priest come to Kevin's bedside, and when he arrived, he gave Kevin his last rites. Kevin lived through that night, and from that point on, every time he reached a new milestone, it was on a Sunday. Two weeks after that, he opened his eyes for the first time. The nurses threw a party when that happened. They were overjoyed.

That whole period of time was a nightmare. One thing led to another. Kevin's hands and feet started to turn black. He had an infection in his blood. He couldn't make urine. He had dialysis every other day. Earlier in my career, I used to work in a senior citizens center, helping people with Alzheimer's. I've dealt with people on their deathbed. They get a particular look on their face, where their lips recede back so their teeth look like they are protruding forward. I looked at Kevin one day when he was getting his dialysis. My beautiful son who had been so big and strong now only weighed about 100 pounds. He looked back at me, and the light from the large hospital window shone on his face. In that moment, he looked like a skeleton. His eyes stared into mine, and he asked me, "Mommy, am I going to die?" How was I supposed to answer that? The nurses used to know me so well. They would come in and grab me when I got upset because I couldn't show him how worried I was. When he said that to me, I almost fell down, so they had to come get me. They took me aside and said, "Come on, Mama, get it together, you can do this." I went back and said, "No, Kevin, you're not going to die. You're going to be fine." Meanwhile, in my heart of hearts, I was on the verge of collapse.

We put up pictures of Kevin all over his room so that the nurses would really see the person who was lying in that hospital bed. Along with pictures of him socializing with his family and his friends, we put up pictures of him with his baseball team. We wanted the nurses to know who they were dealing with. He was such an athlete. This was a kid that you would never expect to use drugs or to overdose. That's what I really need to stress to other people. Don't ever think this can't happen to you. Before all this, I would never have thought in a million years that this could happen to my boy.

My husband and I used to pray together in Kevin's room. Neither of us were very religious before this, but during that time, we prayed to God all the time because there was always something else going wrong. Kevin's lungs collapsed. His kidneys failed. His liver shut down. His fever spiked again and again. I used to rub his hands to get some circulation in them because they had grown to the size of footballs from the swelling, and they were starting to turn black. He got gangrene in his feet. His limbs were breaking down because of the pressers that the doctors gave him to try and save his internal organs. These medications cut off the circulation to his extremities and took blood from his arms and legs. I watched his foot turn black and become rotten. To this day, I can't look at a bad banana because it reminds me too much of Kevin's leg.

It was such a long recovery. As Kevin began to get better, he started craving normal food and drink. We couldn't do much to help him, but we did slip him some Gatorade to try and give him something with flavor. We weren't supposed to do this, so we jokingly called this Gator-Gate, like Watergate. We got in big trouble when the nurses found out because he was leaking sugary fluid out of the hole in his trachea, and he could have aspirated again. Even the most normal activities, like tasting a few sips of Gatorade, were potentially life threatening.

I was in a constant state of emotional whiplash. I remember one morning, I was sitting in his room, when out of nowhere all of these alarms and bells began going off. His monitor lines started going flat and disappearing. I thought, "Oh my God, he's dying!" Doctors and nurses came running in from everywhere. They ushered me out of the room into the waiting area where my husband Gene was sitting. I yelled, "He's dying! He's dying! Quick, get on your knees. We need to pray." We kneeled in front of the waiting room windows, praying to God for my boy to live. I closed my eyes, thinking that my son was going to die for sure. Meanwhile, my husband looked over his shoulder and saw that the nurses were wheeling a machine out of the elevator. The maintenance man rushed over and said, "He's not dying. The machine malfunctioned. We had to bring in new equipment." When those machines malfunction, alarms go off to alert the doctors that they need to bring in a new one. My heart sank into the ground, and then just as quickly it rose again. That was yet another hill on this endless emotional rollercoaster.

I want to acknowledge that we all have family members and friends who have been through addiction struggles. At this point, there isn't a single person out there who hasn't been touched by addiction in some way. Once it happens, people look up and say, "Where was I when this started?" I'll tell you, sometimes it happens very gradually, and sometimes it happens all at once. You can't necessarily tell. The important thing is that there is hope. Kevin has come so far. People need to hear his story because recovery is possible.

The opioid epidemic is truly tragic. So is the related epidemic of bullying. Both of these are widespread problems that have taken countless lives and destroyed so many families. While we were in the ICU one evening, an old friend of mine came into the waiting room. I hadn't seen her for twenty or thirty years, but there she was, surrounded by her whole family. She recognized me, too, and I told her I was here for my son, who was in the ICU. I looked over and saw her sister sitting in the corner, sobbing with tears streaming down her face. She was inconsolable. My friend told me that her niece had jumped in front of a bus. Her sister's daughter was only fifteen years old. I found out that the accident was related to school bullying. Tragically, my friend's niece died a couple of days later.

We are all affected by addiction. It has gotten to the point where we can no longer stigmatize any of this because we will be stigmatizing people that we know and love. Addiction can happen to anyone. It is not biased. It could happen to your daughter, your mother, your son, your brother, your best friend. Lawyers, doctors, baseball players—nobody is immune to it. Addiction doesn't see color, race, social class, or economic background. It is an equal opportunity destroyer. We have to talk about what is going on in this country. It has to be an open dialogue.

I want families to understand how crucial it is to recognize the signs and be involved. I also want them to know how to conduct an intervention—they need to know what to do, and more importantly, what to avoid. An intervention is an effective tool to get through to an addict, but it has to be managed carefully. I also want families to understand how essential it is to be there as a loving presence during the time of recovery. When Kevin was in his coma, he clearly remembered the song I sang to him, so part of him was still there with us, even when it seemed like his brain was gone.

The last thing I want you to know is that I love Kevin with all my heart. I am so proud of him and his recovery. He is doing incredible things with his life, and he is an inspiration for so many. I want you to know that recovery is possible. And I want you to know that I understand what you are going through if you are a parent or a loved one of someone who is struggling with addiction. You are stronger than you know, even if you feel like you won't make it through the day. I don't want to tell you how to get through it because there is no one way to do it. You will find your own path that works for you and your family. Just know that there are many other people who have gone through this before you. You are not alone.

## My Father's Story

I'll start from the day Kevin was thrown out of the house. It was me, his mother Barbara, and his stepmother Debbie at my house, sitting around my kitchen table. Now, Kevin's mom and Debbie insisted that it was time for him to straighten himself out. He could either go to rehab or get thrown out.

A little while before that, I was talking to Kev about putting him away, and he begged and begged me, "No dad, that place is no good, please don't send me there." At that time, I knew exactly what he was talking about, and I was totally against sending him there. What I know about rehab facilities is that they often don't seem to work. Barbara, Debbie, and I went back and forth, back and forth. I obviously lost the argument and told them, "You do what you want if you're not going to listen to me."

I'll fast-forward to Debbie calling me and telling me to come to the emergency room. Debbie used to exaggerate a little bit about Kevin's drug problems, so when she told me, "Kevin OD'd, come to the emergency room," I never in a million years expected to see my son lying there like that. This was the real deal. Kevin looked terrible. I didn't know how bad it was, but it looked really bad.

When I walked in, they were wheeling Kevin out of the emergency room on the way to the ICU. That's when they noticed that his oxygen bottle underneath the gurney was empty. Obviously, the most important thing he needed was oxygen! After that blunder, they finally got the bottle changed and got oxygen flowing again. Then we continued up to the ICU.

When I finally got to see Kevin in the ICU, it was worse than seeing him in the emergency room. He had every machine that they own hooked up to him, and he was in an induced coma. As if that wasn't bad enough, the doctors came over and explained to me that on a scale of 1 to 10, where 10 means you're dead, Kevin was at a 9.5, and if he lived, he would be brain dead.

Then it hit me. I thought to myself, "Oh my God, what did I do? Should I have insisted that Kevin stayed with us all?" I felt this enormous sense of guilt. It was all I could think about. I told myself that I should have taken him to a hotel room for a couple of weeks and let him ride it out. That was one of the things that I had thought about doing at my house, but it was more difficult there, since it wasn't as isolated from Kevin's outside influences. Instead, I gave in too easily. I kept saying to myself, "What did I do to my son?"

After that, it turned into one big, long day. There was no separation between the days and nights. The time just went on and on. We prayed and prayed, and we sat around waiting for a speck of good news. I remember praying so hard, "Please God, I'll do anything. Just let him live." Then I thought, "But God, if he's going to be brain dead after this,

I don't want him to suffer. Please take him." It was an insane back and forth, begging and bargaining for my son's life.

Then out of nowhere, I just decided that there was no way that my son was going to die. I was positive after that. When the doctors would come in and tell me that it wasn't looking good, I would just look at them and say, "There's a lot of praying going on here, and he'll be alright. Believe me." I didn't give up hope when he got worse, when his limbs started to die off, and when his feet turned black. I didn't give up when I had to make one of the hardest decisions in my life—the doctors recommended that they amputate Kevin's leg. His mother wanted to transfer him to another hospital in the city to try and save his leg, but I told her that I didn't think he would survive the trip. He was in such a fragile state. I gave the doctors the okay to amputate. I remember praying to God, "Please, please let it be only one foot." There is a big difference between walking on one prosthetic and walking on two. Although both of Kevin's feet were black with gangrene, the doctor said that the pulse was strong enough in the other foot that it could be saved. That helped me make my decision.

One positive out of all of this was our family and friends coming together. It was nice having visitors at the hospital 24/7, taking turns staying with Kevin. My sisters even made a Thanksgiving dinner up at the ICU. I love them so much. However, some of the friends who came to see my son were pretty controversial. They were definitely not the type of friends that he needed in his life, but I tried my best to keep out of it. I knew that some of them were involved in Kevin's drug use, and I didn't want to bash their heads in right there in the hospital.

It was such a roller coaster. Just when Kevin would seem to get a little bit better, the doctors would come to us with bad news. He had sepsis of the blood, and his blood pressure kept on bottoming out, so there were quite a few times that we had a scare and thought that this was it.

Then they decided to try dialysis to clean his blood. Well, let me tell you, that was the best news we'd had since all this had happened.

One day when I least expected it, Gene came out of Kevin's room and told us that Kevin had woken up. Hallelujah! A miracle had occurred. Kevin had come out of his coma, and his brain seemed to be okay. God gave us that miracle against all odds. I was overwhelmed and so grateful. I prayed, "Thank you, Lord, my son woke up, and he is going to be okay."

I was so happy, but then it struck me—shit, I have to tell him about his foot. I tried to reassure myself that we had time for that because he was still out of it. Day after day, Kevin started to get better and become more coherent. We finally explained everything that happened to him, including his foot. To my surprise, the only thing he was worried about was that he had put us through all this. That was the main thought in his mind, not his foot, not the fact that he had been in a coma, not the fact that he only weighed 97 pounds. He came into the hospital at 200 pounds, but his body had wasted away. The only concern that he had was for what he had put us through. He was so sorry. I was blown away. What a good man my son is.

Now we had to figure out how to rehabilitate his body. He wasn't out of the woods yet, not by a long shot. We were still worried about his brain, but after a few tests, he proved to us that he was okay. He was getting aggravated trying to answer us with a tube still down his throat. His organs had shut down, but they were starting to come back. His lungs were a different story, unfortunately. They had been severely damaged, and he still couldn't breathe on his own. They were the last to recover. He had a couple of operations, and the doctors removed a few pieces of his lung. That seemed to help, and after a while, he was breathing on his own, which was a huge step on the way to recovery.

Another big problem came from having a tube in his rectum. He developed an ulcer that would not heal because his body wasn't working 100%. That was the last major thing that was keeping him in the ICU. The doctors decided to send him down to the vent unit, which I believed was premature.

When you are a father in this kind of situation, you learn your share about the medical problems your son has by listening and reading up on things. I got to know a bit about medicine, and I also developed a sixth sense about Kevin's care. So, now it was Kevin and me in the vent unit, and I noticed that his pulse was getting higher and higher. It had gotten to 200 bpm, and he didn't look good. I told one of the doctors on staff, but he told me that Kevin was fine. I looked down at him, and I could tell that he was fading away. Suddenly, he mouthed, "Help me, dad!" He still had his trach in, and he couldn't talk. I pulled up the sheet, and there was blood everywhere, and I mean a lot of blood. I had to yell at the doctors for them to come over and believe what was going on. After a pint or two of blood transfusions, Kevin was okay. Eventually his ulcer healed. That was such good news. He finally left the ICU, and that's when physical rehabilitation began.

# CHAPTER 12

When I first woke up in the hospital, I was disoriented and confused. I had no idea where I was or what was happening. As I emerged from the dream-like state of my coma, I saw my father, mother, stepfather, stepmother, and brother all surrounding my bed. Trauma had etched deep ridges of worry into their pale faces. Their hair was streaked with strands of grey that I had never seen before. It looked like someone had drained the life out of them, and it dawned on me that this someone was most likely me.

I tried to ask what was going on. I wanted to tell them that I was sorry for whatever I had done. However, as soon as I opened my mouth to plead for their forgiveness, I discovered that I couldn't speak. I tried to lift up my hands to figure out why my voice wasn't working, but for some reason, my arms wouldn't move. I started to panic. My eyes darted around the room, and I realized with a shock that I was hooked up to at least ten different machines that were beeping and whirring around my bed. I had tubes going into my throat and tubes leading out of my gown. I felt a wave of horror as I contemplated what they were for and where they led to. I looked down and saw the outline of my body. I was a withered, skeletal husk of the person I had last seen in the mirror. For a while, I was in disbelief that the stick figure I saw was actually me underneath the gown.

This was one of the most terrifying moments of my life. I couldn't communicate with anybody, and I couldn't move. All I knew was that my loved ones were crying, I was surrounded by machines, and doctors and nurses were running frantically around my room. Finally, one of the doctors came up to my bed and told me that I was in the ICU because I had overdosed. I heard another doctor talking to my parents. He was preparing them for the worst. He said, "Don't get your hopes up. Kevin may not make it through the night." Was I going to die? The doctor continued, "You might want to start making arrangements. Kevin still has a bad infection, and his temperature isn't going down. His brain is on fire. He's sustained brain damage. Even if he pulls through, he is not going to be the son you once knew."

I remember hearing that and thinking to myself, "Do I have brain damage? And if I do, is it reversible?" This was confusing to me because I understood what they were saying. I didn't think my brain was damaged, but then maybe I wouldn't know if it was. All I knew was that I had no ability to communicate that I understood what the doctors were saying. I couldn't make any sounds with my mouth, and I couldn't move my arms. My muscles were completely atrophied. I lay there listening to my bleak prognosis, and I watched helplessly as my family cried over my body.

I remember looking around the room and realizing that the walls were covered in pictures of me from when I was growing up. I could also make out dozens of get-well cards that people must have sent. Those photos and cards filled my mind with memories of the fun times I had spent with my family. I thought to myself, "I want that back. I'm not going to give that up without a fight."

When I woke up from my coma, it was a little before Christmas. My family had adorned the room with ornaments. There were even Christmas stockings. They had succeeded in making the austere hospital room seem festive and lively. My parents told me that my whole family was there at the hospital. Only my immediate family sat by my bedside, but dozens of my extended family members camped out in the waiting room. I have a huge family. My father is one of eleven, and I have nearly seventy cousins. I had my friends on top of that, and the whole clan took over the visitors' area.

People would come into my room in a steady stream. They would hold my hand and talk to me, which was so frustrating because I couldn't respond. I was in so much pain. Both of my lungs were infected and were giving out, my liver was failing, and my kidneys had already failed. My brain was frying up, there was an infection in my blood, and my feet and hands were turning black. I knew that I was dying.

The people who would visit me all wore the same expression. Their faces were filled with a mixture of concern, sadness, and fear. I couldn't even tell them that I didn't have the energy for their worry. All I could do was try to express my exhaustion with my eyes. I was torn between wanting to give up and wanting to fight. On top of the excruciating physical pain that I felt, I was so ashamed about what I had done to my family. I knew that if I did survive, I would be left with irreversible damage to my body. The doctors were discussing the possibility of amputating at least one of my legs, and they thought they might have to take my other limbs as well. They were still concerned that I would sustain lasting brain damage. I didn't know if I really wanted to live a life like that. At that moment, if you had asked me if I wanted to live, I would have said no. I remember praying to God every night and asking Him, "Is this really what the rest of my life is going to be like? If it is, could you just take me now?" Some days when I woke up, I would have a fleeting thought that maybe this was all a nightmare. I would try to pinch myself awake, but I would soon realize that I couldn't move my arms or my hands. Then reality would come rushing back, and I would start to cry.

Most young people have a sense of immortality. They think that something like this couldn't possibly happen to them. I used to believe that I was this crazy gangster who could do anything that I pleased and survive the fallout. I never thought I would suffer life-altering consequences, no matter how dangerous and self-destructive my actions had become. Waking up in the hospital was like a thousand glasses of cold water thrown into the face of that delusion. I was frozen with fear as I came to terms with this stark new reality. The road ahead filled me with horror. I told myself, "This is your life now. You fucked up so bad that you're going to be a brain-dead vegetable with no arms or legs." I realized that I hadn't only destroyed my own life; I had also ruined the lives of all the people who loved me. I felt like I was drowning in a river of shame and guilt. I despised myself for being so selfish.

Christmas finally arrived, which brought more visitors to my bedside. Their looks of pity as they stared at my shriveled, immobile, mute body were the furthest thing I could imagine from Christmas cheer. I remember hoping that I would fall out of my bed in the middle of the night and die on the floor. I was bitter, depressed, and terrified.

I spent New Year's watching the ball drop in my hospital bed. My family tried to commemorate the holiday with as much optimism as they could muster, but I remember thinking to myself, "Why the hell should we celebrate this? This is the worst fucking New Year of my life." I felt like I had been sentenced to hell. The bright new chapter of my life that year would be learning to live in a persistent vegetative state.

Looking back at it now, at least my parents were trying to put a positive spin on the situation. Honestly, someone should have given me a party horn and a balloon because all I was doing was throwing a New Year's pity party for myself.

I felt like I was burning up at all times. My body was trying to fight the infection in my lungs by literally cooking me from the inside. I had a steady 105-degree temperature, but at times, it would spike at 108 degrees. The doctors honestly didn't know how I was still alive. Every one of them expected that I would die. They thought my parents were in denial. A few of them shook their heads in pity when my parents refused to accept that their son was a dead man. They explained what my life would be like in the unlikely chance that I survived. They warned my parents that I would be bedbound, and that I would need round-the-clock care for the rest of my life. One positive thing that I heard from the doctors was, "Not many people wake up from this, and those that do wake up usually don't last long. This kid is an athlete. He's got a fighting will. I'm shocked that he's fought for this long, but it seems like his soul doesn't want to let go." That was the only thing that I had going for me—my spirit—and that was almost broken.

Survival was a double-edged sword. On the one hand, every time I looked into my parents' eyes, I saw how happy they were that I was alive. On the other hand, I was in unbearable pain every moment of every day. When I was with my family, I struggled to live, but whenever they left my bedside at the end of the day, all I wanted was to die. I kept fighting because I didn't want my loved ones to go through the pain of losing me all over again.

I couldn't speak to anybody during this time because of the breathing tube in my throat, so my only conversations were between me and God. You know how they say there are no atheists in a foxhole? Well, that's a true statement. I was never a religious person before my accident. I never prayed, I rarely attended church, and I had only a vague concept of God. The only time I thought about God was when something bad was happening. Then I would curse Him and ask why the world was always out to get me. Let me tell you, when you're alone in a foxhole, and it's just you, yourself, and God, you become a believer. I remember praying to Him every night, "Please God, I've learned my lesson. Please, give me a second chance at life. Let me learn from this experience and let me grow. Let me beat this addiction and live a normal life, as much as I can. If you let me live, I promise I will make a difference in this world." I prayed nonstop. Praying to a higher power shifted the paradigm from "Should I give up?" to "I can't give up!" I finally appreciated that this is my one and only life. This is all that I have. I was meant to overcome this struggle and become a stronger man.

I realized the power of prayer in that hospital bed. I prayed to God for my survival, and I wasn't the only one. My parents had organized a prayer chain around the world. People in forty-seven states and several countries were praying for me every day. That prayer chain brought together people from different nations and different religions. Their prayers changed the energetic frequency of my recovery. I could feel a shift in my perception and my outlook on life. If you had asked any doctor when I was wheeled into the ICU that first day, he would have told you that I had no shot in hell of making it out alive. The odds were around 2% that I would survive. Yet somehow, by the grace and power of God, here I was, beating the odds.

I kept going back and forth between the ICU and the vent unit. The vent unit is where they intubate you on a ventilator. It is usually where they bring people to die. In my case, they had to change out my breathing tube. I still couldn't breathe on my own, and I was dependent on the trach in my throat to keep me alive. During that time, I was having issues with internal bleeding. There is one trip to the vent unit that is seared into my memory. They brought me down because they thought that I was doing better, and they hoped I might be able to start some aspects of rehabilitation. My father came with me that time and thank God he did. He was sitting next to me, watching me in the hospital bed, and he recognized that I was looking worse than normal. I was pale in the face, and the machine monitoring my vital signs was making all sorts of noises. He had been in the hospital long enough to identify when I was having trouble. By that point, my parents were almost like honorary nurses. They would go home and study the treatments that I was receiving so they would know what was going on. Suddenly, I mouthed, "Dad, help me!" My father knew something was very wrong. He lifted up my sheet, and the bed underneath was soaked with my blood. I had nearly bled out. He yelled to the doctors, and they rushed me back to the ICU. They gave me several blood transfusions, but no matter what they did, I kept bleeding out. Finally, they discovered that I had a bleeding ulcer in my colon. They had to perform emergency surgery to cauterize the lesion. That was the day that my father saved my life. If he hadn't alerted the doctors, I would have certainly died.

As bad as things often got, I actually had it pretty good in the hospital. My stepmother Debbie worked there as a PCA, and her mother had worked there for thirty years as a clerk. Everybody adored my step-grandmother, so they made sure to give me extra attention. My aunt Cindy, my father's sister, also worked as a PCA, and a few of my friends had become doctors in other units. I knew at least twenty people there who were family or friends. They kept up on my case and made sure that I received the best care I could get. They gave me extra pillows and blankets and tried to make me as comfortable as possible under the circumstances—anything they could do to keep my spirits lifted. In addition to the medical staff who looked out for me, I had an army of people who camped out in the waiting room in shifts. On any given day, there were at least forty people there to support me and cheer me on.

I still couldn't speak, so I watched movies to pass the time. When my parents would ask me what I wanted to see, I would often mouth, "Scarface." I must have watched *Scarface* over a hundred times. It was like a running joke. My mom would ask, "I wonder what Kev wants to watch today?" I don't exactly know what it was about that movie that inspired me. Maybe it was the hope of being able to come from nothing and reach incredible heights. I wanted to rise up like Tony Montana, of course without getting brutally murdered at the end. I watched other movies, too. My hospital room only had a VCR, so my parents put out a call on Facebook, and their friends brought me dozens of videos. Everybody took such good care of me.

It was still a long road to recovery. When I was in the coma, my eyes had remained partially open for several weeks. The doctors were busy making sure that my organs didn't fail catastrophically, so finding a way to keep my eyes closed was low on their priority list. When I woke up, I had corneal scarring from my eyes drying out and being exposed to the hospital environment. I had also developed severe bedsores from being unable to shift my body in the hospital cot. I had two deep sores on the back of my head, several lesions down my back and on my legs, and a gaping wound on my buttock cheek. I don't blame the doctors at all for this physical deterioration. Like my dried-out eyes, my bleeding sores were triaged down on the list of life-threatening emergencies that I faced every day, which just goes to show how close to death I really was. The bedsores could be healed later, but if my lungs collapsed, that would be the end of me.

One day, a doctor came into my room in the ICU. He said, "Kevin, I've got some good news and bad news. The good news is I think you're going to make it." I thought to myself, "That's amazing news! What could be so bad about the bad news?" He answered my unspoken question. "The bad news, Kevin, is I think we are going to have to take your leg." At the time, I was in such a surreal state from all the painkillers and the fever that I thought, "Take it. I don't care. Just keep me alive." After that, I remember a joke emerging from some dark recess of my brain: "All my bad luck was in that foot anyway. Take that foot, I don't even want it." I've always had a good sense of gallows humor. Of course, amputation was a last resort. The doctors were trying everything they could to save my foot, and my parents were looking into all sorts of alternative treatments, like using maggots and leeches. They called doctors at several hospitals around the country to see if there was any way to save my leg. The fact of the matter was that it was too late—my foot had already rotted from gangrene. If they didn't amputate it soon, the infection would spread to the rest of my body, and I would die from blood poisoning. Cutting off the source of infection would also allow me to keep my other limbs, which were on the verge of becoming gangrenous, as well.

When I woke up from surgery, I wasn't fully aware of what was going on. I was loopy from all the painkillers, and I didn't remember that my leg had been amputated. That blissful obliviousness lasted until the next day. The nurse came in to change me, and she lifted up the sheets. I looked down, and the lower half of my left leg was gone. It was a stump. That's when the reality of my situation finally hit home. It felt like I was in a horror movie, but it was all happening for real. I remember crying and thinking, "God, how can this be my life?" I realized that I would not get out of this journey to hell unscathed. Every action has consequences, and this was my penance for what I had wrought in my life. I would never again be the same person that I used to be. I didn't yet understand what a blessing that would become.

When the painkillers wore off, I was in agony. The pain from my amputation was one of the worst things I had experienced throughout this whole ordeal. I was still suffering from multiple infections, organ failures, and bleeding ulcers, but now I had the mental torment of knowing that the doctors had cut my leg off. My nervous system was in a state of hyperalgesia, which is an enhanced sensitivity to pain caused by injury. I wanted to scream, but the trach down my throat prevented me from making so much as a whisper. Instead, I writhed and thrashed so violently that I ripped open the bedsore on the back of my head. The exposed tissues became so badly infected that the bacteria ate the skin and hair from the back of my head, leaving behind a festering wound. Agony multiplied on top of anguish in an endless mountain of torment, like an Everest of pain.

I was allowed to get pain medicine every two hours. They had me on an absurd amount of intravenous Dilaudid. I think they had me on six milligrams, whereas two milligrams is a standard dose. If a regular person took it, it would kill them, but I was so heavily addicted to painkillers that I had already reached tolerance. I remember staring at the clock, willing the time to pass. My only pleasure in life was realizing that the next two hours were almost up, and I could ask for my next dose. I couldn't speak, so I would mouth to the nurse, "PM! PM!" which was their code for pain meds.

I remember the relief I felt when they would inject Dilaudid into my drip. My arm would get nice and hot, and then the high would rush through the rest of my body. It felt like I was on a slip and slide. I would get shot straight out of my hospital bed into a happy land of pain-free euphoria. It was like the Pink Floyd lyric—"I have become comfortably numb." The Dilaudid would dull the agony of life for a few blissful minutes. Then the pain would inevitably creep back into my body, tearing down the walls of my illusion, and it would deposit me back into my miserable hospital bed. I never shot heroin intravenously, but I imagine that's what it feels like. Heroin can be even stronger than Dilaudid, so I understand how people can get addicted to it so quickly. I know if I had experienced that type of high while I was in active addiction, I probably would have overdosed and died.

After my amputation, the doctors brought in a physical therapist twice a week. They wanted me to be able to sit up by myself in bed, but I could barely move, let alone work my abdominal muscles enough to elevate my torso. They knew that if I didn't start shifting my body, my bedsores wouldn't be able to heal, but even that small amount of movement was nearly impossible. I wasn't even breathing on my own at this point. I had a trach in my throat and tubes in my lungs.

When I threw up and aspirated, the vomit solidified into a crusty mass on the inside of my lungs, which prevented me from taking in oxygen from the air. Vomit is filled with bacteria, so this quickly turned into pneumonia. In order to save my life, the doctors sawed open my ribcage, cut into my lungs, and scraped out this toxic gunk. They even had to remove a piece of my lung that had suffered tissue necrosis and was too damaged to survive.

During that surgery, the doctors put three tubes into my lungs to suck out the fluid that continued to pool from the pneumonia. I couldn't cough, since I had a breathing tube, so a machine effectively coughed for me. This vacuum device would suck out disgusting globs of brown, bacteria-filled phlegm and collect it in a bucket. I was both horrified and fascinated by the technology that was keeping me alive.

As I slowly recovered, my body began to fight back against the pneumonia. The doctors were able to take out two of the chest tubes; however, my lungs weren't yet strong enough for me to breathe on my own. The trach remained in place, and I was still rendered mute.

Weeks passed by in a slogging haze of pain, and eventually my hands and my remaining foot started to regain some blood flow. They were no longer black and gangrenous. The doctors were relieved that they wouldn't have to amputate my hands, but they warned me that I would still have lasting nerve damage and circulation problems.

Now that my remaining limbs were in the clear, the doctors wanted to wean me off of the breathing tube. At the time, the doctors weren't sure if my lungs were ever going to come back because they had sustained so much damage from the pneumonia. Like every treatment that I received in the hospital, the process became a unique form of torture. In the middle of the night, the nurses would lower the oxygen level on the breathing machine. There was just enough oxygen flowing for me to survive, but the amount was so low that I would have to fight for each inhale. For months, my lungs had been controlled by the rhythm of a machine, so I had to relearn how to coordinate my diaphragm, ribcage, and abdominal muscles to get my lungs to expand and contract under my command.

Each night, they would lower the oxygen a little more so that I would be forced to breathe more independently. It felt like I was being waterboarded, or like someone had dropped me at the top of Mount Everest without giving me a chance to acclimate to the altitude. I was getting just enough oxygen to prevent me from dying, but I didn't actually feel like I was breathing. I would gasp and fight for air, and I would panic from the fear that I would suffocate, making me even more breathless. This would go on all night long. At the end of the day, I remember locking eyes with my parents and silently begging them not to leave the room. They had no idea of the horrors I went through while they were gone. They would have stayed with me 24/7, of course, but visitors' hours were strictly controlled, and the doctors wouldn't start this torture until everyone had left. Even though these breathing treatments were a good sign that I was recovering, they were some of the scariest and most traumatizing moments of my entire ordeal in the hospital.

In addition to my nightly breathing therapy, the doctors had me on a twenty-four-hour dialysis because my liver and kidneys had failed. Dialysis is incredibly draining to the body. During these treatments, I remember hallucinating that I was standing in the middle of a boiling, infernal lake. The water level was just above my head, and I had to stand on my tiptoes and gasp for air to keep from drowning. Dialysis made me feel like my body was burning up. It was exhausting, and many times

I just wanted to give up. It took all my energy to keep my head above the water so I wouldn't die.

I was still too weak to move, so in order to shift me in my bed or place me in a wheelchair, the nurses brought in a contraption that wrapped around and picked me up, almost like a crane. It was the most painful transition. The whole time, I would be shaking my head and trying to stop them, but I was too weak to fight back. On some level, I knew that they were doing this for my own good, but at the time it felt like I was in a torture chamber. Finally, the doctors realized that I wasn't just being ornery. They found an abscess the size of a tennis ball in my buttocks. It had eaten its way through my left glute, and it was beginning to eat into the bone of my hip. I went back into emergency surgery for the umpteenth time so they could remove this growing pocket of infection.

When I woke up, I was in for a new round of horrors. In order to suck out all the infection, the doctors had removed some of the surrounding muscle tissue, leaving a large hole in my buttock cheek. They packed this hole with gauze to keep it from getting re-infected. Every morning and night, the nurses had to remove the gauze to clean the wound. The nurses would put me on my stomach and pull out the blood-soaked cotton. It was like watching a magician pull a never-ending red scarf out of a hat. As horrifying as this was, it was worse when they had to stuff fresh gauze back into the hole. It was one of the most uniquely painful things I have ever experienced. It felt like my nerves were on fire. I would lie there with the trach down my throat and wish I could scream.

Everything in the hospital was life or death. It was a test from God to see if I deserved to live. That's what I got from this whole experience. God wanted to test my mettle to find out what I was truly made of. Would I roll over, give up, and let myself drift into oblivion? Or would I fight for my life, learn from my mistakes, and grow from this experience?

After what seemed like an eternity, I finally started to breathe with my own muscles, and my circulation began to come back online. In February, I got my first good omen that I was going to survive. Every Sunday while I was in the hospital, I would watch football. My favorite team growing up was the New York Giants. They won the Superbowl in 1987, the February after I was born. Then they won again in 1991, a few months after my brother Sean was born. When I turned twenty-one, I got a belated birthday present of another Giants win. Then four years later, when I was fighting for my life in that hospital bed, I got to watch the Giants fight their own impossible season. They battled their way from the worst team in the Playoffs to win a spot in the Superbowl, and on February 5th, they beat the heavily favored Patriots. They should never have won that game, yet here they were, Superbowl champions. They were a longshot, just like me. We had both made it despite impossible odds. Their victory gave me hope that maybe my recovery was meant to be. It was a moment of synchronicity that this was all part of a greater plan.

I had a team of amazing doctors there at the hospital. I was one of the most difficult cases they had ever seen. They admitted that when the standard protocols were ineffective, they would sometimes use experimental procedures to keep me on the path to recovery. I was a bit of a guinea pig, but at least I was alive. They threw everything at me plus the kitchen sink because they were determined to find something that worked.

My family also fought hard to keep me at the forefront of the doctors' care. They put up pictures of me in my prime as a way to tell the doctors, "Listen, this kid is important, and we're all going to pull together to keep him alive." The rules didn't exist for my family. The hospital had signs in the visitors' area telling guests that they couldn't come in after a certain hour, but there was no telling my family that they couldn't come in to see me. They brought in blankets and converted the waiting room chairs into makeshift beds. They had Thanksgiving dinner in the waiting room when I first went into the hospital. Their love and belief in me gave me the strength to keep going.

Throughout all of this, my girlfriend stuck with me. She was super supportive. She had been involved in my intervention, and now she was determined to be part of my recovery. I called her Little Bit because she was this petite slip of a woman. She would sneak into my room even when the visitor quota had been reached, and she made sure to be there almost every day. She would climb into my hospital bed and cuddle up against me, even though I probably stunk to high heaven because I hadn't taken a shower in months. She made me feel supported and loved. When she was there with me, I felt hopeful for the future. Hope is a powerful motivator. People can survive excruciating torment so long as they have the hope that something better is waiting for them on the other side.

Being in the hospital is a humiliating experience. I had a catheter in my urethra that allowed me to pee into a bag, but one day it started to get infected. Some of the nurses and PCAs in the hospital were girls that I had known growing up. One of them was still a friend of mine. As if to school me, the universe made sure that these nurses were on call the day that my catheter needed to be removed. Under normal circumstances, if I were single, I would be flirting with these women. Instead, they were leaning over my crotch, painfully yanking a tube out of my penis. I don't think I truly knew what shame was until that day. To add insult to injury, these nurses would come back each day to help me pee. They tried to help me use a urinal, but it didn't work because I couldn't coordinate my hands. My right hand couldn't grasp, and my left arm couldn't lift. I hadn't yet figured out that I could use my right arm to lift my left hand. Instead, I just wet the bed. The nurses put me in diapers, so every day I had the fresh humiliation of these women changing me like a little baby. On top of this, I struggled to have bowel movements. The doctors were concerned about my GI tract and thought that I might need a colostomy bag. Finally, I managed to shit on my own. After that, every time I would have a movement, the nurses would throw a little party and cheer, "Look, he's crapped himself!" Then they would wipe my ass. I was mortified, but at least I wouldn't need to have my colon removed.

After a few days of this, my parents volunteered to take over some of the diapering duties, just as they had when I was a baby. Here I was, a twenty-five-year-old man, and my parents were taking turns changing and wiping me. I was humiliated, but I didn't have a choice. At least, it was better than when the nurses would diaper me. It was a humbling experience having to accept assistance from whoever would help me.

As frustrating as it was to have my butt swaddled like a baby, it was infinitely more difficult to be unable to speak. I still had a trach in my throat, so I couldn't ask for even the simplest of things. Through some cosmic irony, I couldn't write my thoughts either because my hands and arms still didn't work. The only noise I could make was a clucking sound with my tongue. At first, the doctors thought that my clucking was a sign of brain damage, which worried my parents. Fortunately, my PCAs and nurses knew me well enough to realize that I was just trying to get people's attention. Whenever anyone would walk past my room, I would cluck at them to tell them that I needed their help.

I'll never forget this one time. I had a new infection, and I was burning up from a fever. It was the middle of the night, and my diaper was full. I was trying to get out of my gown because it was wet. I had tubes and wires sticking out of me, threatening to tangle me in a web. I could just barely move my right arm. My right hand was frozen in the shape of a claw, and I couldn't get it to grasp. My left arm was dead, and the small amount of grip in my left hand didn't do me much good. I somehow managed to slither part way out of my gown. My diapers would often overflow, so the nurses had started wrapping my lower half in towels to soak up the urine and feces that would escape. As I squirmed there on the bed, I had unknowingly loosened my towels and started spreading this disgusting mixture all over my body. I became tangled in the wires, and I couldn't find the button to call the nurse. I was lying there for two hours covered in my own filth. Finally, one of the nurses came in to check on me. I looked at her like a wet dog caught out in the rain. I clucked at her with my tongue and begged her with my eyes, pleading for her to help me. She shook her head at me, chuckling, "Oh no, you poor baby! What did you do? You look like the most pathetic thing in the whole world." I was burning up from fever and desperately needed a bath. She took care of me and cleaned me up. Here was this girl my age who was treating me like I was a ninety-five-year-old man. Even if I hadn't had a fever, I probably would have burned up from embarrassment.

I learned a lot of humility in the hospital. That experience stripped me of my agency, my autonomy, and my personhood. No matter how caring the nurses were, I felt infantile and incompetent in that setting. It gave me a lot of empathy for people who are elderly or physically disabled and have to deal with this kind of treatment on a daily basis.

As painfully slow as it was, I was starting to regain my functions. It took two and a half months for the doctors to become reasonably sure that I wasn't going to die. I was breathing on my own, the infections were becoming less frequent, and my temperature had lowered to a steady 101 degrees. I had gone two and a half months without eating or drinking anything by mouth. All my nutrition came through an IV. Now I discovered that my appetite had returned. Everybody who came into my room to visit me would bring a snack or a drink, and I would salivate whenever they would open a bag of chips or crack open a can of soda.

The doctors finally stopped moving me between the ICU and the vent unit, and they brought me up to the rehabilitation center. The abscess in my butt had healed, and they could get me into a wheelchair. I still had a low-grade infection in my lungs, and my organs were touch and go, but I was stable enough to start rebuilding my strength. The doctors knew that if they didn't push me now, it would just mean a longer hospital stay. I went to a morning exercise program where I would sit in my wheelchair and try to move my arms and hands. I was on an IV drip for my food, and I still had tubes in my throat, so I couldn't talk, eat, or do anything social. Regardless, the physical therapists got me to interact with people and try to communicate. After that, they began to build up my muscles that would allow me to walk again. My leg was still swollen and painful from the amputation, and I had to put a kind of shrink-wrap around the stump to prepare me for my prosthetic. I had a PT come to my hospital bed every day to get me to do my exercises. I was so tired that without that constant encouragement, I would have just laid there while my muscles continued to atrophy. I was in dire pain, and I felt terrible. All I wanted was a cheeseburger and a comfortable bed.

Several weeks later, the doctors determined that my lungs had healed enough from the pneumonia to remove the remaining tubes and take out my trach. I was ready to breathe entirely on my own. They'd had to leave the trach in longer than the standard protocol, so after it came out, I was left with a hole the size of a silver dollar in my throat. I still couldn't cough on my own, so they would stick a vacuum tube into this throat hole and suck out the phlegm. The doctors put in a temporary trach to plug the hole, and they would only take it out to clean it. They weren't ready to stitch me back up in case I needed to be intubated again.

As my recovery progressed, I found that I was dying all over again, not of infection this time, but of thirst. I wanted to drink something so badly it hurt. My mouth and tongue were as dry as a desert. I hadn't eaten so much as an ice chip for months. Making matters worse, I hadn't brushed my teeth since I had been in the hospital, and the inside of my mouth had crusted over with a sticky film. The doctors were keeping me hydrated with a saline drip, but nothing could quench my thirst. Of course, even after my trach came out, I couldn't eat or drink because I would have choked. I had finally relearned how to breathe, but I didn't remember how to chew my food or swallow it without aspirating. I used to beg my mother and stepfather for ice cubes. I was allowed to have them under the condition that I would suck on them and immediately spit out the water. They also had a sponge that they would dip in cold water and put into my mouth. I would latch onto it like a little turtle, and I wouldn't let go. It felt so good to have liquid in my mouth.

In the rehab wing, I had started working with a speech therapist. Her job wasn't only to teach me how to talk. She was also the person who would help me relearn how to eat, drink, chew, and swallow. I still wasn't allowed to eat or drink anything on my own, but I convinced my family to give me liquids. I couldn't even whisper, so I would mouth to them, "Give me a little bit of water on that sponge." They weren't supposed to do that because I could have aspirated and gotten another case of pneumonia. I knew this, but I couldn't take it anymore. I felt like a man who has walked for months in the desert only to find a source of water that is out of his reach.

One day, my father brought in a bottle of blue Gatorade. I was longing to taste something, so I convinced him to dip the sponge into the blue liquid and let me suck on it. He stared at me skeptically for a moment, but he couldn't resist the pleading look I gave him. I sucked on the little sponge, and let me tell you, I wish I could have caught that on camera because I could have made a million-dollar commercial for Gatorade. I cannot adequately describe the sensation of tasting Gatorade after not tasting anything for three months. The expression on my face could have sold them a million bottles. I probably resembled Homer Simpson eating a bacon cheeseburger with a doughnut for a bun. It was the first time since I had entered the hospital that I felt like I was able to experience the finer pleasures of life.

I started manipulating my mother into giving me Gatorade, too. I would play my parents off of one another, telling them that it was okay because the other one was doing it. I would guzzle Gatorade every chance that I got. It was my new drug of choice. If I could have mainlined it, I would have. One day, my father was giving me red Gatorade, when all of a sudden, my speech pathologist walked in to debride the gauze pad in my trach hole. She looked at my neck, and there was red Gatorade dripping out of my throat. She started to panic, thinking that I had injured myself and was bleeding. She called the nurses to put the trach back in and figure out what was going on. My father and I immediately turned into guilty four-year-old boys. We flushed red and looked down at the ground. We knew we were about to get busted. The nurse yelled, "What the hell did you do?" My father and I looked at each other and then returned our gaze to the floor. The nurse finally realized that the red liquid wasn't blood. She scolded us, "You know you can't do this! What is this?" My father looked shamefaced. He said, "It's Gatorade." The nurse was livid. She berated me, "Do you know how dangerous this is? How could you have done this? Kevin, you were making such good progress! You could have died! Do you want the tubes back in your lungs?" My father looked like he wanted to disappear into the floor, getting yelled at by this young woman in scrubs. After that, we referred to this as Gator-Gate. It was our little conspiracy to bring some basic pleasures into my dreary life at the hospital.

The PTs worked for several months to shrink down my inflamed stump. They would wrap it tightly every day to control the swelling. I was starting to experience terrible phantom limb pain. It is a whole other kind of torture. My remaining foot wasn't doing much better. The skin on the sole of my foot had sloughed off from gangrene, and the muscles in my calf had atrophied. It was little more than skin and bone. The flesh on my foot was fragile and soft, and the nerves were like live wires. I couldn't even touch the bottom of my foot with my finger. That's how sensitive it was. I was just grateful that I still had my foot, and I was determined to do whatever silly exercises the PTs gave me to rehabilitate it. The last thing I wanted was to become a double amputee.

At last, the speech therapist determined that I was ready to speak. The nurses had placed a little valve in my throat to close up the hole, but it kept me from pushing air through my vocal cords. Finally, they took the little valve out, and I was able to use my voice for the first time in nearly four months. I remember my throat was so raspy that it made a bronchitis infection sound like a professional singing voice. The first thing I did was to call my mom on the phone. I rasped out as loud as I could, "I love you!" I remember how excited and happy she was to hear my voice. She hadn't heard me speak in so long. Being able to talk infused me with a sense of pride. For a while, I didn't think I would ever be able to communicate again. I was afraid that I would be trapped in my body for the rest of my life without any means of expressing myself. I would get so frustrated because I wouldn't be able to tell people whether I wanted a pillow, a shot of pain killers, or a diaper change. Communicating my needs was laborious, and I was already exhausted from the constant battle for my life. I would mouth things, of course, but reading lips is a difficult skill, and unless you're trained in it, it is hard to pick up. Some of my family members were good at understanding me when I would mouth requests, but others weren't. When I was finally able to speak, it felt like a giant boulder had been lifted off my chest.

Meanwhile, the PTs had reduced the swelling on my stump enough to fit me for my prosthetic. I remember putting the prosthetic on for the first time and being overcome by the intensity of the pain I felt. In order to keep the prosthetic on my leg, it had to be a tight seal. I didn't think I would ever be able to use it to walk, but the PTs encouraged me to keep trying.

It is amazing the progress you can achieve when you make small, incremental changes every day. When I first put on my prosthetic, I was only able to wear it for about a minute before I had to beg the PTs to take it off. Then the next time, I would be able to keep it on for two minutes, then five minutes. Like learning how to play baseball or football, I went through a process of gradual improvement until I was able to wear the prosthetic for a few hours at a time. Eventually, I was able to go to the gym in the rehab center. They would help me stand out of my wheelchair, and I would use a walker to get around. Every day, I would try to reach a new milestone. I would walk a little farther and a little farther until I was able to do a lap around the gym. Then I would extend my goal to two laps. Next, I started to walk using the walking bars. They had a simulated staircase with three steps, and I learned how to climb up and down. I am a goal-driven person, and once I started making milestones for myself, I began to progress quickly.

At last, the day came when the speech therapist determined that I was ready to relearn how to swallow on my own. The muscles in my larynx had weakened from lack of use, and I had lost the ability to coordinate the movement that blocked off my trachea from my esophagus. I started by swallowing water, then I moved onto pureed food, and eventually I graduated to solid food. After a few weeks of practice, the speech therapist gave me a swallowing test. Based on my score, she gave me a list of approved foods that I was allowed to eat on my own. I was ecstatic.

I will always love my stepmother Debbie. She was like my hype man. She would get so excited for me. She told me, "Kevin, I promise you, when you are able to eat, I am going to make you whatever food you want." The day that I was allowed to eat real food, she made me two pounds of king crab legs, filet mignon, and pasta. My family also ordered Chinese dumplings and several other dishes. There were at least six different entrees for me to enjoy. It was a buffet that would have fed a family of five. It was indulgent, and I enjoyed every bit of it, even though I only managed to eat about two bites before I was stuffed. What we didn't take into account was that I hadn't eaten for three and a half months, so my stomach was probably the size of a baseball.

For the last few weeks that I was in the hospital, I was allowed to eat normally. All four of my parents were determined to get some meat back on my bones, so every day, they would bring me a feast of my favorite food. They spoiled me rotten. They cut up my food for me and helped me get it to my mouth because I could barely move my limbs. My jaw was also incredibly weak, so chewing took a long time. I tried to eat as much as I could, but my digestive system was still becoming accustomed to processing solid food. I could usually manage only a few bites before I couldn't physically swallow another morsel. Despite all this, I remember the pride in my parents' eyes as they watched me eat. With every bite, I was taking back my life.

The best way I can describe the rehabilitation process was that it felt like learning to become a human being from scratch. I was like an infant the size of a grown man. This made it even harder because I was bigger and heavier than a child, and I had more needs than a baby. I remember that my stepfather Gene would give me sponge baths so that my girlfriend would be able to sleep next to me in my hospital bed. I stank like a barnyard by then, and she was finding it difficult to be physically close to me. I appreciated his care, but I also felt embarrassed to receive it. I was still too weak to move, so there was no way I could bathe myself. My family would shave me and change my diaper, and I felt like a baby most days.

Near the end of my rehabilitation, my stepfather said, "You deserve to take a nice, hot shower." I rasped to him, "How are we going to do that?" He said, "Don't you worry. I've got this." He went back home and got a bathing suit. When he returned, he changed into his swim trunks, picked me up, and carried me over his shoulder into the private shower next to my room. He washed my whole body in the bath while he struggled to hold me up. I was basically a 120-pound dead weight at that time. Afterwards, he was so proud of himself. As much as I still felt resistance to accepting help, it was refreshing to finally be clean for the first time in so many months. One of the nurses came into my room a few minutes later and said, "Well, don't you look fresh and clean." My stepfather said proudly, "Yes, I carried him into the shower. I washed him myself." The nurse looked incredulous. She said, "Why did you do all that? We have a wheel-in shower. All you have to do is put him in the wheelchair, and you can wash him with the detachable shower head." We laughed about that for a while after. We had made it a whole complicated thing when the hospital had a much easier system. No matter, it was a bonding moment for the two of us.

There were times in that hospital that I didn't think I would survive, and there were other times when I didn't think that I wanted to survive. As time passed, however, and I kept clinging to life, I came to realize that I am a tough son of a gun, and I can survive almost anything.

My experience in the hospital taught me to recognize small victories. I learned to celebrate being able to take a step, swallow a gulp of water, and tell my mom "I love you." I came to understand how precious it is to have the personal autonomy to brush my teeth, wipe my ass, and shift in my bed. There were so many things in my life that I had taken for granted until they were stripped away.

I also learned the importance of having a support system. No one has to go through life alone. We can all assemble a team of people that wants to see us succeed. If I had been on my own through this ordeal, I would not have survived. It's as simple as that. I learned that there are people in my life who love me and are cheering me on every step of the way. Even when I wanted to give up, I knew I wouldn't because my family and friends were there. I had people all around the world who were praying for me. They were all looking at me and saying, "You better make it, Kevin. We're counting on you to keep fighting." Recovery is an act of accountability. I wasn't just recovering for myself; I recognized that people were willing me back to health, and I knew I couldn't let them down. There were many times in my life when I expected other people to hold me accountable when I messed up. My recovery taught me that I am the only one who is responsible for me, so I need to step up and take charge of my life.

My time in the hospital stripped me back to the basics. I'm glad that it happened the way it did because it allowed me to start from scratch. It was a necessary evil. It ripped away a lot of my ego and gave me an opportunity to create a new life for myself. When I reached my rock bottom, I recognized that I had nothing. I was an infant, naked in the cold. At that moment, I made a choice. I realized that I wanted to rebuild myself. All of the things I had used to construct my identity had been taken away. Now, I had a cleaner slate to work from. I could either go forward or I could stop, and I didn't want to end my life. I wanted to live a life that was rich with experience, a life that I had been dulling all these years with drugs.

These are four months of life-or-death moments compressed into one chapter. There is no way that I can ever possibly convey all the twists and turns of my journey to hell and back. I hope that I am at least able to convey the emotion of that experience. I want you to appreciate the gravity of what I went through because of my addiction so that you can understand the mountain that I have climbed to get to where I am now.

# CHAPTER 13

⟳

I had spent four long, hard months just surviving. It was a grueling ordeal to be stuck in a hospital room for that long. Even at the end of my recovery, I still couldn't drink, eat, or use the bathroom by myself. I could barely speak, let alone socialize like a normal twenty-five-year-old. On the day that the doctors finally discharged me, I remember my family wheeled me out the front door, and I winced at the blinding radiance of the sun. I had corneal scarring on my eyes, and I had grown accustomed to the artificial brightness of the fluorescent lighting. I had to squeeze my eyes shut to protect them from the pain of sunlight. I fashioned a shirt into a makeshift blindfold, and I put my hood up to keep the sun off my face. I was quite a sight to behold.

My father pushed my wheelchair across the parking lot over to my stepdad's car, and my mother, father, and stepdad all helped me stand and hobble toward the passenger door. It took the three of them to maneuver me into the car and sit me down. As we drove, I felt every bump jar my body as I hunched in the backseat, still holding the blindfold over my face so my eyes wouldn't be burned by the sun.

When we arrived at my stepdad's house, he opened the door, and then it took all three of them again to pull me out of the car. I was only about 120 pounds at the time. My muscles were still atrophied, and I could barely move my body. I remember looking at the front steps of my house, thinking, "How the hell am I going to climb those?" I realized that stairs had suddenly become a major obstacle for me. It took me about twenty minutes to get up the steps into my house, and in the end my parents had to carry me most of the way.

We finally got to the front door' and I hobbled into the house. I had a momentary sense of relief, but that was short lived. My bedroom was on the second floor, and I felt anxiety, shame, and exhaustion overtake me as I realized that I would need my parents' help to climb a much longer flight of stairs up to my bed. Once again, my parents carried me up the staircase, while I took steps where I could. When I got to my room, a wave of genuine relief washed over me. At last, I was in my space, not some impersonal hospital room. As my parents lowered me onto my bed, I finally felt at home.

My girlfriend came over later that day to see me. She had given me so much support and care in the hospital while I was recovering. I was looking forward to being able to lie down with her in my own bed and feel her love and warmth. She spent the evening with me, but I could feel that something was wrong. Before we went to bed, I asked her what was going on. She looked at me, a withdrawn expression on her face, and told me, "You know it's been a really hard time these past four months. And you know that I love you. But I just can't do this anymore. I'm going to have to figure out what's going on in my life and get myself back together because this has been very traumatic for me, too."

I understood, but I was heartbroken. I thought that I had somebody by my side for this fight. She slept over that first night, and in the morning, we parted ways. That's when it really hit me. I realized I was completely broken down. I had only one leg. I couldn't move my right hand. I couldn't lift my left arm or take care of myself. And now this woman who I thought would be my partner in recovery was gone. I had no friends left because the people I hung out with were addicts. I felt profoundly alone, and it seemed to me that my life no longer had any purpose.

In the first week of my recovery at home, I was unable to leave my bed, not even to use the bathroom. I had a setup which allowed me to relieve myself in my bed. My right hand didn't work, and neither did my left arm, so I had to coordinate my right arm and left hand in order to do my business. I had to relearn how to do everything with my left hand. I was like a kid, figuring out how to eat with utensils, write with a pen, and clean myself up. It was exhausting and difficult, and often extremely embarrassing.

As the days wore on, I slid into a deep depression. There were a lot of people who came by to see if I was okay, but they were mostly coming out of curiosity. It seemed like everybody felt bad for me. They had sympathy for me, but it was laced with pity and other negative emotions. I internalized their looks of condescending condolence, and I threw a little pity party for myself that lasted about two weeks. I thought to myself, "Poor me, I am useless, I'm a burden to everybody, and I'm never going to be able to do anything with my life. I have no job, I have no girlfriend, and have no friends, period. I have no social life, I'm ugly, I have only one leg and a huge hole in my throat. I have no voice, I can barely see, and my entire body is in excruciating pain. My life is going nowhere. I'm going to spend the rest of my days in my bed with my mom taking care of me."

Eventually I had to get out of bed and have my parents carry me down the stairs because I had a doctor's appointment. The doctor examined me and told me it was going to take me two years to relearn how to walk. This drove me deeper into despair. I was overwhelmed by negative emotions, and for those first couple of weeks, I spent my time lying in bed, watching TV, and feeling sorry for myself.

As the days and nights wore on, however, I slowly shifted my perspective on my situation. I realized that I could either give up and die, or I could fight. I finally accepted that the only person who was going to get me out of this was me. My "poor me" mentality was not serving me or getting me anywhere; it was just sealing my fate as a vegetable. I remember praying to God and bartering with Him. I begged Him: "Please get me out of this alive. If I get out of this, I promise You that I'm going to make a difference in this world." The answer that came back to me was, "Kevin, you're not going to make a difference in this world as a vegetable lying in a bed. You're not going to make a difference accepting your fate as a person who can't function in society." Even though I still had huge obstacles in front of me, I decided to take action.

I wrote a list of all the things I thought I would never be able to do. I started my list with: "Walking, playing sports, going swimming, running along the beach, finding someone who will love me, finding a purpose in life, enjoying life as a normal person." I filled up a whole page, back to front, with the things that seemed unattainable to me now that I had hit rock bottom. As I looked at this list, I understood that I wasn't going to achieve everything in one move. I had to figure out what my first steps would be, and then go from there.

I realized that my first obstacle was my physical being. I needed to regain my ability to walk, I needed to move my right hand and my left arm, and I needed to gain back my weight and my strength. Every day, I sat on my bed and did exercises to strengthen my muscles. I pushed myself to get up on my prosthetic, even though each step I took caused me excruciating pain. When I first got my prosthetic, I remember looking at it like, "There's no way I'm ever going to be able to walk on this thing. It looks impossible." Now my mantra was, "To hell with impossible. I'm going to walk again." As I started to move on my new leg, I realized that I had lost a lot of my flexibility and balance. At first, I was unable to touch my toes, and I worked each day to bend closer and closer to the ground.

Every morning, I promised myself that I would make at least one improvement in my life. I would accomplish one thing that I was unable to do the day before. I would overcome one obstacle, so I could expand my growth and rehabilitate myself. Each day, I found a way to break out of my comfort zone.

At first, I could barely move my right hand. I could get a little movement out of my fingertips, and that was it. I would stare at my hand for hours at a time, willing it to move. I would tell my hand that I had been moving it my entire life. I would yell at it, "You can do this! I'm not giving up until you start moving." Then slowly but surely, my hand started responding. It moved a little more each day, until with great effort, I was able to slowly curl and straighten my fingers. I couldn't open and close my hand all the way, but I now knew that I would get there eventually.

One day, I decided that I was going to try to get down the stairs on my own. That first time, I went down on my butt, using my arms and my remaining leg to scoot myself from one stair to the next. I felt like a toddler who has found a way to climb down the staircase without falling. At last, I reached the first floor, and I walked around the house for a little while to celebrate. I knew that this job was only half over, and I would have to figure out a way to climb back up, which would be much harder. This time, I walked on my legs, one step at a time, pausing after each stair to catch my breath and try to process the pain. I braced myself with my arms as best I could, using the railing and the wall. Finally, I scaled the final stair and reached the landing. It felt like I had just climbed up a mountain. It took me twenty minutes, but when I got to the top, I recognized I had accomplished a major milestone. No matter how painful this might be, no matter how slowly I might move, I was back in control of my body.

My family was worried that I was going too fast. I remember sensing that they felt bad for me, and they wanted to give me a copout so I wouldn't have to work so hard. I refused to accept it. I didn't want any helping hand that I didn't need. I was done feeling sorry for myself, and I didn't want anyone else's pity, either. After about two or three weeks, I walked into the prosthesis doctor's office with just a cane. The nurses were shocked. They said, "What are you doing walking with just that cane? Someone grab a hold of him, help him out!" I held my hand up and said, "Don't touch me, I'm okay." My doctor was amazed at my progress. He had written me off, and he never thought I would be able to get so far this quickly. I walked around with the cane for another few weeks, and by the end of that month I was able to put the cane down. I was walking free.

I could see that my family was inspired by my progress, especially my mother and my little brother. I realized that if I overcame the obstacles that lay before me, not only would I prove my self-worth to myself, but I would be able to inspire others by showing them what's truly possible. I started walking for longer periods of time without the cane, and now I set my sights on my next goal. I was going to learn how to run on my prosthetic. The doctors had told me that I would probably never be able to run or even jog again, and that made me even more determined to do it. Their doubt fueled me, and I knew that I was going to prove them wrong. Around the two-month mark, I asked my brother Sean to come outside and make a video of me. He was going to film me, and I was going to run. I wanted him there to document this moment and to hold me accountable. With him standing there recording me, there was no way I was going to chicken out. It was agonizingly painful, but I did it—I ran. I decided to post the video to Facebook. Everyone kept asking me how I was doing, and I wanted to show them my progress. I needed them to know that I was fighting. Even though my odds of failure were astronomically high, I was going to win this battle.

I am an athlete through and through, so regaining my ability to run gave me a boost of confidence. I now knew that I could push myself like I used to when I played baseball and football and that my body would respond. I started eating more, and slowly I began regaining some muscle. Even though there was still a steep uphill climb that remained ahead of me, I was no longer so scrawny and atrophied.

When I was in the hospital, the doctors put me on methadone so I wouldn't have withdrawal symptoms. Once I got out, I decided there was no way I wanted to do this for the rest of my life. I could have gone the traditional route and detoxed in a rehab clinic, but I decided to go cold turkey. Just straight willpower. I took suboxone for a few weeks to get off the methadone, and then I locked myself in my room for about a month. I sweated, threw up, and had constant diarrhea. I was suddenly super sensitive to everything because my body was used to being numbed by drugs. Even a light breeze felt physically painful. I realized that I had been numbing my entire existence. I had used drugs for more than half my life, and they had muted everything about me. They had taken away my zeal for life, and they had dulled me mentally, physically, emotionally, and spiritually. Suddenly I felt like a raw, exposed nerve. Everything was on fire—burning and throbbing. The pain was unimaginable, but somehow it was refreshing because I felt like I was alive again. I was feeling things for the first time in more than a decade, and in my mind, I was starting to experience a newfound clarity. Even though it was still early in my recovery, I knew that I would never again want to grab a pill to get me through the day.

During this time, I had to force myself to drink a lot of water and eat healthy food, no matter how sick I got. Staying in bed was no longer what my body needed, so I had to work exercise and stretching into my days even though I felt like hell. I started to realize the vital importance of physical activity and healthy eating habits. For so long, I had eaten whatever I liked and done whatever felt good, and I had completely stopped taking care of myself. Now I understood that I had only one body—this was my second chance, and I probably wasn't going to get another one. No more screwups, not this time. This was my opportunity to take back my life.

Dealing with all this pain without painkillers was horrible, but it was the only way I was going to survive. The pain of recovery was layered on top of the chronic neck and back pain from my car accident, and my whole body went into a state of hyperalgesia. The nerves in my remaining foot were shot. It was so bad that I still couldn't touch the bottom of my foot without screaming in agony. I couldn't walk barefoot; I had to wear a shoe at all times, or the pain would be unbearable. Still, I knew that I was not going to be helpless. I kept pushing myself to do things physically that I thought I wouldn't be able to achieve. I purposefully fell down in the middle of the floor and figured out how to get back up. I didn't want to be like one of those Life Alert commercials. I wasn't ninety years old, and I knew I had to take care of myself.

Sometimes I would get out of bed in the morning, and I would forget that I had no leg. On those days, I would try to take a step, and I would fall over and smash into the bureau or knock over my bedside table. Just because I had lost my leg didn't mean I had lost the sensation in it. I had a lot of phantom limb pain. To this day, I still get itches between toes that I will never be able to scratch and bolts of electricity that shoot down a leg that is no longer there. It comes in waves, and there's nothing I can do about it. I have learned to accept it as the new normal.

Putting on my prosthetic leg was incredibly painful because the stump was still swollen. It was about twice the size it is now, and it stayed inflamed like that for about six months. I accepted the pain because I wanted to be able to do all the things I had done before. I wanted to walk and run, and I wanted to drive. My stepdad was impressed by my progress, and he wanted me to get behind the wheel again. He let me drive his car while he rode shotgun. As I sat in the driver's seat, I could barely see out in front of me because my corneal scarring was still severe. I couldn't lift my left arm or use my right hand to steer, so I held the bottom of the wheel with my left hand and placed my right hand on top. It was probably one of the scariest things I had done, but my stepdad trusted me. I almost crashed about five times, and we were just driving around the block.

There were so many limitations that I had to overcome. If I wanted to bathe myself, I would use my right arm to pick up my left hand to use the scrubber. I would have to sit on a chair in the shower to clean myself because if I stood on one foot on the slippery surface, I could fall and hurt myself. It was extremely difficult to use the toilet. From that squat position, I found it nearly impossible to stand back up. My stepdad realized this and installed a disability toilet, which was a bit higher. It was also difficult for me to sit on people's sofas—I was still relearning to coordinate my legs, and my limbs weren't strong enough for me to haul myself up from the squishy couch cushions. My remaining calf muscles had atrophied while I was in the hospital, and it was going to be a long road to rebuild them to where they had been before. My balance was wobbly. When you learn how to walk on a prosthetic leg, it's like walking around on stilts, only the stilt is on your knee, so it's not natural at all. My hand-eye coordination was also off, partly because of my vision and partly because my hands and arms were still damaged. I couldn't carry anything that involved two hands. Although I hated doing it, I frequently asked my family to carry my things for me. My voice was super raspy because I'd had a trach in my throat for almost three months. I had also developed sleep apnea from having tubes down my throat for so long. The muscles in my larynx had weakened, so when I fell asleep at night, they would pinch closed. I had to wear an oxygen mask when I slept or else I could suffocate.

I was frustrated that my right hand and left arm hadn't regained the mobility they'd had before. I had a device from occupational therapy that I always wore around my right wrist. It held my fingers and hand open and trained them to stay in that position. My nerve damage was severe, and my brain was still having trouble communicating with my muscles. I had been going to physical and occupational therapy three times a week for months on end, and I was finally starting to see some little improvements. Some days my progress felt like it was going at a snail's pace, but bit by bit, my body was coming back.

A few months into my rehabilitation, I went to see the neurologist. He assessed me and told me that I was never going to move my right hand like I'd been able to before. I'd had enough of doctors looking at me and giving me their dismal opinions of my recovery. I looked at him and said, "Doc, I respect your opinion, but don't tell me what I can do. I can do anything." I made it a personal vendetta to show this doctor that I was going to be able to move my hand normally again.

I continued rebuilding my muscles. I would slowly rotate my right wrist and let gravity be the weight. I would do sets of reps until I started building strength back in my hand and forearm. I would take my left hand and walk my fingers up a wall so I could regain mobility in my left arm. I started exercising with 20 oz coke bottles and then moved onto bigger and bigger weights. It took nine months of pain and strained willpower, but I was finally able to prove that doctor wrong by regaining full mobility in my right hand and raising up my left arm all on its own.

I think the hardest part of my recovery, harder even than rebuilding my body, was learning how to socialize again. I needed to find my place in this world. I didn't have many true friends. Most of the guys that I used to hang out with before were still in active addiction, so it wasn't safe for me to be around them. The last thing I needed was to be pulled back into that world again. My social skills were stunted, I had no real hobbies, I lacked job skills, and I didn't have a college degree. Even though I had gotten a new lease on life, I didn't know what I was going to do with the rest of my days. I felt completely directionless. I used to be the life of the party in social gatherings, but I didn't know how to socialize sober. What self-worth I had was based on being everyone's drug connection. I realized I would need to relearn how to relate to people, and that prospect was daunting.

Ever since my accident, my confidence around women had plummeted. I hadn't felt this insecure since middle school. It didn't help that my girlfriend had dumped me as soon as I'd gotten home. It made me feel like she had been sticking with me out of pity. I remember thinking to myself over and over, "Who is going to love a man with one leg? There are millions of men out there who are healthy and have two legs, so what woman is ever going to love me?" I saw myself as this undesirable, ugly creature, and I believed I had nothing to offer anyone. I did a great job of convincing myself that I would be rejected the moment I told a woman I liked her. I felt disgusted by my physical appearance, and I was scared of seeing that disgust mirrored back at me by a woman I was attracted to, so I isolated myself romantically for a long time.

Even though my self-image was completely shot, that period of recovery at home brought me closer to my family than I had been in years. I made sure to tell my family that I loved them whenever I had the chance. To this day, I tell my family members that I love them at the end of every phone call because you never know whether you're going to see them again. It's important to let people know how much they mean to you.

I started to have a higher appreciation for life. I felt truly lucky that I got to have a second chance. I experienced love from people around me, and I gave them love back in return. That was really everything I needed in life. That was the void I had been trying to fill all those years with drugs. It's so vital to have a good support network. Those people don't all have to be family, but they have to be people who love you and cherish you. No matter how much I wanted to be a loner, I realized that I couldn't do this on my own. The love I had from my support network was my biggest weapon in my recovery. If I didn't have them, I probably wouldn't be here today.

My little brother Sean is one of the most upstanding people I know. He helped me get out of my rut and got me back into the social world by adopting me into his friend group. He took me to social gatherings and brought me out of my shell. My brother is an incredibly popular guy. He's like the mayor of Staten Island. Everybody in my town knows who he is and holds him in high regard. For the first time in a long time, I was treated with respect because he was there to vouch for me. I had been so lost, but little by little, I started to gain more social skills. Suddenly, people wanted to be my friend, which was a big deal for me. You know what they say—you are who your five closest friends are, and for so long, I had been surrounded by people who were caught up in cycles of toxic behavior.

My little brother looks up to me so much—he has ever since we were kids. He was my number one fan during my recovery. He became my protector, which is kind of ironic in the grand scheme of things. He wouldn't let anyone hurt me or talk badly about me. He was my guardian, and I love him dearly for that. He did so many things to help me, and I will be forever grateful to him.

I remember one time when my brother and I were hanging out and having a few drinks at a bar. He looked at me and said, "Kevin, I'm so proud of you. I love you, and you are my biggest inspiration. You give me so much strength. I look up to you more than you could ever imagine. You think I'm strong, but I think you're the strongest person I ever met in my whole life." That was the moment when I realized that I was still worthy of respect. My lack of self-confidence was just in my head. I could see that I was inspiring people and motivating them by showing them that the impossible is possible.

My mom, my stepdad, my father, and my stepmother were all extremely supportive. I couldn't have recovered as quickly as I did without such a great family around me. Soon I started to recognize that my family was also drawing strength from my will to survive. Everybody encounters obstacles in their lives that make them want to give up. There were people in my family who were dealing with their own battles, and when they saw how hard I was fighting, it made them want to keep going.

During my recovery, my stepmother Debbie had been battling stage four cancer. You wouldn't have known she was so ill when I was in the hospital because she just forgot about herself and focused on me. When I started to recover, however, she got really sick. I would visit her in the hospital, and she never lost her ability to make me feel like a worthwhile and capable person, not even when she was dying. I would sit by her hospital bed, and she would tell me, "Keven, God spared you for a reason. He gave you a purpose. You are going to save people. You are going to inspire people and motivate them and transform their lives. You are going to write a book, and you are going to mentor young people who need your help."

At the time, I had trouble believing her because my self-image was still so poorly defined. I was just starting to figure out who I was, so how was I going to help other people? She never lost faith in me, though. Hearing her speak with such conviction made part of me start to believe her predictions about me.

She passed away on my birthday. My brother, my father, and I were grabbing a couple of drinks to celebrate, and we got the call that she was dying. We rushed over to the hospital, and I remember on her deathbed, she asked me to promise her that I was going to make the most out of my life. She told me that it was my calling to help other people and make a difference in this world because I was a bright light and an inspiration. I promised her that I would help others, especially people who were going through the same kinds of trauma that I had suffered. I knew that I would keep that promise. I had made a pledge to my stepmother, who loved me as dearly as my own mother. I couldn't let her down because she would be watching over me for the rest of my life. If I didn't keep my word, I knew she would bust my ass, even from heaven. I want to dedicate what I do to her. She has always been a big part of my confidence in every part of my life. That oath she made me swear to help others was one of her most profound gifts to me.

My stepmother helped me realize that my actions ripple out further than myself, and I have the ability to affect everybody around me. I began to appreciate the power of a positive attitude and the drive to do the best you can with the resources you have. When I realized that my efforts were not only saving my own life but were making my family's lives better too, I was inspired to work as hard as I could to achieve my goals.

Friends and acquaintances started coming up to me and saying things like, "Kevin, I love you so much, your strength is inspiring to me, I can't believe how strong you are," and they meant it from the bottom of their hearts. It wasn't just a shallow statement like, "Hey, you're a tough kid," like I'd gotten when I was younger. It was a genuine compliment from their soul, and it was so rewarding to me. It was the first time I really understood the profoundly positive impact that my actions could have on people outside of my family.

These experiences fed me and gave me gratitude for what I was accomplishing because I still kind of hated myself for what I had done. I had a lot of guilt and shame, and I would internally scream at myself, "Why the hell did I do this? What a stupid idiot I am! I ruined my entire life." But when I saw how much my recovery was helping other people, it gave me a taste of joy, and it made me thank God that I was alive so I could have some positive influence on someone other than myself.

Several months into my recovery, my mother was finally able to smile, relax, and start loving life again. I had put her through hell, and I felt horrible for it. I still remembered when I saw my father break down for the first time. It was traumatizing to see that I had hurt my loved ones so deeply. When they started returning to their old day-to-day routines, it gave me hope that I was on the right track.

By the grace of God, I was turning my life around, but I know that not everyone is able to escape the clutches of addiction. When I was in the hospital, my friend Daniel had come to visit me. At the time, I didn't want to see him—I was still upset with him for stealing from me when I was clinically dead. When I came home, I continued to keep my distance from him. His addiction was destroying him and his family, and I knew that I couldn't be around him when he was so sick. It was hard to cut myself off from my friend, but I was so fresh in my sobriety that hanging out with Daniel could have jeopardized my recovery. I couldn't yet risk letting him back into my life.

About five months after I returned home, I got a hideous shock. Daniel's mom called to tell me that Daniel had died. I was heartbroken. I felt incredibly guilty that we weren't on speaking terms when his addiction had robbed him of his life. I never got a chance to say goodbye to my first true best friend.

Daniel's mom asked me to read the eulogy at his funeral. I agreed, even though I didn't know what I would say. I felt numb and confused. I had been just as lost in my addiction as Daniel. Why had God spared my life? What did He mean for me to learn from this?

When I arrived at the wake, I looked around to see who else was there, and my jaw dropped. There were only about five other people at the funeral who weren't members of Daniel's immediate family. Daniel had been one of the most popular kids at our high school. My eyes grew misty as I remembered how we had all voted to make him our prom king even though he was failing out of school. He was smart, funny, handsome, and charming. Everyone loved him. Yet here he was, lying in a casket, nearly abandoned by his friends. Many of his friends had distanced themselves from him as his substance abuse continued to escalate. Now there were practically none of us left to pay tribute to his life. Daniel had so much potential, but drugs took everything from him. They ate away at his very existence. They robbed him of his dignity and self-respect. They stole his connections with the people close to him. They destroyed his legacy. When he died, he was alone and forgotten.

I was grief-stricken, but I was also filled with immense gratitude to God for saving me. That could just as easily have been me lying in the coffin. I was determined to do something meaningful with my second chance at life. Daniel was no longer here to contribute to this world, so it was up to me to make a difference for the both of us.

I was obsessed with proving myself to all the people who thought I wasn't worth saving, that I was just a worthless junkie who had tried to throw my life away. I wanted the world to see that every time I achieved something that people thought I couldn't accomplish, I opened doors to new opportunities and inspired others to realize what was truly possible. I stepped outside of my comfort zone and expanded my self-definition. I even started cleaning up my language. After I left the hospital, I felt inspired to clear the profanity from my life. I made an intentional choice to avoid cursing and throwing around F-bombs every other sentence. I have tried to keep that pact with myself to this day. Even now, when I catch myself cursing, I feel a bit embarrassed about it. These little victories helped me grow stronger and wiser every day. Before I knew it, I looked around and realized that I had traveled a long way from the person I had been when I was clinging to life in the hospital. It was so uplifting to see the proof that small, incremental changes can add up to create a profound transformation.

I learned the true meaning of the phrase, "How do you eat an elephant? One bite at a time!" When I felt like I wasn't accomplishing much in a day, I would look a week or a month behind, and I couldn't believe how much progress I had made. If I tried to look at the whole picture, I would get overwhelmed, so I would focus on the individual pieces that I could accomplish. Otherwise, I would start to feel like a loser who hadn't achieved anything at all because my overall goal was so huge. By narrowing my scope, I could concentrate on one task and then the next, and I would do it to the best of my ability in the moment. It was like laying bricks. When I stacked those accomplishments one on top of the other, I could see that I had built a huge, solid wall.

After about six months of being out of the hospital, I started drinking and smoking cigarettes again. At first, I thought this was my addiction relapsing, but then I noticed that when I drank or smoked, I stopped craving harder drugs. I have a huge Irish family, and we have a lot of family parties where alcohol is served. Everyone drinks socially. I'd been worried about the prospect of never picking up another glass of alcohol, since in my family, being a teetotaler makes it a lot harder to socialize. It seemed unnecessarily cruel to deny myself the ability to bond with someone over a beer. I had to give myself kudos, though, because now when I drank, I knew when to stop, and more importantly, I didn't want to do cocaine, snort heroin, or pop a painkiller.

I took up smoking for a time because I had a ton of social anxiety. I was still worried about not fitting in. Cigarettes were bad for me because I had serious lung issues, but again they were the lesser of evils, and they kept me away from the stronger stuff.

I was still in a great deal of legitimate pain, and I knew that at any point I could have gone to a new doctor, lied about my history with addiction, shown them my leg, and they would have prescribed me painkillers in a second. Even though it was sometimes a temptation, I found the strength and the willpower not to do that. This was a constant struggle because every single day of my life, even today, I am in pain.

I would sometimes cry to myself and say, "How am I going to get through the rest of my life if the pain keeps getting worse and worse?" Then I would just suck it up and focus on the joy and gratitude I feel for being alive. God gave me a second chance, and I'm not going to throw it away or hurt my family like that ever again.

My willpower is one of my greatest strengths. I'd needed painkillers to deal with my back injuries even before my amputation. Now I had ten times that pain, and I felt proud that I was managing it naturally with physical therapy, exercise, and eating right.

I'm a big advocate of compromise and moderation during recovery. I was able to scale back my use of alcohol and cigarettes to the point where I was using them as tools, and not as addictions like I had before. Eventually, I no longer needed cigarettes to help me manage my social anxiety, and I was able to quit smoking entirely. I still drank socially, but I didn't get hammered like I had before.

Several months into my recovery, Hurricane Sandy hit our community. I live about seven blocks from the beach, and we had ten feet of water in our streets. My family helped save our next-door neighbors. There was a lady living in a house adjacent to ours who was dying, and my father swam out and saved her. Luckily, our house had three stories, so we were relatively safe. It was a terrible and awe-inspiring experience to watch a river float down our block. Some of my friends rowed out in canoes to save people.

I knew that I wanted to help people however I could. I jumped into the rescue effort. I volunteered to get people out of their houses and to help recover their valuables. I fed people and ensured they had bottled water to drink. I brought new clothes to people who had lost everything. I checked in on friends and family and made sure they were safe. It was an incredibly rewarding part of my life. I got to see how much love there is when people come together selflessly to help one another. Even though it sometimes takes a natural disaster or a tragic event for people to form community like that, we can still incorporate that kind of selfless love into our everyday lives.

About a month after Sandy hit, we celebrated Halloween. There's a fun Halloween party scene down by the shore that I liked to go to, but it was my first Halloween without a leg, and I was incredibly self-conscious. I didn't know what outfit I was going to wear, so I went to a Halloween store. As I was looking through the costumes, inspiration struck. I chose a pirate outfit. I couldn't believe it—it was perfect. When I got home, I cut off the pant leg at the knee, and my mother dressed up my prosthetic to look like a peg leg. And that was the beginning of Parker the Peg Leg Pirate. I went to two different bars that weekend to celebrate with my friends. I had the most amazing time, and everybody loved my outfit. They thought it was the coolest, most creative costume they'd ever seen. I won both of the costume contests I entered. My confidence was soaring. Slowly but surely, I was rebuilding my self-image.

I met a beautiful woman that night as I was celebrating out on the shore. She came up to me, and we danced and talked for a while. At the end of the dance, she kissed me. I was taken by surprise in the best possible way. It was just a kiss, but it carried a deeper significance for me. I thought to myself, "Wow, I can do this! Women still like me. I'm not going to be alone for the rest of my life."

That was the definitive point where I decided to own it. To completely own it. I decided I was going to be comfortable in my skin. I was no longer going to see my leg as a weakness, but rather as my best attribute, my X Factor, the thing that's going to make me stand out in a crowd and shine brighter than anyone else. Before that point, I saw my leg as a disability, as something that would hold me back. However, when I was having fun at that Halloween party, cheerful and sure of myself, it was clear that people were drawn to me. They were drawn to me because of my leg, and not in spite of it. This experience showed me the power of confidence and embracing yourself for who you are. No one saw me as a crippled guy, the way I'd been imagining myself in my mind's eye all those months. They saw me as Parker the Peg Leg Pirate, at the bar with a drink in my hand, having a great time being myself and owning it.

I often come back to Wayne Dyer's famous quote about perception: "If you change the way you look at things, the things you look at change." Through my experiences, I have come to realize that it is absolutely true. The way you look at your reality and the way you see yourself will shape your life and the lives of everybody that you interact with. It's amazing the exponential effect that it has.

That evening was the moment when I decided to become a warrior. Not just a survivor, not just a fighter—a warrior. I announced to the world, "I am who I am, and I can do anything. There's nothing I can't achieve if I set my mind to it. Let me make the best of this life. Let me shine and stand out and be someone that people remember after they meet me. Let me be a beacon of hope and a source of strength for people who are going through difficult times."

On that night, I learned one of my most important life lessons. I'm going to share it with you, and I want you to remember it: If you can turn your biggest weakness into your greatest strength, you will become truly unstoppable. Let me repeat that: *If you can turn your biggest weakness into your greatest strength, you will become truly unstoppable.* Now repeat it to yourself and believe it.

# CHAPTER 14

⟋⟍

As my recovery progressed, I found myself doing a lot of soul searching. I still felt inadequate. I didn't know who I was or where I fit in, and I didn't feel like I was accomplishing much. I was looking for my purpose in life. What was I good at? What kind of career would I have? What work would I be able to do given the nature of my physical disabilities? I was unsure of my place in society.

I returned to college. I thought that getting a degree would make it easier for me to work in a field where I could help other people. I started as a business major, and then I changed to biology because I wanted to become a physical therapist. I knew I could relate to people that were going through the same struggles that I had experienced in the hospital. My initial excitement soon turned to dismay when I found out how many years of schooling it would take to get a doctorate degree in physical therapy, not to mention how much debt I would incur in the process. It didn't make sense for me to go to grad school for ten years and take out $200,000 in student loans in order to make a starting salary of $60,000 a year. I wouldn't even be guaranteed a job once I graduated. It would take me more than a decade of full-time work to climb out of that hole. To put this in perspective, I was making more than 60-grand a year when I was in the union, and that was without a degree or the burden of student loans hanging around my neck. I knew I still wanted to help people, but I didn't want to be in a worse financial position than I'd been in when I was still in active addiction.

I decided to change my academic focus to becoming a physician's assistant. I followed that route for a few months, but then I did some job research and realized that being a PA is the end of the line for that career track. It would limit my job opportunities and salary within the medical field. I switched gears again and looked into nursing. That seemed more promising in terms of career growth, especially as a male, so I shifted my focus to becoming an RN or an NP. My overall goal was still to carve a path for myself that allowed me to help other people recover.

Meanwhile, I was introduced to network marketing, which helped me in my self-development. It gave me the confidence that I could be my own boss, and it showed me that the sky really was the limit in how much money I could make. I wouldn't have the same income caps that were present in the medical field. That was when I decided that I didn't want to work to make someone else's dream come true. I wanted to work for myself and create something that would be lasting. I still didn't know exactly how I was going to do that, but I was on the way.

I got sales and business training through network marketing. It was the easiest way to become successful and make good money while also having the flexibility to make my own schedule. Planning my own work hours was essential for me, as it is for many people with disabilities. The disability that I have means that I often can't be on my feet for a normal eight-hour day. Some mornings when I wake up, my leg is so swollen and painful that I can't walk on my prosthesis. When this happens, I am able to hop around for short periods of time, but it would make it difficult to work full-time in a physically demanding job like nursing.

I knew that there must be a path for me, but it was obscured by my own self-doubt. Many days, I felt lost, and I questioned what God wanted me to do with my second chance at life. The answer came to me as I began to hear more and more stories about the opioid crisis. Each week, I read about people dying awful, preventable deaths from drug overdoses. I decided to write my story of survival and recovery for a local newspaper. I submitted it, and soon after, I got an email back from the editor. He told me that it was one of the most inspiring accounts that he had ever read, and he wanted to publish it that month. A week later, I opened the newspaper, and my jaw dropped. My article was featured on the front page. From there, my story went viral in my Staten Island community. People shared it on Twitter and Facebook by the thousands. In all, it reached more than 30,000 people. After that, organizations began reaching out to me, inviting me to present my story to their members. One of these organizations was called Addiction Angels. I connected with the organizer, and she invited me to speak at one of their meetings.

Addiction Angels had a "scared straight" program for teens and young adults struggling with addiction. I picked up a pen, and I wrote out my story long-hand on pieces of notebook paper. I tried to memorize it, but my nerves got the better of me. I was terrified of public speaking at that time, and no matter how hard I tried to commit my speech to memory, the words seemed to slip from my mind like water through my fingers. I decided that I would read my story from the sheets of paper, which were now smudged by my sweaty, anxious hands. This was difficult because my corneas were still scarred from my ordeal in the hospital. Nevertheless, I stood firm and kept going. On the day of my speech, I walked onto the stage of a large auditorium, looking out at a sea of more than 300 people. I was petrified. My legs were shaking, sweat was beading on my forehead, and my glasses were beginning to fog up. I held my crumpled pieces of paper in my trembling hands as I tried to speak the words I had written. I think I stuttered my way through most of my speech. All throughout my presentation, I kept thinking to myself, "I can't believe I'm doing this. I can't believe I'm doing this."

As I came to the end of my talk, I looked up at the crowd, and the entire auditorium rose to its feet. The audience gave me a standing ovation. I saw that many people were wiping away tears. A few were openly weeping. Everyone started cheering for me. I was stunned. I had no idea that my story would affect people in this way. After I left the stage, a group of teens and parents lined up to thank me. They told me that I had inspired and motivated them. I had opened their eyes to the consequences of addiction, and I had touched their hearts with my story of perseverance. That was the moment I realized that my stepmother Debbie was right. I have a purpose. Everything clicked into place. In an instant, I knew why God made me, and I knew why he saved me when I should have died. I was put here on this earth to inspire people and motivate them to keep moving forward, no matter what struggles they might be going through.

I started giving regular speeches and presentations. My fear soon vanished, and public speaking became one of the things I looked forward to most. I loved being able to use my story to help young people choose a different path. Every time I posted on social media about the work I was doing, someone would reach out and tell me that they had been able to turn their life around because they had attended one of my speeches or read one of my articles. Even in my interpersonal relationships, I realized that I had a knack for bringing out the best in people. I loved helping others understand their own power and recognize what they're truly capable of achieving.

My first real girlfriend after losing my leg was a sweet, beautiful, Jamaican woman. I met her on my birthday. She went to NYU for acting, and she was one of the smartest, most creative people I've ever met. Through her, I came to understand the importance of following your dreams. I saw how passionate she was about acting and theatre. She would direct, produce, and star in shows in the city, and I loved how she would light up with excitement when she started working on a new production. A few months after we started dating, she graduated from NYU. When she got out of school, she didn't know what her next move should be. She was still doing plays in the city, but she wasn't sure how to go further in her career. I asked her if she wanted some help, and she said yes. I helped her brainstorm her unique qualities and talents. We went through a process of defining what she was good at and what she loved to do. At the time, she was looking for work, and she came across a job listing for a production assistant on the Maury Show. I told her to go for it. I knew that the position would be perfect for her. She was incredibly nervous, but I coached her through it. She applied for the job even though she was sure she wouldn't get it. She went to the interview, and she rocked it. They loved her, and they hired her on the spot. That showed me the power of belief. I saw the potential in her even when she didn't have full confidence in herself. It was amazing to me to see how her self-belief grew with some motivation and a support system. Coaches have the insight to guide you along your path when the way seems unclear.

I learned a lot from my girlfriend. She taught me about different cultures, and she gave me the empathy and compassion to understand where she was coming from. When I first met her, I was fairly ignorant about racism. I hadn't experienced it firsthand, so I didn't fully understand what people of color go through. She opened my eyes to the reality that everybody lives their own truth, and she showed me that I have to meet people where they are. If you choose ignorance over understanding, you cut yourself off from your connection with other people.

Along my path to becoming a coach, I helped a few of my cousins who were dealing with addiction. One of my cousins was incarcerated, and I would write to him in jail. He heard how well I was doing in recovery, and it gave him strength to overcome his addiction. He had a daughter on the way, and he decided to get clean for his child. It was rewarding to know that I had helped him through one of the darkest times in his life just by living my life by example. I realized that my recovery had a butterfly effect. I was able to become a beacon of hope and show others what was possible in their own lives. I began to teach what I had learned in the long months of my recovery—you can accomplish pretty much whatever you set your mind to so long as you don't give up.

My newfound sense of responsibility gave me the motivation to live on the up and up. I was going to school, I was maintaining steady employment, and I was doing what I had to do to stay clean. I read dozens of self-development books, and I started working out again to strengthen my body. I reached out to another one of my cousins who was in active addiction. I dragged him along with me to the gym every day. I saw the potential within him to recover, and I never abandoned my belief in him. I didn't fully realize it at the time, but I was coaching him. Back then, I didn't even know what recovery coaching was. All I knew was that I had a natural gift for pointing people in the right direction in life. Before I knew it, my cousin was clean. To this day, he says that I'm one of the reasons he quit. He needed someone's help, and I was right there with an outstretched hand. Nowadays, he's doing amazing. He's ten times stronger than me at the gym. He became a workout junkie. See, we're all addicts. The trick is to get addicted to something healthy. He's an incredible guy. He has so many skills and talents. I'm so grateful to see him thrive and come into his own. He gets to appreciate all that he has to offer this world.

Helping people made me feel more empowered than I had ever felt in my life, even though I still couldn't quite put my finger on what I was doing right. I kept on trucking and moving forward, and my progress inspired the people around me. They were watching this stubborn kid who would not give up and kept striving for excellence. In my mind, I thought I was a bit of a hot mess, but I still put one foot in front of the other. Even though my progress was slow, my consistency allowed me to move toward my goals.

A few years into my recovery, my brother Sean opened up a bar a block away from my house. I was a little hesitant to get involved because I was still a recovering addict, and I was concerned about what could happen if I returned to that kind of environment. If I hung out regularly in my brother's bar, would I relapse? It turned out that the warrior mentality that I had developed during my recovery gave me the strength to be honest with myself. I was able to sit at the bar, drink a beer, and tell myself when to stop. It felt amazing to have a few drinks with my family and friends without escalating into drug use.

I will tell you, some people judged me for this. In their minds, that's not what someone in recovery should do. This is one area where I don't entirely agree with the conventional notions about sobriety. Don't get me wrong—absolute abstinence is the best possible outcome for physical, mental, and spiritual growth. It is proven that 12-step programs can change a person's life for the better when they are dealing with the demons of addiction. I wholeheartedly believe that there is a need for this path to recovery. I think that everyone should explore the 12-step model, but I also know that it is not a paradigm that works universally. Sobriety looks different for each individual, and there are many roads that lead to that ultimate goal. For me, alcohol and weed are no longer triggers to do harder drugs. It would actually be detrimental for me to be a teetotaler because almost everyone I know drinks socially. My family and friends would of course support me if I chose that path, but I know that I would feel isolated if I decided never to pick up a drink again. I am not alone in this. Many people stay trapped in active addiction because they believe that complete abstinence from all substances is the only way to recover, and they know this is not feasible for them.

If this is you, I want you to know that there is a middle ground. If you are currently figuring out what long-term recovery looks like for you, or if you are a family member supporting a recovering addict, I want you to hear these words: there is no one "right" way to recover. To my critics, I say this: you don't know what I have had to overcome or how amazing my life is right now. If I want to have a drink with my family at a wedding or a celebration, go mind your own business.

My brother's bar became the place to be. His friends would hang out there, and my brother made sure that I was welcomed into their circle. At this point, I was still socially isolated and starving for human connection. I didn't really have a place in society, and I was trying to find out who I was. The bar became a safe haven where I could enjoy people's company and develop my social skills after years spent living like an animal. I was also able to ask my brother to watch out for me and hold me accountable in case I made decisions that jeopardized my recovery.

After my body had healed enough to travel, I went on vacation. My friend Richie was going on a cruise with his family, and he invited me to be his guest. I had never been on a cruise before, so I was both nervous and excited. On our first day out at sea, the DJ decided to organize a sexy leg contest for the men. The women were designated as the judges. A lot of the guys on board were into it. They were all oiled up and muscle-bound surfer types, and each of them were sure they were going to win. I figured I probably didn't have a snowball's chance in hell of winning, but I thought to myself, there is no way I'm going to sit this one out—I got this.

During the competition, the guys lined up, and one by one, they walked up the catwalk and grinded on the women judging them. Some of the guys even turned it into a lap dance. The women loved it. I shook my head. How on earth was I going to compete with these guys? Then it hit me—boom! I knew what I was going to do. My song came on. It was

"Right Round" by Flo Rida. I got up on the catwalk and did a little swagger, a little wiggle, and then I reached down to my left leg. I pressed the button and took off the prosthesis. I swung my leg around above my head, and I hopped down the catwalk on one foot. I gyrated to the lyrics while I spun my leg above my head: "You spin my head right round, right round, when you go down, when you go down down..." At the end of the song, I put my leg back on and walked off the catwalk. The judges whooped and cheered, and the rest of the crowd went wild. The woman serving as the lead judge jumped up, ran over to me, and literally gave me a bear hug. I looked around at everyone cheering me on, and I realized that in that moment, I had gotten everyone's respect.

This experience taught me that no matter what you are doing in life, no matter how ridiculous you might feel, it's your job to own it. Let me say that again: You Must Own It. When you walk with unstoppable confidence, you elevate yourself physically, mentally, emotionally, sexually, and spiritually. Charisma radiates from the core of your being. It starts with accepting and owning who you are. When you do that, you can accomplish anything.

That experience on the cruise helped me respect and value the person that I was becoming. For the first time, I was consistently saying Yes to life. If an opportunity crossed my path, I would grab a hold and go with it. I was booking frequent public speaking engagements. My favorite presentations were the ones I got to give at schools. Helping just one kid turn their life around made everything I went through feel worth it, let alone the hundreds of kids that I was able to connect with. I was nearly done with college, which was something that I felt incredibly proud of. I was about to graduate with a psychology degree with a minor in biology. I didn't know exactly what I wanted to do, but my long-term plan was still to become a nurse practitioner. Unfortunately, I continued to carry around some of my old self-doubt and small-minded thinking because I didn't yet believe that I could turn my public speaking into a career.

During my final months in college, I met another girl who changed my life. She was gentle and loving, and she reminded me how wonderful it was to be cared for by a woman. She also had a history of drug and alcohol use, and I think that was part of what attracted me to her. I knew she could understand what I had been through. When I first met her, she was dealing with a difficult family situation. She was living in her mother's basement, and her mother was physically and emotionally abusing her. Her mother would get blackout drunk, storm down into the basement, and become physically violent.

My girlfriend was a nurturer. She had a huge heart, and she wanted to take care of people. She recognized that her relationship with her mother was toxic, but she didn't know how to get out of it without hurting her family. She was paralyzed by the trauma that she was dealing with on a daily basis. I had a real soft spot for her. I wanted to get her out of that situation, but I didn't know where to start. I realized that I would need to develop a game plan. I decided to focus on helping her save money. She was a chain smoker, and she drank energy drinks all day long. I knew that if I could help her cut back, she would have a few hundred extra dollars each month that she could put toward renting her own apartment. With my help, she kicked her cigarette habit, and she stopped buying energy drinks. Still, she was afraid to live on her own. I convinced her that if she got rid of the toxicity in her life, she would have more energy to confront those fears. I never told her what to do; I just asked her the right questions so she could come to the conclusions on her own. As I continued to guide her, she made the decision that it was time to move out. She moved into her own apartment, and her life opened up. She was finally able to live the way that she wanted to without the constant trauma of her mother's abuse.

Eventually, we both moved on to seeing other people, but a year later, she reached out to me and told me how thankful she was that I had been there when she needed me most. She told me that without my help, she would never have moved out. She could have been stuck in that abusive cycle for years. Even though I had no formal coaching experience, I saw the power that one human has to help another. I will always cherish my relationship with her. She helped me move forward along the path that God had set out for me.

At last, I graduated and got my degree in psychology with a minor in biology. I applied to Wagner College, which has an accelerated, sixteen-month nursing program. Then I sat back and waited for them to tell me if I had been accepted. I was expecting it to be like in the movies, where the college sends you a letter in the mail. You sit at the kitchen table and open the letter with trembling hands while your family looks on and silently prays for good news. I waited for months, but no letter ever came. After a while, I figured that they had rejected my application and didn't bother to tell me. I felt somewhat dejected, but I decided that it wasn't meant to be. I had to keep moving forward along my path.

I had bought a ticket to attend Tony Robbins' Unleash the Power Within, and I was preparing myself for this next step in my self-development journey. Right before I went to UPW, I decided to call Wagner College. I was expecting them to tell me that my application had been rejected, but instead they informed me that I had been accepted into the program. The catch was that they had sent the acceptance letter by email, and since I hadn't responded to it, they had given away my spot. I remember yelling in disbelief, "Noooo!" I rushed over to the school's admissions office and asked them if there was anything that they could do to let me in that year. The administrator shook her head sadly. She told me, "Listen Kevin, I read your letter personally, and it made me cry. I was so honored to have you apply to our program. But the rules are the rules. You didn't inform us that you had accepted our invitation, so someone from our waitlist got your spot. I can't give someone else your place in our program and then take it back. But I want you to know that if anything opens up, you will be the first person that we invite."

I was devastated. A few days later, I went to UPW. I felt lost. I didn't know what I was going to do. I'd been given a chance to pursue my goal of becoming a nurse, and I'd let it slip through my fingers. Tony was standing on the stage, talking about living your dreams and finding your passion and purpose in life. Meanwhile, I was sitting in the audience thinking to myself, "What does it mean to live my dreams? I don't even know what that looks like anymore." After the first day, however, something shifted within me. I started getting into the event. I was jumping around and dancing with everyone as Tony inspired us and filled us with motivation. Tony is famous for his stories, and toward the end of the event, he told us an anecdote that changed my life. If you have ever been to a Tony Robbins event, you will know the story and how transformational it can be.

Once long ago, there was a general who sailed with his fleet of ships to attack an island kingdom. His soldiers knew that they were outnumbered by the enemy, and they were afraid that they wouldn't win. The general saw this, and as soon as his men had landed, he ordered them to burn their own boats. Now they were left with only two options: either they take this beach and win the battle, or they die. Tony explained that in order to move forward in life, you have to take away the security blanket that keeps you trapped in fear and really commit to pursuing your dreams.

As Tony was telling this story, my day job called me and left a message. They thanked me for being a dedicated worker, but they told me that my position was on the chopping block. The company was downsizing, so I could either come in and work a few extra shifts that week, or I would be laid off. I called them back and thanked them for the opportunity, but I told them to give the extra shifts to someone else. I let go of my scarcity mindset, and I realized that I was now free to pursue whatever I wanted to do in life. I came to the epiphany that I wanted to pursue my public speaking as a career. I loved speaking to teens and young adults, I loved working with people in addiction, and I wanted to do what Tony Robbins did. I wanted to empower people. I wanted to show people what they are truly capable of, not just in recovery, but in life. Everybody has an amazing gift to offer this world. Everyone is unique in their own right. I wanted to be the guy that helps people figure out exactly what God has put them here on earth to do. That was the day I made the decision to become an empowerment coach, even though I didn't know how I would get there. I burned my boats, and I ran like a true warrior into the unknown.

Everything started clicking into place. I looked back at the years since I had emerged from my rebirth in the hospital. I thought about everyone that I had helped along my own path of recovery. I had given them the courage to overcome their own obstacles and challenges. I knew that I had the ability to help anyone triumph over just about anything that life threw at them.

I still didn't know exactly what I was doing, but I knew that I needed to take bold action. At UPW, I signed up for Date With Destiny, which is Tony's most intensive self-development seminar. Through UPW and Date With Destiny, I learned that self-development immersion courses are the fastest way to change your life for the better. You get so much out of them, just in the networking alone. You get to be in the company of other enlightened people and learn what is possible from their success stories. Buying stock in yourself is the best investment you can make. I didn't yet know where I was going to get the money to afford this training, but I had a dream and a belief that this would elevate me to where I wanted to be in life.

At UPW, I walked across hot coals. This process of firewalking is Tony's way of showing you that your body is capable of achieving anything that your mind decides it can do. If you tell yourself with the full power of your conviction that you can walk barefoot across hot coals without getting burned, your body will make it happen. I was one man in a crowd of 10,000 people, all marching toward lanes of hot coals to the rhythm of: "Yes! Yes! Yes!" As I approached my lane, I knew that it was smoldering at a cozy 2,000 degrees. I used Tony's self-hypnosis techniques to elevate the workings of my mind and body, and both my right foot and my prosthetic left foot survived unscathed. It showed me that I can believe anything into existence.

Six months later, I went to Date With Destiny, and it forever altered the course of my life. It is a multifaceted program that rewires your brain for success. I changed my goals, my values, and the way I looked at relationships. I embraced happiness, love, and gratitude. It was seven days of inspiring, motivating, life-changing learning. My experience there confirmed my desire to work in self-development and public speaking. There was no longer any doubt that this was my path. I released my goal of becoming a nurse. I would not spend any more time in college earning an advanced degree, nor would I be saddled with hundreds of thousands of dollars of academic debt. My path was clear. From here on out, my education would consist of coaching certification courses and programs of self-study.

At Date With Destiny, I made a plan for the next few years of my life. I would become a recovery warrior, and I would develop a coaching program that would certify other recovery warriors, as well. I would create a community of like-minded people who would empower one another to become their strongest selves. I also decided that I was going to write my life story, which is the book that you are holding in your hands right now. I knew that as soon as someone read my story, they would be inspired to work with me. This beautiful vision for the future was the first time I had ever created a definitive picture of what I wanted to do.

There is an old Chinese proverb that sums up this time in my life. You have probably heard it, but it bears repeating. It's important to remember that not getting what you want can sometimes be a blessing in disguise. In a remote village, there was a wise old man who owned a prized stallion. One day, his horse escaped the stable and ran off into the countryside. His neighbor exclaimed, "What terrible luck to lose your horse!" The old man shrugged his shoulders and said, "Maybe so, maybe not. We'll see." A few days later, the horse returned, accompanied by a large mare. The old man's neighbor exclaimed, "Your horse has come back, and now you have two horses to plough your field! What great luck!" The old man shrugged his shoulders and said, "Maybe so, maybe not. We'll see." Later that week, the old man's son was trying to train the new mare, but she threw him off her back, breaking his leg. The neighbor ran to the old man, yelling, "Your son has broken his leg falling off your new horse! What terrible luck!" As the old man tended to his son's wounds, he turned to his neighbor and replied, "Maybe so, maybe not. We'll see." A few weeks later, the national army marched into town and conscripted all the able-bodied young men in the village. The old man's son was spared because he was still recovering from his injury. Most of these young men died in battle, but the old man's son grew up to carry on his father's name.

I knew that I had missed my opportunity to become a nurse for a reason. I was meant to do something else with my life. Although I was devastated at the time, scrolling past my acceptance email turned out to be the best thing that could have happened to me. It allowed me to start the next phase of my life. God had saved me so that I could transform other people's lives and steer them away from the dark path that had nearly consumed me. I was meant to be a coach. This new adventure awaited me, and I embraced it with open arms and an emphatic exclamation of "Yes!"

# CHAPTER 15

❧

After I returned from Date With Destiny, I wanted to leap directly into my formal education to become a coach. Unfortunately, I was still dealing with my old mentality of scarcity and lack, and I didn't believe that I would be a success. As I had done so many times before, I failed forward into the next chapter of my life. I decided to try and make some quick money leasing cars. I told myself that I was saving up for my training program, but deep down I knew that I was just stalling. I was afraid that I would never make a living as a coach, and I didn't want to add to my long list of blunders. It would have been especially painful to fail at something that I wanted so badly.

My brother Sean had set up the arrangement. He knew a guy who had a leasing company and owned a body shop. The guy wanted to establish a leasing business with my brother, and he invited me to come on as a third partner. It was exciting in the beginning because I loved the idea of working in a company with my brother and becoming successful together. The problem was that neither of us really knew what we were doing. We didn't have enough experience managing the business side of things. Still, I was wrapped up in the dream of being a partner in this company and making lots of money. The plan was that we would hire people to be our downstream. They would go out and work for us, and we would take a cut of what each of them made. In theory, this business would be very lucrative for us, but in reality, we never got it off the ground.

I had jumped in with both feet without knowing enough about the leasing industry, and now I was just trying not to drown. It was exhausting. I was spending all my energy doing something that was getting me nowhere. I felt helpless. To make matters worse, the expenses were starting to outweigh the profit, and I began to go into debt. I realized that I hated leasing cars, but I kept telling myself that it was a safer career move than coaching and public speaking. I felt further from my passion and purpose than I had at any point since waking from my coma in the hospital. I was lost, and I became incredibly depressed. The road ahead of me was murky, like I was driving through a dense fog. That's when it dawned on me. I was experiencing the consequences of abandoning my dreams. God was showing me that this was not the path for me. It didn't matter that leasing cars was theoretically more financially viable than becoming a coach. It wouldn't make a difference how much money I was earning if I were stuck in a job that made me miserable. Money by itself cannot buy happiness. I needed to pursue my true calling.

My brother and I dissolved the business. Despite the financial loss, I think we were both relieved to be out of it. We were normally thick as thieves; however, being business partners in a sinking company had put a strain on our relationship. This experience turned out to be a great life lesson—it is always a wiser investment to do what you love, no matter how much money you could earn doing something you hate.

At last, I began my formal training to become a coach. The first course I took was with the John Maxwell Coaching Program. Through this school, I became certified in life coaching, and I got formal training in public speaking. The education I received opened my eyes to the power of coaching, and it strengthened my desire to help other people. It gave me the tools I needed to create the life of my dreams.

I was determined to be my own boss. I promised myself that I would never again return to a 9–5 job where I dreaded Mondays and lived for the weekends. I wanted to have the freedom to help people without being tied to a profession that made me trade my hours for dollars in order to fulfill someone else's vision. I was ready to take the leap into the unknown where I could live a life of purpose.

Full disclosure here—at this point in my life, I was also afraid to make too much money. Because of my amputation, I was on Social Security Disability Insurance (SSDI), and if my income were too high, I would lose my disability benefits. SSDI is a broken system. It gives you just enough money to survive, but it comes with an earned income limit. If you make more than about $1,000 per month, you will be kicked off the program. SSDI was set up for people who can't work due to a short-term disability, like a broken leg. They get benefits during the few months of their recovery, and then they resume their job immediately afterwards. The system doesn't work for people with life-long disabilities. When you have no endpoint to your disability, working a normal 9–5 job often isn't feasible; however, if you take a part-time job that lets you work around your disability, you stand the chance of earning too much to keep your benefits. SSDI may be a lifeline, but it also encourages disabled people to stay trapped in a cycle of poverty and unemployment.

SSDI was holding me back from excelling and going after the life of my dreams. I had debt that I needed to handle, but I was afraid to earn the money I would need to pay it off. I was stuck in a scarcity mindset around my finances. Even after I made the decision to sell the leasing company and pursue my goals of becoming a coach and a speaker, I felt unable to move forward financially. I was teaching people, speaking at events, and making a difference in people's lives, yet I still felt like I was treading water.

I learned a great lesson from this time in my recovery: the comforts in your life are often the chains that bind you. My newfound sense of contentment, at least relative to what my life had been before, was keeping me stuck in the mud. People kept praising me for the work that I was doing to help others recover. They thanked me for saving their life, saving their marriage, or saving their children from addiction. It was clear that I was having a positive impact on the community I served, but I couldn't see beyond my own scarcity mindset. Although I was adding value to other people's lives, I still wasn't creating a life for myself that I loved to live. At thirty-one, I was disabled, tens of thousands of dollars in debt, and living with my parents. No matter how high I had climbed in my recovery, my debt kept me trapped in a seeming abyss of failure.

I knew that I would have to make a change. For a long time, I'd had a mental block around asking people to pay for my coaching and public speaking. Part of me felt guilty for charging people money to help them, since it was something that I would gladly do for free. I did some soul searching, and I realized that giving my time without receiving adequate compensation meant that I would always be pouring from an empty cup. If I were spread too thin, I wouldn't be of service to anyone else, let alone myself. This would limit me in the number of people I could help. Money is just an energy exchange, after all. I was always giving of myself without allowing others to give back, and that is a kind of selfishness. Eventually, I started charging what I was worth—my ego and my SSDI benefits be damned.

Next, I needed to handle the crippling situation I was in with my debt. It had kept me stymied in my life for long enough. I explored many different options, and I decided that the best path for me was to declare bankruptcy. In one move, I washed away $40,000 worth of credit card debt. I still had $60,000 in student loans, but that was more manageable. Declaring bankruptcy turned out to be one of the most liberating experiences of my life. I got to start from scratch. I wasn't drowning anymore. Once my bankruptcy went through, my coaching business began to flourish. As soon as the money started flowing in, I reached out to the SSDI office and told them that I would no longer need their assistance. I freed myself from their chains. Finally, I owned my own self again. Then, as Tony Robbins puts it, I burned the boats. I threw off the safety net that was holding me prisoner, and I went full speed ahead into building my coaching practice.

I decided to seek out additional training so I could become certified as a recovery coach. I was already working as a life coach to help people in addiction, so it was a natural decision to marry that modality with recovery coaching. I decided to train under Dr. Cali Estes. She is a world-renowned celebrity addictions coach who runs the Addictions Academy. Studying at the Addictions Academy was the best move I could have made. It is an incredible training program, and through it, I received certifications in recovery coaching, drug intervention, and family coaching.

Dr. Estes is a brilliant teacher. She must have seen something in me because she took me under her wing and became one of my greatest mentors. In her program, I learned many different modalities for recovery, including the moderation and harm reduction approach that I use for my own sobriety. I made a choice that my addiction wasn't going to own me, and neither was my recovery. I was going to be in charge of both. I was going to follow my own path, not one that was prescribed for me. That goes for everyone recovering from addiction. It's important to find a route to sobriety that fits your unique needs, wants, and goals.

My training allows me to help people at any stage of addiction, whether they are in active addiction, newly in recovery, or several years clean. No matter where someone is in their recovery, I can relate to them. I also resonate with kids who are getting interested in drugs. I have gotten many teens back on the right path just by showing them my leg and recounting what I went through in the hospital. I now teach recovery coaching classes at the Addictions Academy to train new coaches. My goal is to be a one stop shop for helping to cure this epidemic that we have in our society.

One of the most valuable parts of my coaching education was reflecting on the life lessons that I learned during my addiction and recovery. I realized that I needed to forgive myself in order to move forward. I carried a lot of resentment toward myself for all the terrible things I had done to my body. I also held decades-old anger for the tormentors who bullied me as a kid. I harbored so much bitterness in my heart. When I started writing this book and getting it all out on paper, I realized that I had to let go of the hatred, animosity, and guilt in order to grow into someone that I was proud to become.

Another important life lesson was discovering that recovery can become just another addiction. The conventional wisdom in recovery is that if you take one drink or one hit, you've got to reverse your clock back to zero. You are back to square one, and you have to admit to a group of people that it has been zero days since you messed up. You are constantly beating yourself down. I know plenty of people in recovery who believe that they are weaker than most people because of their addiction.

For instance, let's say you are a cocaine addict, and you have been clean for three months. One night, you have a few drinks and wind up doing a line of cocaine. You might want to throw your hands up and say, "I've failed! I'm a failure. I'm a cokehead again." But it was just one night, a single wrong decision, a temporary lapse in judgment. Don't beat yourself up. Come back to the present moment. The only thing you have is Right Now. It doesn't help you or anyone else to use up the present feeling guilty about the past or afraid of the future. If you're six months clean and you got high once, that means you've been clean for 180 days. Stay focused on the prize. Don't throw it all away because you had one bad day. Throughout my years of sobriety, I've had a few days where I reflect back the next morning and think, "Oh man, I shouldn't have done that." Then I realize I just won't do that again, and I move on.

Let me be clear, I'm not discrediting complete abstinence programs. They are the ideal for achieving sobriety. I just don't connect with the mindset of believing that you are forever helpless to your addiction. In my philosophy, I don't believe that you have to identify as an addict for the rest of your life in order to be successful in recovery, nor do I think you have failed at your sobriety if you don't regularly attend meetings. Now, I have brought many people to 12-step meetings at the beginning of their recovery. I think that meetings are a phenomenal tool for combatting addiction; however, they don't work for everyone. The construct of having a strong support system and sober social circle is absolutely vital, but it doesn't have to come from an organized meeting. I say, seek out people who add value to your life and who push you to strive for success.

I do not define myself as powerless to my addiction, nor am I a victim to it. I beat my addiction. Sure, I have an addictive personality, but that isn't the sum total of my identity. My self-definition is based on being the strongest guy I know. I am a warrior. So are you. You can do anything. If you are struggling with addiction, just know that you are incredibly strong, resourceful, and creative. You have so many hidden talents. When you get clean, you still keep all those skills and abilities, but now you get to use them as a productive member of society.

Addiction is a social disease. It includes the people you hang out with, the places you go, and the feelings you harbor. The path to recovery is also social. It involves taking responsibility for your contribution to this world. Be a leader. Take care of yourself physically, mentally, and emotionally. Seek out your passion and purpose in life. Fill your soul with spiritual guidance. Choose love over bitterness and resentment. This is the path that I have chosen to follow.

You see, the more I have sought to add value to my community and live my life in service to others, the less I have felt tempted to engage in behaviors that could lead me back to addiction. There is an inverse correlation between happiness and substance abuse. When one goes up, the other goes down. The more my heart is filled with gratitude and joy, the less inclined I feel to have a few drinks, pick up a joint, or binge watch a TV show.

I know I have an addictive personality—that will never change, nor would I want it to. I now see it as one of my greatest assets. It is what has allowed me to become a recovery warrior. Without it, I would not work as hard as I do to help others become the best version of themselves. The only time my addictive nature becomes an issue is when I am feeling unfulfilled. If my contribution doesn't feel meaningful, if I don't feel passionate about what I'm doing, if I don't feel like I'm adding enough value to other people's lives, I am more likely to overindulge in ways that are unhealthy.

I am not alone in this. In fact, lack of fulfillment is a frequent social predictor of addiction. Addicts often start using because they are trying to fill a void within themselves. This feeling of emptiness often stems from three fundamental fears that we all experience: feeling like we are unloved, feeling as if we are not enough, and feeling uncomfortable in our own skin. The euphoria of addiction can seem fulfilling in the moment, but it will never satisfy the needs of the soul. In order to show you why this is, I want to share a psychological model that I learned at UPW and Date With Destiny. These seminars taught me one of the most important lessons that I have come to understand about addictive behavior. In his work in practical psychology, Tony Robbins explains that we all have six core human needs that we must fulfill in order to feel genuinely happy.

Tony calls the first four human needs "the Needs of the Personality." They are:

- Certainty: the need for safety, comfort, order, predictability, and control.

- Variety: the need for excitement, surprises, change, adventure, and novelty.
- Significance: the need to feel special, needed, wanted, valued, and worthy of love.
- Love & Connection: the need to communicate and reciprocate a loving connection with others.

Tony calls the last two human needs "the Needs of the Spirit." They are:

- Growth: the need for emotional, intellectual, and spiritual development.
- Contribution: the need to give beyond oneself in order to protect and serve others.

We can survive by fulfilling only the first four human needs, but we will always feel a sense of emptiness. If we don't satisfy the Needs of the Spirit, we will feel that something is missing. In the absence of Growth and Contribution, we will seek to fill that void within ourselves by doubling down on the Needs of the Personality. Once we find something that reliably satisfies even three of our four basic human needs, we will gravitate toward that thing. We may even form a dependence on it. Any time our mind perceives that doing, believing, or feeling something meets at least three of our core human needs, we can become addicted to that action, thought, or experience.

Here's the thing, you can become addicted to the experience of addiction itself, independent of the drugs that are used. In fact, addiction fulfills all four of the Needs of the Personality. Let me show you how. Back when I was in the height of my addiction, whether I was using weed, Percocet, or porn, I had Certainty from anticipating the pleasure I was about to experience; I had Variety from the risk and excitement of using; I had Significance from the feeling of grandeur I got when I was high; and I had Love and Connection from the sensation of being in tune with the universe. All I needed to do was snort a line of coke or take a hit of ecstasy, and my basic needs would be satisfied. What was worse, I had no desire or motivation to seek out anything to replace my addiction because it so reliably met those first four needs.

No matter how powerful it may be, addiction can never fulfill the Needs of the Spirit, and that is why it is ultimately such an empty, self-centered experience. No amount of drugs, sex, or cash will lead to Growth and Contribution. Spiritual needs are greater than yourself. They are gratifying and joyous. They allow you to direct your focus outward toward the betterment of the world instead of on the indulgence of your own ego.

As I have had time to reflect back on my life, I can see that my addictions only ever gave me short-term comfort. The high would soon wear off, and I would feel even worse than before. Then I would seek out another shot of adrenaline. The greater the high, the harder the crash, and each crash buried me deeper until I had dug my own hole to hell.

When I used to feel unfulfilled as an addict, I would look for a new drug to fill me up. Now, I look for opportunities to serve others and to grow spiritually. I have learned how to navigate my life to avoid harmful vices like coke, ecstasy, and opiates. My mind doesn't even consider them as an option anymore. I still have an impulsive, addictive personality, but I have learned how to channel it into spontaneity, passion, and persistence.

I find that it's important to understand your personal makeup and then direct yourself toward things that give you an intensity of experience in a safe way. You are not going to fundamentally change your nature. If you try to deny who you are, your addictive tendencies may come out in ways that you are unable to control. I also encourage you to be forgiving of yourself. If you have more drinks than you should, don't beat yourself up about it. Don't use guilt and shame as self-control tactics. Just know that you are in control of moderating your behavior, and next time, you are going to be honest with yourself and stop before you get wasted. You will learn your limitations through experience.

I want you to know that you are not on this journey alone. You have people in your corner who will champion your recovery goals. It is your responsibility to figure out who these people are and to invite them into your inner circle. This necessarily means that there are also some people that you will need to release from your life. Understand that part of recovery is clearing house and removing the people that are dragging you down. Look for people who will hold you accountable. Your job is to build a strong team that can support you in your sobriety, whatever that looks like to you. Like the saying goes, you are the amalgamation of the five people that you spend the most time with, both in person and on social media. If you don't like where you are in life, look to your left and right. Figure out who you need to distance yourself from and who you need to get closer to. You can build a better future by changing your social circle. When you bring people into your life who have an achievement mindset, you can't help but be elevated by that.

Social accountability needs to start early on. We are social beings, and we rely on the satisfaction of hearing "good job" or "atta boy." We also need to feel other people's concern for our wellbeing when we go astray. I don't think that anyone is 100% self-motivated. We all strive for love and acceptance from the people around us, and we depend on them to help us act in accordance with the better angels of our nature. When I was in high school, almost everyone gave me a pass for my actions. Few people held me accountable, whether it was my classmates, my teachers, or even my school administrators. If someone I had respected had expressed high expectations of me, I think I would have elevated my own self-expectations to match. Because of this, I feel that I have a responsibility to connect with teens who are going down the same path that nearly destroyed my life. I say to them, "Listen, you're obviously a bright kid. You're an entrepreneur, and you've got a head for business. You can do better than this. Direct your intelligence to legitimate business, and you will earn more money than you could ever make dealing drugs."

If you are a teacher or work with kids, I want you to pay special attention to this strategy. If you are trying to reach a kid who is having behavioral challenges in school, don't try to shut them down or punish them until they comply. Instead, give them responsibility. Tell them, "You're really smart. You do good work. I heard that you're a leader in this class. The way you handle yourself impacts the rest of the class because they look up to you. That's a big responsibility, and I have faith in you. I'm looking forward to having you in my class. You are going to help make this a good year for everyone."

Just by saying this to a child, you can change their paradigm of school. When you move from an attitude of blame to an attitude of responsibility, you give a kid with behavioral challenges an opportunity to contribute to something bigger than themselves. Returning to Tony Robbins' model of the Six Human Needs, you are showing that child how to find fulfillment through prosocial actions, instead of seeking clout through antisocial behavior.

When a kid becomes a school bully or class clown, they get the Certainty of being in charge, the Significance of making people fear them, and the Variety of not knowing who they will target next, but they have no Connection, Contribution, or Growth. They have only the three lowest human needs met. It is just enough to make their behavior addicting, but not enough to make them happy or fulfilled in life.

Now imagine the following scenario: as this student Contributes responsibly to the classroom, he gets to experience prosocial Growth. He builds a Connection with his teacher and the other students, and he feels the Significance of being a leader. He gets Variety in his life because he is learning new ways of interacting with his peers, and he has Certainty because he is in charge. He has all six human needs met, just like that. Using this model, you really can shift a student with behavioral issues into a superstar. From that point on, he might even become an honor roll student. That is the power of coaching.

# CHAPTER 16

N o matter how traumatic the years leading up to my recovery have been, I can honestly say that I wouldn't change a thing. My journey through addiction has shaped who I am, and I draw on these experiences to become a better coach, public speaker, and all-around recovery warrior. The road may be winding at times, but I am never going back to the hell that I inhabited for so many years. When I woke from my coma in the hospital, I made a commitment to God that I would follow a spiritual path, and that has been my saving grace.

I was never into religion or spirituality as a kid. I was raised Catholic, but it didn't resonate with me. I felt judged when I went to church, and I was uncomfortable trying to fit in with my family's congregation. When I was in the hospital, my parents brought a priest to baptize me and read me my last rites. Catholicism was not the route that I chose to take in my recovery, though it is still part of my story. My awakening started when I reached out to God and pleaded for my life. In that moment, I made a pact. I promised God that I would end my quest for self-destruction. I would open my heart and allow His grace to save me. He answered my prayers, for it was truly a miracle that I survived that ordeal.

After I left the hospital, I set out on a path of spiritual exploration. I prayed and meditated, and I sought out everything from Native American rituals to Buddhist practice to Christian services. When I began my search for God, I didn't know where to look. The closest thing that I was able to cling to at the time was the Law of Attraction. I sought to influence the universe in order to create the things that I wanted in life. I wanted to be the higher power that I was searching for. I saw God in the intelligent design of the world, and that brought me a sense of peace and security. I kept searching for other manifestations of God, and that is what led me to prayer. At first, I didn't really know who I was praying to or if I was doing it right. All I knew was that I was praying for God's help because I couldn't continue living with the delusion that I had all the answers. I recognized that I couldn't do it all on my own. Prayer changed my life.

As I continued my journey, I decided to explore a Native American spiritual path. I attended moon ceremonies and sweat lodges. Then I decided to try San Pedro and Ayahuasca ceremonies. During these experiences, I received profound messages about who I truly am. In order to partake in an Ayahuasca ceremony, you have to start preparing at least a month in advance. During that time, you must simplify your diet to remove meat, preservatives, salt, and sugar. You can't watch TV or engage in any sexual encounters. You have to go right back to the basics. At the ceremony, the shaman gives you Ayahuasca tea, which is a brew infused with a natural hallucinogenic plant from the Amazon. It is a medicine that has spirit to it. During the ritual, the vibrations of the music, prayer, dance, and singing create a vortex of energy. It feels like you are peeling back the layers of your ego. You unwind yourself until you figure out who you are at the core. You delve into your primal consciousness and awareness.

I saw the egotistical mask of bullshit that I had learned to hide behind throughout my life. I undid years of cultural brainwashing and stripped away the expectations of friends, family, and society. I realized that the people in charge feed us black and white narratives to keep us at each other's throats. The angrier we are, the easier we are to manipulate. People are always fighting and feuding, whether it's about money, politics, religion, or anything else that we are fed each day by the news. In life, there are never two sides to anything—there are always a million different perspectives. Our leaders are not working for us; they are just here to control us. Revelations like these came to me quickly, like I was seeing the world for the first time. It was a wild experience. Afterwards, I felt like a newborn. I didn't care what people had to say about my life. I just wanted to lead a happy, fulfilled, and purposeful existence. That's what life is all about.

As I went through this spiritual odyssey, I opened my third eye and allowed my intuition to speak to me. I received messages from a higher consciousness, whether you want to call it God, energy, or the universe. The veil was lifted, and I saw fundamental truths about life. It was at once exquisitely beautiful and overwhelmingly profound.

Ayahuasca is not a recreational drug. It is a medicine that opens you up to a new perspective. It allowed me to explore an entirely new dimension. I saw things that I never thought existed in this reality. It showed me that the possibilities in this universe are endless. There is no limit to potential. It was like the dimensions of reality split themselves into a million pieces, and I saw them all with my own eyes.

I don't regret doing it because it expanded my understanding about the world that we all share. It showed me that we are truly all one. I gained so much more compassion and empathy for other people because I realized that they are just another piece of me, as I am a piece of them. Each one of us is merely a handful of atoms in this vast universe, and we are all created from the same stardust. We experience different viewpoints of conscious awareness within the same frame of reality.

I got what I needed from these experiences. They were medicinal and therapeutic encounters. I was always in controlled environments with shamans and medicine men. These journeys furthered my path into self-development. I learned to live a life that is rich and full of gratitude. I made true connections with people who were on their own quest for enlightenment. I solidified in my soul who I am and who I want to grow to become. I want to live a life full of passion and purpose, to be in service to others, and to make a difference in this world. I want to fill up my cup with adventures that I will be excited to look back on when I am eighty years old.

I continued my journey into faith. I read books on Buddhist duality, and I learned that there is always a little bit of good in all that is bad and a little bit of bad in all that is good. According to their philosophy, wisdom comes from the lessons you learn working through the inevitable pain of life. I also read about Islam and Judaism. Judaism resonated with me because of the one God of creation. I even read the Torah. These experiences had a significant impact on my life, and I am where I am today because of this spiritual exploration. I found that each of these religious beliefs had pieces of truth within them; however, I felt that something was always missing. I knew I felt whole having God in my life. It gave me comfort knowing that there is something bigger than what I can see, hear, and feel. I was on this quest for about seven years. Eventually, all roads that I traveled led me to Christ. When I accepted Jesus as my Lord and Savior, my entire life was transformed. I found the conviction to live in a righteous way. All it took was faith.

I now know that it was God who transformed me in my beliefs. He made me into the man that I was meant to become. I am not nearly the person I thought I was going to be when I was young. The metamorphosis that I went through wasn't of my doing; it was of the Holy Spirit. It was a beautiful journey, although it was painful at times. I experienced the tearing of the flesh from the spirit as I released my desires to fornicate and overindulge in harmful vices. Those impulses were taken over by the spiritual aspects of kindness, gratitude, joy, and all the things that money and power can never buy. I shed many parts of my life that were not serving me. My journey in faith was a challenging but ultimately wondrous experience.

I advocate that you too search for spirituality in your life in whatever way feels right. Christ was it for me. He was the truth that I was looking for. For someone else, that truth might be Judaism, Buddhism, Hinduism, or New Age mysticism. If you had a religious upbringing, I encourage you to seek out an individual expression of faith that is meaningful for you. Claim your faith with intention, whether that means committing to the religion you were raised in or opening your heart to a new spiritual expression. Be mindful and consistent in your practice and find what resonates with you.

When I lived as an atheist, I worshipped things that would never fulfill me. I worshipped money, drugs, popularity, and the power I got from being a dealer. Here is a lesson I learned in my recovery: As human beings, it is part of our fundamental nature to worship. We experience great solace when we worship the eternal and unchanging; however, many of us project our worship onto worldly things. When we worship material commodities, it leads to possessiveness, obsession, and overindulgence. Anything impermanent can be taken from us, and so we crave it. Take wealth and influence—if you worship these things, you will never be rich enough or powerful enough to satisfy your thirst. That is why the love of money and power is at the root of all evil. It will make you do filthy things to obtain and keep it.

Spirituality fills the void within that we too often try to satisfy with power, possessions, prestige, and other materialistic experiences. Those things will all decay and die, leaving you feeling empty. The tighter you grasp them, the faster they slip through your fingers. God is eternal. When you pray to Him, you connect with a power that is everlasting.

We are all designed to worship something. It is up to each of us to worship mindfully and choose a higher power that is enduring and fulfilling. Through my recovery, I have finally found the truth that I sought for so many years. I have discovered the way to my relationship with God through Jesus Christ. I know that if you embrace this quest for spirituality and God, you too will find the truth that you seek. I invite you to open your heart, let in the Divine, and inspire others to do the same.

# CHAPTER 17

---

fter spending thirteen years in active addiction, I knew that I needed to find a way to give back. There were so many people that I had hurt, and I looked for a means to atone for that. I wanted to contribute to this world instead of merely taking from it. Becoming a coach allowed me to do that. I was able to transform myself into a force for good in people's lives. Coaching gave me the means to empower others to overcome their own traumas and discover their passions. Nowadays, I help people find their "YOU factor" that allows them to achieve success. I love this process because when people discover their purpose, they start to create a life of fulfillment and joy.

I have trained in three different modalities of coaching. I am certified in the John Maxwell Coaching Program, I have studied under Tony Robbins, and I have been certified as a coach by the Addictions Academy. I now train future recovery coaches at the Addictions Academy, and I love that I can multiply what I am able to do in society and help more people than I could reach by myself. I have certifications in recovery coaching, life coaching, empowerment coaching, family coaching, nutrition coaching, and drug interventions. The way I approach coaching is multifaceted and customizable. I tailor the way I implement these modalities to help me reach each individual client that I serve. There is no single objective, strategy, or blueprint that I use because everyone has different capabilities, talents, skills, and goals.

I specialize in helping people that are getting out of rehab. When you are newly out of a recovery program, you feel empty and scared, and you are searching for your place in the world. Happy people don't do drugs. You don't wake up one day and say, "I think I'm going to get addicted to cocaine." The gateway to addiction is trauma, and the road to recovery is through empowerment. As a coach, I help my clients discover and utilize what makes them uniquely amazing.

I have learned to take my clients from exactly where they are and bring them to exactly where they want to be. I take a physical, mental, emotional, and spiritual approach to this. I honor my clients' goals and beliefs. It is not my place to superimpose my beliefs onto theirs. I look at what they desire and what they are trying to obtain because the coaching process is not about me. It's not about my judgment or my opinions. I coach to each client's unique criteria. My goal is to help them figure out what they genuinely want in life.

My coaching is strengths-based. I have clients that come to me for overcoming trauma, improving self-confidence, mastering anxiety and depression, and recovering from addiction. I work with people who want to take back their lives. They feel unfulfilled, and they need some structure and stability. They need to get into a physical, mental, and emotional state of greatness. I show them how to cultivate these resources that they have inside, and I help them become the most empowered version of themselves.

When you work with me as a client, I help you discover your strengths and understand your weaknesses. I show you how to create a life that is built around your abilities, and I teach you to sort through the baggage that slows you down. That is my overarching model. I help you create and design a life that you love to live, whatever that looks like for you.

I am trained to help you see different perspectives. You learn to challenge old patterns and cultivate new ones. Just by switching your paradigm, you can change your entire life. As you learn new models, you unlock skills, resources, and inner greatness that you never knew were there.

The power of coaching is that all the answers lie inside of you already. As a coach, I help unlock that inner wisdom. I am here to help you navigate uncharted waters. I give you safe passage through this crazy ocean of life.

I wish I'd had a coach when I was young, and it is my goal to be that person for someone else in need. If I'd had someone like me when I was struggling, I know I wouldn't have suffered the way that I did.

I've helped people from scientists to drug addicts, from stay-at-home moms to celebrities. There really is no limit to the people who can be helped by coaching. I'll tell you, my absolute favorite clients are the ones that truly want it. I don't take clients unless they commit to the process. I interview them to assess if I am a good fit for what they need. I won't work with somebody if I think that I'm not the right person to help them. I'm not here to take people's money. I am here to change lives.

I have the best job in the world because I give people the tools to break through blockages that have held them back for years. I live for the "aha" moments where they change their whole perspective on life in an instant. Some of my clients have even been able to put down drugs after decades of use.

I work with people all over the country. I coach many of my clients over video conferencing. Some of my clients need more intense, in-person coaching. I have even stayed with clients for up to a month at a time as a sober living companion. I watch them in real life and see how they interact in their environment. This helps us figure out their triggers, identify their weaknesses, and most importantly, build on their strengths. I help them create life skills from the ground up, from cooking to cleaning to budgeting to working out. I establish a secure base for them, which allows them to step outside their comfort zone. I want them to see that they can accomplish anything they put their mind to.

I like to do fun activities with my clients because life is not all about struggle. It is about creating the fire within you that drives you to keep going even when you feel like giving up. I want my clients to push their limits in a safe and controlled environment. If I can get them to stretch their wings while doing something that they enjoy, the positive changes are cumulative and lasting. After the program, they are twice or three times the person they were when they started.

As I have described, I use a harm reduction model to help people overcome addiction. My perspective is that if hard drug use is keeping you from living a full life, and you feel that it's important for your social rehabilitation to drink responsibly at family gatherings, then sobriety is first and foremost about recovering from the drug use. It is not about creating strictures that will make relapse more likely.

I let my clients lead the process and define what sobriety looks like for them. Obviously, if a client says they want to do heroin or meth on the street, I walk them down off that ledge because those are illegal, irresponsible, and self-destructive behaviors. Also, if they are addicted to a legal drug like alcohol and they can't use it responsibly, then we have to come up with a recovery plan that includes abstinence from that drug. Recovery and sobriety are about responsibility to yourself and the people around you. Still, I always give my clients the benefit of the doubt. It is my goal to help them create a life that works for them and is conducive for their success. As a coach, I'm not judgmental. I'm not here to condemn anybody. As you know from this book, I have been through the ringer myself. I give my clients a comfortable environment to open up and be truthful. They know they can share their struggles with me. I am here to help them find solutions that are sustainable in the long-term.

As a coach, I have worked with many different clients. In working with them, each has provided a unique set of challenges and rewards. I want to tell you about some of the amazing clients that I have had the privilege to serve in my career.

**Life Coaching:**

One of my most memorable life coaching clients was an engineer who struggled with social interaction. He had a lot of insecurity around communication. He was an introvert and didn't have strong relationships with his family, friends, or co-workers. I remember that he seemed very sad. He was a genius in his own right, but it was a challenge for him to build a meaningful life for himself. He didn't have a significant other, and he'd never had close friendships. He struggled to find confidence day to day.

Throughout the course of the coaching process, I got him to evaluate his life, and he realized that he actually had everything that he needed. He just didn't believe in himself.

I helped him stretch past his comfort zone, and I worked with him to cultivate relationships. He recognized that he spent all his time, energy, and resources on his work. His emotional bank account was empty. We worked to strengthen the relationships in his life. He discovered that he had friends who cared about him, but he had been shutting them out. He started connecting more with his family, and he made more time for his friends.

I assessed that his nutrition was poor. I recommended supplements to him for brain health, and he started to improve. His anxiety around communication started to dissipate. So many issues can be solved simply with good brain nutrition. Then I got him to begin a workout routine. He started working out every day, and he got into good shape. I also noticed that he was eating garbage, so I recommended a change in his diet. He started eating right and putting good food into his body. I like to say, garbage in, garbage out, but when we eat clean, we live clean.

We did a physical, mental, emotional, and spiritual cleansing of his body and his life. He threw out the self-loathing thoughts that he had been poisoning himself with for so many years. He affirmed that he is a strong, intelligent, likeable person. It was a three-month process, and he was unrecognizable as his former self at the end of that time. He was smiling and confident, and he was excited to create new relationships in his life. At the end of those three months, he walked with a swagger that the man he had been before would never have thought possible.

**Intervention:**

I am often hired to stage interventions to help families communicate with their loved ones who are struggling in active addiction. Families contact me from all over the country, so it is not uncommon for me to get on a plane and fly hundreds of miles to help someone in need.

This time, I flew all the way across the country. The woman I was helping was heavily addicted to crack and heroin, and the family was at their wit's end. They didn't know what to do, and they put the process in my hands.

I do things a bit differently than many interventionists. I conduct a pre-intervention. Starting two weeks before the actual intervention, I learn everything I possibly can about the client. This allows me to get to know them before I even meet them. I study their Facebook and their

Instagram. I get information from their loved ones, and I interview their friends. I find out what kind of clothes they wear and what music they listen to. This allows me to build rapport with them as soon as I walk through the door. Not only am I the professional and the authority figure in the room, but I know everything about them and their dynamics within the family.

I control every aspect of the interventions that I lead, down to the way that people are sitting in the room. I choose three different facilities that the client can go to, and I find out how to sell the facilities to them and their family based on their individual needs, wants, and desires.

In this intervention, I knew to sell the client on the rehab facility itself. I described the massage sessions, yoga classes, and exercise center that the facility offered. Even the food was phenomenal. I knew from studying her that she would refuse to go to any place that felt like an institution. Then I sold her family on the clinical aspect of the facility. It had great staff and a good reputation.

When we set up the intervention, she tried to run out. This is common, so I had somebody remove her car keys so she couldn't leave. I had someone else confiscate her phone. She threw a temper tantrum, which is also common. She told me, "You don't understand what I'm going through. I can't just quit. I can't do this." I looked at her straight in the eyes. Then I took my leg off and put it on the table. I said, "I do understand." I told her my story. I described in brutal detail all the horrific things that I had endured. She was clearly moved, and I used this as leverage. I told her, "You have this one opportunity not to go through something even worse than what I experienced. Because if you're in the same shoes that I was in, you're not going to be so lucky. I was a miracle. I'm going to do everything in my power to help you avoid what I went through, because it was hell."

I told her, "You have two options. I've instructed your family to change the locks on the door. I have gathered up all your stuff in a big black bag near the door. Next to that bag is a suitcase. Option One: I've got an amazing facility for you right now. It's ready to go. Your plane ticket is booked. Everything's ready. We can pack whatever you want to bring in your suitcase, and you can go there and get clean. I will coach you when you get out so that you're able to maintain your sobriety. In the meantime, I'll work with your family, so they are more understanding of what you're going through. When you get back, they'll give you the resources and support you need to get through this. You will be able to create a life that you love to live. We are going to get through this together, and I'm going to make it as painless as possible."

Then I clearly laid out her choices for her. I explained, "You have to make this decision right now. Either you go to this program, or you choose Option Two: you take all your stuff that is packed in that black bag, and you leave this house. The locks have been changed, and you don't have the new key. I have coached your parents, and they're not going to let you back in. They're not doing this because they hate you. They're not doing this because they're trying to punish you. The reality is, they can't sit here and watch you kill yourself. If you're going to do that, you're going to do it on your own. If you want to get help, if you want to live a life with family and love and support, we are here for you, and we're all in. We're going to give you everything you possibly need. But you have to get on that plane today."

She looked at me, and she looked at the bags. She said, "Well, you're not giving me much of a choice." I told her, "No, I'm giving you all the choices in the world right now. But I'm making it very clear what your choices are. You can die in the streets by yourself. That is a choice, and it is eventually what's going to happen if you keep going down this road. Nobody in your family wants to see that. Or you can choose to have all the love and support that you need. We can fix this today. What's it going to be?"

Ultimately, she took my offer. She decided to go into the program that day. She is now a year and a half clean, and she is loving her life.

Now, I need to stress this next point. She stayed clean when she got home because she had the right kind of support. A lot of families believe that detox or rehab facilities will cure their loved one of their addiction. They think that when an addict comes back home, they are fixed. The reality is that when an addict returns to their familiar surroundings, they are one trigger away from going back into active addiction. If the people, places, and things in their life don't change, the statistics show that they are 91% likely to relapse. The addict and their family need to have a plan in place for when they return, which includes professional support.

The most effective strategy is to hire a sober living companion and a recovery coach. It is a one-two punch that works. When you take drugs out of somebody's life, there is a huge, empty void that is left behind. They have been filling that void with their addiction, and without their familiar substances and social interactions, they feel completely lost. If an addict returns home without support, relapse is almost guaranteed, and suicide is common. To beat these odds, hire a sober companion to live in their home, and make sure this person can stay with them for at least thirty days. This should not be a family member or a friend. It needs to be a trained professional who is separate from the dynamic of the family system. Have a recovery coach lined up and begin sessions as soon as the individual returns home. These sessions need to be ongoing because each person has their own timeline for recovery. Having this support established ahead of time helps the addict figure out how to reintegrate into society without drugs.

**Sober Living Companion:**

Because of my background and training, families often hire me as a sober living companion to help their loved ones achieve or maintain sobriety. One time, a family flew me thousands of miles to live in their private compound. From a certain perspective, it was idyllic. I lived in a guest house on a beautifully maintained estate. I had my own pool and all the amenities I could ask for. As comfortable as it was, this was no vacation. I was there to help this family's eldest daughter recover from a decade-long addiction to heroin and meth. She was skin and bones when I met her. Her addiction had all but consumed her. She was highly intelligent, as many addicts are, but her entire life had been taken over by drugs.

My job was to live with her and help her get her life back together. As I usually do, I started with physical health. I looked at what she was putting into her body. We went through her kitchen and threw out everything in the fridge and cupboards. Then we started from scratch. I took her to the supermarket, and I taught her about perimeter shopping. That is when you shop on the outside aisles of the supermarket and fill your cart with healthy produce. I taught her how to prepare her food and how to appreciate her own cooking.

Next, I taught her how to work out. I would accompany her to the gym every single morning, and I taught her a healthy and sustainable exercise routine. She had returned to work at this time, so every day when she got home, I would give her a coaching session. I served as both a recovery coach and a life coach. I helped her set her intentions for that month, and I worked with her to establish a routine that she could maintain after I was gone. At the beginning of each week, I would sit with her as she wrote down her goals for the next seven days, and I would help her define reasonable goals for each day. In my coaching, I don't want my clients to feel overwhelmed by what they think they *have* to do. My aim is always to help people feel motivated by what they *get* to do.

During this coaching process, I helped her figure out what she had too much of in her life and what she felt was lacking. We looked at what was making her feel sad and afraid. She discovered that depression and anxiety were two of her biggest triggers to use drugs. As she started to figure that out, we also made a list of the people in her life that she had used drugs with. We went down that list, and I helped her distance herself from the people that were no good for her sobriety and her future.

As we removed negative things from her life that might trigger her to relapse, we began adding in positive things to take their place. My goal was to help her develop an enriched daily, weekly, and monthly practice that would fill the void that drugs had occupied. She decided that she wanted to start attending church again, so I accompanied her to her congregation each Sunday.

She started to step into her strength physically, mentally, emotionally, and spiritually. I coached her through each problem that came up, whether it was family dynamics issues with her parents, relationship issues with her boyfriend, or interpersonal issues at her workplace.

There was only one slip up during the four-week process. She got a hold of some meth, and she used it. It turned out to be a good learning experience because she got to observe her triggers from a place of personal insight. I always tell my clients, failure is the best source of information you can ever get. Every time you fall down, you learn so much about yourself. The only time a failure is actually a failure is if you don't learn from it. Learning turns failure into a motive force that drives you forward. So, when she did fail, we diagnosed the situation. We looked at what factors went together to cause her to use, and we figured out what she could do differently next time.

At the end of the month, I worked with her to create a contract that stated that she would maintain her sobriety after I left. Then I had her sign it. She held herself to that contract to the letter. She has been clean since.

**Recovery Coaching:**

Recovery coaching is a powerful tool to help someone reframe the factors that trigger their addiction. One of my clients was a man who was profoundly bored with his life. In order to alleviate his boredom, he would use large quantities of cocaine. When he started working with me, he was spending about $1,500 a week on cocaine. He had maxed out his credit cards, and he had lost a mortgage on his house. He was in a really bad place, but he couldn't stop himself when it came to his addiction. When I started coaching him, it became clear that he had very little fulfillment in his life. His job was incredibly tedious for him, he had ADHD, and he was starving for excitement. As I assessed how I could help him, I knew that I needed to provide him with an activity that would give him the same excitement as cocaine, but in a relatively safe and controlled environment. I decided to take him skydiving. As soon as he was in the air, he fell in love with it.

In the process of the recovery coaching, we also discovered that he hated his job and he felt stifled in his relationship with his fiancée. I worked with him to improve his mental state by optimizing his diet and exercise routine. Once he was healthier and more focused, we looked at his personal and workplace relationships. He decided to break things off with his fiancée, which removed a lot of toxicity in his life. Then we looked at his job. He decided to train to become a skydiving instructor, and once he was certified, he quit his other job and started skydiving for a living.

When he focused all that energy and passion on something that he genuinely loved, he finally found fulfillment. He stopped using cocaine, and he hasn't relapsed. He replaced his unhealthy addiction with something that is healthier and safer. Not only that, but it also puts money into his bank account instead of drawing money out of it.

I still see him from time to time, and it is wonderful to see how much he enjoys his job. He is grateful for being able to take back his life and find something that he truly loves doing. It is a beautiful thing to watch people find their power zone.

**Discovering Your "YOU Factor":**

I want you to understand that we are all addicts to pleasure. We are wired for it. Just because your flavor of pleasure is different than mine does not make you any better than me. That said, it is up to each of us as responsible members of society to learn how to harness those addictions in a constructive manner. If you like adrenaline, then find something that gives you that rush, but also make sure that it is good for you. My job as a coach is to help my clients figure out their personal brand of thrill and excitement, and then find healthy, fulfilling ways to achieve that in their lives.

Your job is to discover your "YOU factor" that allows you to achieve success. That doesn't mean being an overachiever or pushing other people down to reach the top. Nor does it mean trying to become the next Michael Jordan. If that is how you define success for yourself, I can pretty much guarantee that you are setting yourself up to fail. If you measure a fish by how well it climbs trees, you are always going to see it as a failure. So, you have to find out what your passion is, because God put everybody on this planet to do at least one amazing thing. Your job in life is to figure out your unique skills and talents, and then share them with those around you. Say YES to life. Jump at your chance to help others. I love coaching because you get where you want to go much faster than you can alone. In just a few sessions, coaching can cut out a decade of trial and error. If you are struggling to carve out your path in life, find a coach who can give you a shortcut.

There are so many resources out there that will help you become a better, stronger, and wiser person. Seek out your strengths and your God-given gifts and develop them. You have so much value that you can add to other people's lives. Through my struggles and my triumphs, I discovered that my gift is inspiring and motivating others to become the best versions of themselves. It is my calling. It is what God saved me from near death to do. When I reach people through my coaching and my public speaking, I see them start to realize how amazing this world really is, and that is the greatest gift of all.

# CHAPTER 18

As I come to the conclusion of my memoir, there is a final story of addiction and recovery that I want to share. For many years, my brother Tim and I traveled separate, parallel paths through our addiction. The traumas that drove us to substance abuse created an emotional rift between us. It has taken us a long time, but we are finally starting to heal those wounds of the past. I am blessed to say that Tim and I now share a stronger bond than we have at any other point in our lives. Addiction may have ripped us apart, but in recovery, we are learning to build on each other's strengths and become better men than we could have alone. As I was finishing my book, I reached out to Tim and asked him to share his story. He graciously agreed and allowed me to interview him for this chapter.

Family dynamics are complex, and substance abuse makes them infinitely more difficult and painful. Drugs can create a civil war within a family, turning brother against brother. I want you to know that it is possible to mend those relationships that addiction has torn asunder. I hope that Tim's story gives you the inspiration and courage to keep hoping for a better tomorrow. Don't give up on those that are still caught in the clutches of addiction. Keep rooting for your loved ones and have faith that when they are ready, they will step up to the plate of life, swing hard, and hit a home run.

## Tim's Story

When I was a little boy, I was attacked by a wolf-dog hybrid. It was a mixture between a wolf and a husky, and it was a huge animal. I lost my right ear and the majority of my scalp in the attack. For most of my life up until I was sixteen years old, I had constant surgeries and doctor's appointments. Even though I was on painkillers, I was always in a ton of pain. I was scared of the surgeries, but I think my greatest fear was not being accepted. I was always picked on because of the way I looked, and that drove me to become a mean and bitter little kid. At the time, I didn't understand why I did the things I did. Nowadays, I know that my relationships with Kevin and the rest of my peers were strained because I was always frustrated, angry, and afraid.

Everything in my life stemmed from that one incident. I went through more medical trauma as a kid than most people experience in a lifetime. I had eight rounds of skin stretching balloons inflated in my scalp so that the doctors could reconstruct my injuries. Each one of those surgeries took me six months to recover from. During the procedure, they would stick me in the back of the neck with a long needle and pump saltwater into the balloons in my scalp. When they were done, I would look like an alien from *Star Trek* with giant growths on my head. They would wait until the skin was stretched out, and then they would cut out the scar tissue to merge the parts of my head with hair on it. They also tried to reconstruct my ear using skin grafts and cartilage from my rib. It was medical horror, as bad as anything you would see in the *Saw* movies. To make matters worse, I had lost so much of my scalp in the attack that the doctors weren't able to reconstruct my head so that it looked normal. To this day, I wear hats and bandanas to cover my scars, which makes it hard to fit in within a workplace, let me tell you. But I'm getting ahead of myself.

Throughout my life, I have dealt with the social ramifications of looking different. A lot of people have been pretty awful to me because of the way my scalp looks. When I was a kid, my defensive strategy was to become a bully. I didn't feel like anyone liked me, so I hit back first. I was nasty and violent. If people didn't want me, I decided that I would force my way into their lives. Nobody would dare tell me that they didn't want to hang out with me because they would be too afraid to.

All of this social fallout from my injury put a big strain on my relationship with Kevin. He was like a model child when we were little. He did what he was supposed to, he was good in school, and he was pretty straight-edge. Family dynamics are always hard, especially in a blended family. I was dealing with medical trauma, bullying from other kids, and then I had this brother who was labeled as the "good kid." Rather than be happy for him, I was envious of his success. I could and should have followed in his footsteps, but instead I just kind of backed away from that path.

When I was sixteen, I refused to get any more surgeries. I supposedly had the best doctors in the country working on me, and they kept promising me that they could fix my scalp, but after a certain point, the procedures didn't do me any good. They just caused me pain, and they took six months to heal. Let me tell you, it is incredibly demoralizing to look in the mirror after six months of hell and realize that you look exactly the same as you did before the doctors cut you open. Why put myself through that if all I got was a bad result? I felt defeated, and I gave up on the whole thing. At that point, I just accepted that I am what I am.

By then, drugs were already a big part of my life. As I left my teens and arrived in my twenties, drugs were so ever present that I didn't even see them as a problem. I was there when everything happened with Kevin. I saw him on his deathbed, and even that didn't wake me up. I watched one of the most important people in my life almost die from drugs, and still I did nothing to change my way of thinking or my behavior. I did whatever I wanted, and I wasn't worried about the repercussions of it.

Substance abuse takes your brain out and it puts another brain in its place. Sometimes it takes everything falling apart before you can wake up enough to make a change. At that point in my life, I know I wasn't ready to change yet. The rewards of the substance have to become less than the rewards of stopping, and addiction tricks you into believing that getting that next high is the most important thing in the universe.

My addiction went as far as you can possibly imagine. I took every drug that you can possibly name, except acid. I smoked crack. I injected meth, heroin, and coke. I did all of the worst drugs that you can do, and I did them as often as possible to the point where I barely even looked like a human being.

I didn't care about consequences. In fact, I didn't really care about anything. I traveled from state to state, from New York to Florida, buying and selling drugs and guns. Nowadays, I can see how awful this was, but at the time, it ran my life.

I remember one time I was driving somewhere in the South. I was riding in a car with some guys that I didn't really know. I was going to buy a few ounces of meth from a dealer. I didn't realize it at the time, but the people I was riding with were intending to rob me. After the drug deal went down, we drove back to the motel where we were staying. As I sat there using some of the meth that I had just bought, I couldn't help hearing the other guys shouting a few rooms away. The walls were paper thin, and I could hear everything that was going on. I remember feeling shocked when I heard that the guys were plotting to kill me. I decided to barricade myself in my motel room. I pushed the bed in front of the door, and I crouched down on the floor behind it with a .40 caliber gripped in my hand. I lay there, pointing my gun at the doorway so that when they kicked the door in, I could shoot at them. Eventually, they burst through the door, and I found myself locked in a stalemate, aiming my gun at some guy who was pointing his gun at me. I came as close as I possibly could to ending my life, and it was over $600 worth of drugs. These people were willing to take another person's life to steal some meth that would last them only a couple days.

As for me, I was risking my life every day for my addiction. I wasn't just dependent on drugs; I was hooked on the lifestyle. The world of addiction is immersive and enthralling. It sucks you in and quickly becomes your reality. I made insane amounts of money and got to get high every day.

As harrowing as that experience was, it wasn't enough to get me to stop. It didn't matter to my addiction that my family and friends had distanced themselves from me. It didn't matter that I had lost property and possessions. It didn't matter that I had destroyed my health and ravaged my physical appearance. Nothing was enough to stop me, not even the threat of losing my life.

I had no willpower to stop, so the law had to stop me. At the time, I was affiliated with the organized crime industry. One of the guys must have gotten into trouble for heroin distribution. I was traveling state to state selling meth and firearms, and this meant that I was a bigger score for the police. So, in order to get themselves out of trouble, some of these guys turned me over to the DA. They introduced me to an undercover police officer, who they told me was a friend of the family. After three sales, the police arrested me. Those mob guys hit me when I was down. I was homeless at the time, going from motel to motel. I lived in the streets in the total grip of addiction. I was finally arrested in 2019 and sentenced to jail. They charged me with nine different crimes, including possession of a controlled substance on four separate occasions, possession of a loaded firearm, sale of a loaded firearm, and sale of a controlled substance both over and under a certain amount. These were all class B and C felonies. Even though I didn't sell them the gun knowing that they were going to use it in a murder, it is still a violent crime. I was looking at serving ten months and twenty-two days of every year that I would be receiving. Since I already had one prior felony for possession of a controlled substance over a certain amount, I could have been hit with the book. The judge could have sentenced me to anywhere from six and a half to twelve years.

Once I got to jail, I stopped using for the first time since I was a teenager. They drug tested me to make sure I stayed clean, and they put me on suboxone for a few days. Then I went through withdrawal, which was brutal, but there wasn't much I could do about it. Of course, you can score drugs in jail if you are willing to pay exorbitant prices and risk getting caught, but that wasn't really an option for me at the time.

When I was in jail, 90% of the inmates were there for drugs. They would rob people, houses, stores, even churches to get money to feed their habit. One way or another, everything goes back to drug abuse. People like me that sold those substances prey on other people's weaknesses. When you sell people drugs, you are benefitting from the loss of somebody else's life.

Everything about jail is awful. There is nothing good about it. You come to appreciate the most meager blessings when you're in there. I didn't get to go outside at all when I was there, but I was allowed to play handball and basketball in their little gym. Another blessing was that I was a big, scary looking guy, so I wasn't someone that the other inmates tried to pick on.

There is a pecking order in jail that you have to obey. When you get there, the other inmates tell you which toilets you can poop in, what shower you can use, and what telephone you can call from. I was able to walk my own line more than some of the other guys because of my stature and my scars. I don't look like someone you want to mess with. They probably thought I got my scars from fighting. Little did they know that I had never been in a fight that was bad enough to leave a permanent mark. I was as scared as they come, but I was damned if I would show it because once you show it, they'll prey on you, steal from you, and beat you.

Jail isn't good for anybody. It doesn't rehabilitate anyone. All the guys I talked to in there told me that as soon as they got out, they planned to go right back to the lifestyle. They don't know any other life. I was the exception, really. I went to AA and NA meetings when I was there. I had two or three a week that I was able to go to. The meetings gave me just enough sobriety to keep me humane and make me feel like there was a good reason for me to do the right thing.

While I was there, I took part in a program called Scared Straight. It's for these twelve and thirteen-year-old kids who are getting into drugs. The guards march them through the jail, and let's just say, they don't discourage the inmates from banging on the doors and screaming at the kids. They don't want you to curse or say anything too crazy, but they want you to put fear into the kids and make them realize just how bad things can be. They did this specifically in my pod. They brought in a new class of kids every other Wednesday. A hundred students would walk through, and the guards would goad us to scare them.

The guards there were as dangerous as the prisoners. Once they got you off camera, it was your word against theirs, and you're a criminal, so no one was going to believe you. During the time I was there, they killed several of the inmates. Several other inmates committed suicide.

Throughout my time in jail, I tried to stay focused on the understanding that what I was going through was a result of my own actions. Everything that was happening was because of something that I had done. I had to grow up and make a change.

I wound up doing 242 days with five years' probation. I was on edge the entire time I was in jail, but I kept my head down and got through it. Every day I was there, I did the best I could to make sure that I didn't end up staying in this place. As awful as that experience was, it finally woke me up. As I sat there, surrounded by child molesters, murderers, and others who truly deserve to be locked up, I realized that if I didn't turn my life around, I was headed in one of two directions: long-term incarceration or an early grave. At last, the pain of using outweighed the pleasure, and I decided to change course.

Thank God I had my father. He got me a really good lawyer. If I had been stuck with a public defender, I would 100% be upstate in prison right now with another five years to go. My lawyer argued that if anybody deserved a second chance, I did. I deserved an opportunity to get out and do the right thing. Thank God he was able to get the court to see that. But while you're in there, it's hard not to lose hope. They kept pushing my court date back, and no matter how much my lawyer kept telling me to keep the faith, the outlook seemed more grim each day. Many times, I felt overwhelmed by self-hatred and anger at what I had done to myself. I was consumed by so many negative emotions that it was hard not to lash out and wind up hitting somebody or doing something to make the situation worse. Even with a good lawyer, I was one misstep away from spending the rest of my life in prison.

Going to jail was the thing that allowed me to rebuild my relationship with Kevin. Kevin came to visit me while I was inside. He was my only sibling who came to see me. When someone comes to see you in there, it brings you back to reality. It gives you the perspective of life being good again. That's something that Kevin did for me, and it brought us closer together than we had ever been. Kevin has been a role model to me. He has changed his life. He wasn't as bad into his addiction as I was, but he wasn't far off. That one mistake that he made was an accumulation of God knows how many others. It was honestly a miracle that I didn't end up overdosing, too. There were a thousand times that I should have. Not too many people shoot heroin fifty times in a week and live to tell the story. I was more than deserving of the same circumstances that he ended up finding himself in, but somehow, I never wound up there.

Kevin and I now have similar experiences with medical trauma and the loss of a physical attribute. The fact is that his injury is more extreme than mine. Maybe it was a little easier for him to come to a place of acceptance because he was older when it happened. When you're young, you don't understand the context around the things that make you different. It is so much more traumatic for a kid to go through something like what I went through. Not to say that people who go through an ordeal like mine as adults aren't affected—obviously, they are—but they can build more context around it. They can frame their recovery in terms of personal growth instead of trauma.

Kevin was able to look at his injury from a more adult perspective and with a more intelligent mindset than I could have. To this day, I still wear a hat and a bandana to cover my scars, and yet my brother is able to walk around in a pair of shorts that shows his prosthetic leg and still feel confident. It's inspiring to see that someone can have something like that happen and become stronger because of it. After he lost his leg, he became even more outgoing than he had been before. I know that what he went through ultimately had a positive influence on him and everyone around him. He makes me feel more comfortable with myself. When I look at what he can do with what he's been given, it puts things in perspective for me. It makes me able to say, "I can." There's no reason for me to be ashamed or to hide what happened to me when Kevin can embrace his life experiences like that.

When I was finally released from jail, I was a changed man. At 6'3", I was almost 275 pounds. I worked out as often as I could in the jail's gym, and I had gotten really big. I couldn't even fit into my old clothes that I had come in with. When my dad came to pick me up at the facility, I had to wrap myself in garbage bags to walk to his car. It was such a relief to be home, but at the same time, it was like walking a tightrope. At first, everybody was afraid that I would go right back to using, which was understandable because that was what I had always done. They wanted to do whatever they could to keep me clean, but the reality was that no one could stop me from using but me. It was my responsibility to maintain my sobriety. This time it was different. I knew that jail was not where I wanted to be. It did not make me happy, and there was nothing good that would come from going back. I had been given a second chance at life, and I realized that I needed to choose a different path.

When I came home, I had my father, Kevin, and Barbara for support. Kevin was probably the least skeptical of all of them. He showed the most confidence that I would stay sober. I think that a lot of people in my life assumed that it was just a matter of time before I relapsed and went back to jail. Kevin believed in me, and that made me gravitate toward him. He believed that I was ready to do the right thing in my life, and he trusted that I would. More than ever, I needed his faith in me.

As soon as I was home, Kevin helped me get my separation game down. As an addict, you have to be honest with yourself about who you can be around and who you can't. I can't be around anybody anymore who does messed up stuff. If you're still in that life, I can say hi, shake your hand, and talk to you for twenty minutes, but then I have to go.

In 2020 when the COVID-19 pandemic hit, it actually helped me simplify my life. The pandemic began just a few months after I got out of jail. I couldn't go outside or meet up with people, so I didn't have any opportunities to get myself in trouble. It reinforced my sobriety and gave me nearly another year of staying on the straight and narrow. Recovery has started to become a way of life for me. I am learning to avoid bad situations, and I am involving myself with better people.

One of the things that brings a ton of meaning to my life now is coaching baseball. I was an all-star baseball player when I was a kid. Playing ball was my favorite activity. I was really good at it, too, and that gave me a sense of self-worth and purpose. I think another reason I gravitated to it so strongly was because it gave me a reason to wear a hat every day. Baseball literally covered my head. It let me excel at something, but more importantly, it let me be normal. I was tall and big enough to play football or basketball, but neither of those sports had a hat associated with them, so I didn't even consider them. For me, baseball was the perfect sport.

My father was an incredible athlete and a great baseball coach, and he taught me to be what I am. I am not bragging when I say that if you let me walk onto a Major League field and practice against Major League players, in a few months, I would be able to hold my own. I am genuinely good at the game.

If it hadn't been for drugs, if I hadn't allowed myself to fall into that abyss, at this point in my life, I know I wouldn't be talking to you from inside my father's house. I would be talking to you from my mansion that I'd bought in cash from whatever Major League team had hired me. As hard as that is for me to swallow sometimes, that is a fact about my life. I know that I put myself where I am, and I take responsibility for what I have done and failed to do because of my addiction.

My brother-in-law has a traveling baseball team for twelve to thirteen-year-old boys, and it's making the transition from Little League to Babe Ruth. That's a big difference in the game. They're going from 50-foot bases to 90-foot bases. My brother-in-law invited me to coach these kids, and it has been a tremendously positive part of my recovery. It gives me a lot of meaning and purpose to help these kids excel. When you're in recovery, you've got to find things that make you happy. For me, that's being involved in baseball. I have a knowledge and a love for the sport that outshines any love I have for anything in the world. Coaching is as good for me as it is for the kids that I help. Even though I can't play professionally myself, maybe I can help one of my students get there.

I have to thank God that I was blessed with the opportunity to do this. I get to use my experiences and abilities to benefit these kids. If they want to learn, if they want to improve, if they love the game, then I will move mountains for them. That's why I'm there. As time goes on, I plan to steer them in the right direction. I'll be able to teach them about choices and consequences. I'm an example of what happens if you choose to do the wrong thing. Now that I'm choosing to do the right thing, opportunities have started opening up for me. I feel blessed that I am now physically, mentally, and emotionally capable of seizing those chances as they present themselves.

Today as I am talking to you, it is my birthday. Tonight at 6:00, I am going to go to baseball practice and train my students. I'm going to be with them for two hours. That's two hours that I get to do something I care about. After that, I'll spend the evening with my family and my brother and enjoy my life. I get to celebrate the first genuinely good birthday that I have had in God knows how long. Two years ago on my birthday, I was at a random hotel in some other state with a needle in my arm. Last year, I was in jail. Those have been the kinds of birthdays that I have celebrated for the past decade. Now I get to wake up in my own bed, have a bacon egg and cheese, and hang out with my brother. That's not just good. It's not just great. It's awesome. It all comes down to me deciding to be the person that I truly am, the person that I was all along underneath all the trauma and addiction. I own my mistakes, but I am not my mistakes. I thank God that I now have the opportunity to be happy in my life.

# EPILOGUE

L ife is an odyssey. There is no endgame, no final chapter written in stone. It is a journey of exploration in which we create a never-ending story that we love to tell. Life is a process of finding our purpose and our place in this world.

I found my purpose when I chose to become a recovery warrior. That is my calling. I am a true warrior, but I am not the only one. Anybody can do what I did. If you want something badly enough, you can accomplish it. You must make the decision and commit to change. After all, your life is the culmination of the decisions you make. You have tremendous power within you to make new choices and build the life of your dreams.

Look deep inside yourself. Ask yourself, what is your calling? What gets you up in the morning? What brings you fulfillment, gratitude, and joy? When you find that source of passion, life starts there. Fill your environment with the people, places, and experiences that empower you and inspire you to grow. Search for things that motivate you to become the best version of yourself.

At the same time, recognize that your experiences are neither good nor bad. They are what you make of them. Your paradigm determines your perception. When you change the way you see your life, you change your reality. There is value in everything, but sometimes you have to change your viewpoint in order to see it. You can change your life in an instant if you change the way you model your experience.

If I could change my life, so can you. It is my belief that if one person can learn to do something, anybody can follow in their footsteps. My job as a coach is to help you to figure out the "how" of it. Not everybody can become Oprah, but everyone can learn the power of connecting authentically with people. We can all learn to listen and add value in the way that she does. Maybe you won't be the next Oprah, but you can use the tools that you develop along the way to become the best YOU that you can be.

I am a true warrior now, but when I was in addiction, I was a follower. If I had the opportunity to cop out or take the easy route, I usually took it. I didn't do my homework. I used drugs when somebody offered them to me. I did whatever made me comfortable in the moment. I made stupid decisions because it was the path of least resistance. When my choices were narrowed to changing my life or losing my life, I chose to take the tough road and find out what I was truly made of. Even though the route to success was excruciating at times, I knew I had to walk that path. I wasn't going to give up on myself again.

There was never just one answer to the success that I had in my recovery. Before my accident, any time that I was winning in one area of my life, I was usually lacking in another. I didn't find true happiness and greatness until I found balance. I learned to balance the good with the bad, the light with the dark. Without that contrast in life, you don't appreciate its opposite.

Learn from my mistakes. You can continue on a path to rock bottom like I did, or you can choose to change your life now when you have more resources at your disposal. That is where coaching comes in. A coach helps you climb out of the darkness before you are lost with nothing but a thin flame of hope to guide your way. Take it from me—you don't have to journey all the way into the abyss before you turn your life around. Right now, in this very moment, you can choose to become a leader. You can step up, or you can give up—those are your two paths. When you are faced with the choice to prevail or die, you have an opportunity to grab the reins and take control. You start by leading yourself through the fire, and then you can become a leader for others.

Use your biggest weakness and turn it into your greatest strength. Don't look at your challenges as hardships. Instead, look at them as resources. Your challenges give you the power to fight for your success, fulfillment, and joy.

Champions are made when all seems lost. In the moment when the last flame of hope starts to fade, that is where you will find your resolve. When you choose not to give up, your path becomes clear. Yes, the road may be hard. It may be rough and painful, but you can do it. I believe in you. When you find yourself in the trenches with no hope left, have faith that you can white knuckle it and give it everything you've got.

If there is one thing that I have learned on my journey, it is the importance of having faith. All the glory goes to God for me. Without His guidance and love, I would never have been able to survive the things that I endured. Now that I have tapped into the power of faith, I feel truly unstoppable. Having faith in something greater than myself reassures me that no matter how bad a given day might be, there will always be a better tomorrow. God created me as a perfect design for what I am intended to do. Even though the path was grueling, He put me through these trials to toughen me into the man I was meant to become.

Faith seems to be at a premium these days. There is a lot of cynicism in the world. But here's the thing—whether you are religious or not, you need faith in something. We all do. Without faith, our hearts grow hollow. Faith fills a void within us and kindles our hope for the future.

Trust that God is guiding you and know that you are exactly where you are supposed to be at this moment. Some days it may feel like you are driving through dense fog with one headlight out, but keep your eyes looking forward and focus on the goal. If you focus behind you and keep looking to the past, you will be stuck in a loop, living the same old patterns over and over. No matter what challenges may lie ahead of you, have faith in your direction and fail forward.

As I have traveled along my spiritual path, I have studied every major religion, and I appreciate all that I have learned. The one constant in all spiritual experience is worship. Humans were created to worship. It is as fundamental to the human condition as eating and sleeping. Having faith in a higher power allows us to channel our worship in a fulfilling way. We each experience God differently based on our own understanding and perception, but worship is universal. Worship is the reassurance that there is something bigger in the universe than ourselves.

Worship is enthralling. It consumes you. No matter the subject of your worship, you will never be able to get enough of it. I know I've said this before, but it bears repeating: if you devote your worship to something that is impermanent and worldly, you will ultimately feel empty. If you worship money, you will never be rich enough to satisfy your desire. If you worship celebrity, you will always feel ugly by comparison. If you worship people's respect, you will feel crushed if anyone expresses a negative opinion of you. The material world will always break, disappoint, and fade. That emptiness leads to anxiety and depression, and too many of us try to fill that void with addiction.

If you worship something infinite and abundant—whether you call that God, the universe, or a higher power—it can never be taken away from you. Directing your faith to something greater than you creates strength and stability in your life.

My final message to you is this: You are born perfect and whole, but you are also born into a broken world. Society tries to convince you that you are not enough. It tells you that you must fill yourself with materialistic possessions and experiences to feel complete. I want you to know that you are beautiful exactly the way you were designed. Don't let anyone tell you otherwise. You are made of stardust and brought to life with the breath of God, and you are created in the image of the Divine. God put you on this earth to contribute at least one extraordinary thing in your life, and I have faith that you will live up to that greatness.

# ABOUT THE AUTHOR

Kevin Parker has a bachelor's degree in psychology and more than twenty years of experience with addiction. He spent thirteen years in active addiction, using everything from cocaine to opiates and anything else he could get his hands on. When he was twenty-five, his drug use put him in a coma, costing him his leg and nearly his life. He has been clean ever since. His brush with death set him on a spiritual path, and he has dedicated his life to helping others achieve sobriety. He is now a public speaker, recovery coach, professional interventionist, and published author.

Kevin is certified in many modalities of coaching and has studied with top leaders in self-development. He uses his expertise with addiction to help his clients reach their recovery goals. He volunteers in hospitals to help overdose patients and amputees assimilate back into society. Some of his favorite work includes speaking at schools to deter kids and teens from using drugs. Kevin's mission is to inspire people to discover their passion and purpose and create the life of their dreams.

Contact Kevin through his website at
www.TrueWarriorSuccess.com

Made in the USA
Middletown, DE
08 August 2021